RISK AND REDEMPTION

SURVIVING THE NETWORK NEWS WARS

ARTHUR KENT

Interstellar Inc.

Interstellar Inc.

Abbott Building, Main Street
P.O. Box 3186
Tortola
British Virgin Islands

ISBN 976-8056-08-8

First published 1996 by Penguin Books Canada Ltd.

Printed in Canada

*This book is dedicated
to the men and women
who bring home the world's news*

Contents

Foreword

IT WAS SUNSET, the photographer's "golden hour," and as we filmed the graceful arc of buildings glowing in the soft light along the Grand Canal, I began to wonder: Is it only voyeurism that brings people to places like Venice? Are human beings merely tantalized, entertained by places like this? Or is it comfort we're really seeking here, a safe illusion of ourselves through the window of humanity's past, the history of its habits and beliefs, its great crimes and wonderful achievements?

After all, the past, unlike the present, can't leap out and harm us, erupt all around us with unexpected fury and destroy the lives we try to lead. The past just stands there—impassive, unthreatening, a story long since finished and told, and retold. And in the case of Venice, the past stands magically, beautifully, in the splendid forms of ancient buildings appearing to drift on a lazy sea.

We were there, the four of us, for both the magic and the peace. Leon Ferguson, our tape editor, had flown down from Paris. I'd come in from London in my new role of executive producer. Max Matteoli and Stefano Generali, on camera and sound, had come up from Rome, the city where the four of us, for a few wonderful years, had lived and worked together.

We were starting over. Reuniting in the relative serenity of this museum-city after a brief but painful encounter in the television industry with present-day 1990s realism—namely turmoil, confusion and unnecessary waste. We had survived our collision with the darker forces of the here and now, and this project in Venice, a long, languid, bountifully financed documentary, was meant to be a kind of celebration of that survival.

And for me, Venice was something more. A place to reflect, to try to make sense of all the changes and upheaval around me. A chance to bring together the many twisting currents that had landed me there on the verge of that ancient lagoon in the forty-first year of my life.

The setting was a perfect counterpoint to our earlier work. Our film would not have violence as its centerpiece. The only war we might come across was an environmental one, the only refugees, families fleeing unemployment and inflation. No bodies, no blood. We would no doubt return to all that soon enough, with a few dreams of Venice, if we were lucky, to relieve some of the old nightmares of our previous postings.

You see, the boys and I had served together in the Rome bureau of NBC News. The company had once been a world-class provider of international news, and our little team had been one of its most widely traveled front-line coverage units. We'd won our share of awards, too. But then in the early nineties NBC News was transformed into a company dominated by entertainment-influenced, tabloid-style programs. That led to the dismantling of our hard-news operation in Rome, the unceremonious firing and dispersal of our team across Europe, and a very public legal battle between our former corporate bosses and me.

After eighteen months of litigation my lawyers and I won that battle. Evidence revealed that NBC management had wrongfully dismissed me and then tried to destroy my reputation. In a whirlwind reversal of the fortunes of the media wars, my legal victory gave me the means to become an independent producer. A free operator, able to finance my own journalism from story selection through production to the sale of finished programs. Professionally, I felt reborn.

"Catching lightning in a bottle." That's how my attorney, Brian Lysaght, describes our victory. And there was plenty of electricity at our celebrations—all five of them, in London, New York, Los Angeles and Toronto, the cities where much of our evidence had been gathered, and in my home town, Calgary. Along with the many friends and colleagues who had given testimony and support to our case, we ate and drank not only to our success but to the symbolic victory of journalistic integrity over corporate expediency.

The case had beamed a spotlight on to the business of journalism, and had given definition to the craft of reporting—a discipline surprisingly short on leather-bound volumes about ethics. Above all, it dragged into open court a group of media power brokers who were forced to defend their concepts of television news economics. They stood accused of gross ineptitude and misconduct, and during eighteen months of pre-trial discovery of evidence, my lawyers and I gradually built the case against them, fact by fact.

Along the way, we found out exactly how and why one of America's proudest news companies had been transformed into a purveyor of glossy, exploitative sensationalism. And I rediscovered the investigative tradecraft that got me hooked on reporting in the first place—from the time I first tried my luck on my father's typewriter to the day I took on the misguided management of NBC.

CHAPTER ONE

Your Reputation Is No Longer Valid

Arthur is one of our best foreign correspondents.
> —NBC *News press release, February 21, 1991*

Arthur Kent has been unable to deal with any level of management. His actions are unfortunate and bizarre. He has consistently been unable to work within a supervisory and collaborative environment.
> —NBC *News press release, August 17, 1992*

We are unable to reach an amicable resolution of our differences with Arthur Kent. In light of Arthur's repeated breaches of his agreement with NBC, his employment has been terminated effective immediately.
> —NBC *News press release, August 21, 1992*

Arthur Kent is and always has been a talented and courageous journalist who is highly regarded within NBC... Arthur conducted himself fully in accord with his contractual obligations...[and] is always welcome to return... Litigation has been dismissed in return for a fair and appropriate payment by NBC News to Mr. Kent...
> —NBC *News press release, March 16, 1994*

Arthur's got looks, he's got talent...why shouldn't the bugger have money, too!
> —*Adrian Hamilton, of the* Observer, London

AH, ADRIAN. Hardly a man to shower his reporters with empty praise. But even if he hadn't uttered this champagne-induced tribute to our success in the U.S. courts, I would introduce him to you as one of the finest editors (that is, "boss" or "chief" or "grown-up") I've ever had the pleasure to work for.

Adrian Hamilton knows how to inspire a correspondent into action, especially bold, risky, or surreptitious action. He even knows how to coax that most dreaded thing–a rewrite–out of his most temperamental and stubborn scribes.

1

Like the day I first walked into the newsroom of the *Observer* in London to place before Adrian a 1,200-word story of which I was especially proud. "Hmm," he said, frowning, as he flipped through the typewritten pages. He stood, showed me his friendly open smile, and then handed the story back to me.

"You've got something there. Just once more through the type-writer, don't you think?"

Just...once more...through the typewriter. During which journey my scrambled phrases would presumably take on a little more clarity, a bit more punch. I got the picture. He wasn't out to mangle the facts. He just wanted his readers to be able to understand them. I complied, and so this outsider, this colonial, this itinerant field reporter from the world of television news, made it on to the pages of Britain's finest, if at times financially troubled, Sunday newspaper.

I wasn't there for the money. TV has more of that. I was there for the tradition of excellence that pervades the British Sundays. George Orwell wrote for the *Observer* in the forties, when David Astor was editing "The World's Oldest Sunday Newspaper" in its heyday. Anthony Burgess was writing literary reviews for the paper during the years my stories on the Afghan war were splashed across the foreign pages. I was forced to compete for space with much better writers, and that gave me something to strive for. And I'd been taught that striving for something better, from your-self and your story, was vital to good journalism.

For their part, Adrian and my other colleagues at the *Observer* didn't really know what to make of my main "daytime" gig–being an on-air staff correspondent for NBC. I think they were always slightly suspicious of the big money and notoriety thrown around in the American network news business. And although *Observer* staffers were no strangers to management upheaval, editorial crises and sagging morale, even the most seasoned hacks among them were startled by the scope and bitterness of my showdown with the management and ownership of NBC News, as illustrated by the harsh, rapid swing from praise to condemn-ation and back again in the company's official statements about me.

"It's amazing," I remember Adrian saying when the initial

blow-up occurred. "They're really trying to erase your face from the crowd on Lenin's Tomb!"

He had a point–on the surface, the sudden switch in NBC's publicity resembled the practices of Soviet propagandists during the Cold War. Whenever a Communist Party luminary fell out of favor and disappeared, his image, too, was simply removed from old photographs of the Party leadership's annual get-togethers atop Lenin's mausoleum in Red Square.

But a *journalist* getting the air-brush treatment by his network *news* bosses? In the *nineties*?

"You haven't deflowered the chief executive's daughter, have you, Arthur?"

I think I disappointed Adrian slightly when I replied that things had come to a head in a much more mundane way–through an editorial disagreement. I had wanted to continue reporting hard news, while NBC's newly appointed programming wizards had tried to coerce me into the realm of entertainment.

"And they left you no way out?"

Only the one I'd been pushed through–the open window of the network's head office in New York, where the company's publicists were busy disseminating lies about me to every influential TV writer in North America.

Nothing in my experience or training as a journalist had prepared me for this unexpected fall into the Twilight Zone. The chief executives of one of America's most respected news agencies had set themselves about the task of blackening my reputation. If I wouldn't work for them, their way, I wouldn't work for anyone.

It was as if I had stepped through the looking-glass. Now the reporter had become the subject of scandal; the investigator had fallen under a cloud of suspicion. NBC management told the public and my peers in journalism that I had refused a legitimate assignment, had broken the terms of my employment agreement. For good measure they implied that I was a coward, a shirker who had turned tail and run from the front lines of our profession.

This from the company that had been, for years, my only real lifeline to the outside world. From Afghanistan through the blood-drenched streets of Bucharest to the battlefields of the Gulf, NBC News had been one of my principal sources of protection should the violence we regularly beamed home via satellite engulf our aggressive but vulnerable little corps of reporters, camera teams and technicians.

Suddenly, I became immersed in the unfamiliar forms and cadences of legalese. Motions and counter-motions, interrogatories and responses, depositions and transcripts and document demands. Not to mention bills–legal bills–a not inconsiderable worry, since I would be competing, ultimately, with the resources of the mammoth parent of NBC News, the General Electric Company, with more than $130 billion in annual combined sales from all its divisions and subsidiary companies. General Electric, at this writing America's second-largest industrial giant (and its most profitable), with close to 300,000 employees in more than one hundred countries. General Electric, whose chief executive, Jack Welch, as the evolution of my action, Kent v. NBC, clearly proves, enforced a rigid unwritten policy among the attorneys protecting his corporate empire in the many lawsuits and investigations launched against it: never admit fault in litigation, however damning the evidence against the company. And never, ever settle a lawsuit in favor of an adversary of GE until every attempt has been made to exhaust that adversary's ability to reach trial.

A GE subsidiary held NBC's libel-insurance policy. The chief executive of NBC television, Robert Wright, was a GE appointee and a key target of our investigation. Mr. Wright, we learned, personally directed his general counsel and vice-president of legal affairs, Richard Cotton, in the company's defense of my lawsuit. And evidence revealed that Mr. Cotton and his subordinates were very much involved in management's initial actions against me and in the eighteen-month effort to conceal the nature and extent of those actions.

So the officers at GE and NBC had a lot to hide and plenty of spare change to help them do it. They had a platoon of in-house lawyers and hired an outside litigation specialist from one of the most expensive law firms in the U.S. My lawyers, I quickly discovered, had the edge in ability and street-smarts, but before the contest was over I was forced to risk every dollar, pound sterling and Italian lire I had, plus every material possession I owned in life.

On top of the expense, it was all very public. Easily a six-point-

nine on the litigation Richter scale. It was loud and con-
tentious, a most unseemly wrangle in the opinion of those closest
to me, my family of journalists, jurists and editors. The Kent family, you see, is not given to garish displays of venom and
vengeance. But we stick together, and my family supported me
as I fought to restore my reputation and teach a corporate giant a
lesson in accountability and law.

* * *

Especially now, as I recount it to you, the story of how NBC management switched from toasting to targeting me goes down better
with generous measures of dry white wine. To put it concisely,
after years of hard labor on the foreign news trail, most of it spent
in blissful anonymity, I was suddenly summoned by NBC's top
news executives to the inner sanctum itself: the third floor of
Manhattan's 30 Rockefeller Plaza. (This is the splendid old RCA
building, now inscribed with the giant initials "GE" since Mr.
Welch bought out RCA, and with it NBC, in 1986.)

"Welcome to the 'NBC Family,'" one wag on the New York
desk greeted me – "the Addams Family."

A prophetic remark. Black comedy would soon engulf us all as
management set about redefining our company and its products.
Our leaders, that summer of 1992, thought it would be a good idea
if I sat in for a couple of weeks as co-host of the "Today Show" and
substitute anchor for "Nightly News." At no time had I requested
these high-profile anchor gigs on the network's two main news
shows, and I had never seen myself as a studio animal.

I was a field correspondent. A reporter who could use a camera
as well as a typewriter, microphone or computer keyboard. I had
been all over the world for NBC. Afghanistan, Russia, China,
Eastern Europe and the Middle East. But a studio? In New York?
Hardly ever.

But what good TV reporter would turn down the opportunity?
Something unexpected might happen. I might like it. Fate might
intervene in a curious, wonderful way. Just the way fate had a year
earlier, when it fell upon me in the shape of an incoming rocket.

It had been pure chance that I was standing on a certain
rooftop in Saudi Arabia in the opening hours of the Gulf War,

when SCUD missiles, the jalopies of mid-twentieth century rocketry, began falling from the sky. As Saddam Hussein's missiles scorched in at us, live television pictures extended their range around the world and into the living rooms of America, with me, a reporter on the scene, visible beneath the rocket trails, explaining what was going on.

Most of us at NBC's Dhahran news bureau had braced ourselves for an attack. We'd managed to contain the fear–fear of the unknown, fear of what might be in the warheads, fear of how many rockets would fall, fear that might have ended our broadcast before it began. As well, we had been frustrated by severe military censorship–to an unprecedented degree, the Pentagon was trying to control the international news media's access to the war. But now, with a story literally falling down on our heads, unmanaged by the censors, we wanted and needed to hold our ground and report freely, accurately.

It was spectacular–the first-ever live broadcast of missile versus anti-missile warfare, with U.S. Patriots blasting off and deflecting the Iraqi rockets before their nosecones could smash with full explosive force into military or civilian targets on the ground.

By coincidence, one of the first attacks came while a huge audience in the U.S. was watching the AFC final on NBC. The Buffalo Bills had the game clinched well before half-time. Since our own play-by-play of SCUD intercepts provided far more thrills than anything going on in the stadium, the network repeatedly cut away from the game to let us tell people at home what was happening on the other side of the world.

We were astonished by viewer reaction. It was immediate and intense, and suddenly a correspondent who had only two years earlier been a camera-packing extra on the ragged edge of the business was being cast as a leading man. To me this was full of what one of my favorite authors, Graham Greene, called "the confused comedy of our lives." Only two years before the Gulf, in the winter of 1989, I had been ducking bombs and artillery shells while shooting my own stories alone in the Afghan wilderness. Now, backed by a team of forty people, I was reporting live on a twenty-four-hour-a-day satellite link to the United States, with faxes and phone calls from our viewers giving instant feedback on our work.

"While the war is still very frightening," wrote the third-grade class of Mount Carmel Elementary School in Douglasville, Georgia, "because of you, we don't have to live with the fear of the unknown." They concluded, "Know that you are in our thoughts and prayers."

"Beats starring in a paternity suit," quipped one of our veteran cameramen, Brian Calvert, to that one. Brian was shooting SCUD reports with me at the time, and he meant it when he added, "Thank heaven someone's actually *watching* us, Art."

And were they watching. Women faxed Valentines to me. Fan clubs had been formed with chapters in at least four major U.S. cities. My name was mentioned in comic strips; my caricature appeared in the pages of the *New Yorker*, and *People* magazine scrambled to put my story into print.

This quality and quantity of feedback was a ball we could run with. I think our reporting became sharper and more aggressive with the power of public interest behind us. In this kind of spotlight no one wanted to screw up—or let up on the authorities, who were severely restricting coverage of the war.

I was able to use the support of housewives, schoolkids, even breathless young women to press home our counterattack against censorship on the air, which put me at odds with our bosses in New York, who couldn't see any ratings dividends in biting the hand that was feeding them all that great bombing footage from Baghdad and Kuwait—the Pentagon.

Sadly, overall, Pentagon strategists and the White House had us outgunned and outmaneuvered in the fight over reporting restrictions. We couldn't hope to break through the wall of censorship, or even dent it, unless we got some backing from people at the top of the network news business in New York. But there was little chance of that.

The Bush administration frightened our executives with opinion polls. The American public, they claimed, supported the government, not the press. Our company's management bowed to this. And soon these same executives would usher NBC News into controversy and disgrace with their strange programming experiments, blending news with entertainment.

For me, other, more dangerous wars lay just ahead of the Gulf, both on and off camera. There would be Bosnian battlefields to photograph, New York executive suites to survive, Los Angeles courtrooms to win over—all destinations a long, long way from home.

CHAPTER TWO

Wanted:
An Adventurous Life

Arthur Kent comes from a family steeped in the business of journalism. Just as there are military families in which all members wind up in the armed services, and perhaps legal families where all members wind up practising law, this was a family of journalists and all members of it took the responsibilities and privileges of being a journalist very seriously.

–Opening trial remarks by Brian Lysaght,
Attorney for the Plaintiff, Kent v. NBC

Can you believe it? The guy gets all this amazing exposure in the war, and what happens? He says: "I don't want to be a TV star. I want to be a reporter."

–An NBC executive overheard at an industry dinner

GROWING UP in the province of Alberta, Canada, my siblings and I were acutely aware that A. Parker Kent, head of the family, was one of the leading newspaper columnists on our hometown paper, the *Calgary Herald*. I remember, as a child, answering the phone one evening: "Hello?"

"MRS KENT!" (I was insulted, but my broadcast news voice was still a dozen years away.) "PUT YOUR HUSBAND ON THE PHONE!" I thought I recognized the angry man's voice. From television, I thought.

"Yes?" My father generally spoke quietly, except in debate, into which he gladly entered with anyone. He winced at the violent crackle coming down the phone at him and held the receiver away from his ear. When the tirade subsided, he said, "I'm glad you've read my column, Mr. Mayor. Let's talk about it *tomorrow*. When I'll be in my *office*." He hung up, loudly.

"Calling me at home?" he said quietly. "Who does he think he is – the *mayor*?"

I laughed. Journalism looked like good fun. But I was cautioned by my father many times as I grew older. Don't punish your readers with your opinions, he would tell me. Disturb them with facts. Stimulate thought and get them angry, outraged if you can, but

9

not by bludgeoning them with strident language. Instead, serve them up a reasoned, truthful presentation of events and persuade them to get off their backsides and vote or write letters or simply think about their lives and their communities.

Journalism seemed to be a kind of mission, when he spoke about it that way – a crusade. I liked that idea a lot. Thinking back, almost all my childhood games were about riding to the rescue. If I was a soldier, I was rounding up Hitler's SS in the back yard. My best friend Dale and I would play Whirlybirds– helicopter pilots, after a TV serial of those days–which consisted of dropping in to save imaginary girls-in-distress from bad guys of all description. When it was Cops and Robbers, though, I was heavily into John Dillinger and Al Capone. Only when Eliot Ness came along, looking even meaner than his gangster-prey on "The Untouchables," did lawmen seem cool to me.

Sure, I was a child of early sixties television, most of it American TV series recycled on the CBC, filling up air time between hockey games among the original six National Hockey League teams. I had plenty of Canadian heroes, too, though. Men like John A. Macdonald, Canada's eloquent, hard-drinking, iron-willed first prime minister; Samuel de Champlain, the explorer; Louis Riel, western Canada's great revolutionary; and, of course, Eddie "Clear the Track" Shack, tough guy of the Toronto Maple Leafs, a human steamroller on skates.

Eddie's high-sticking came by way of television, too, and it was a graphic weekly display of rough justice. Beat up on my team-mates, his hawk-faced scowl suggested, and I'll smear your features into the ice. I liked Eddie a lot. His message came in loud and clear. He was crude but somehow honorable. And when he smiled into the TV cameras after creaming someone, the broken teeth told me that he'd taken as much abuse in his long career as he had dished out. But he always came back for more. That took heart, and I took early notice of heart.

And of the strange wonderful appeal of being an outsider, a rebel with a cause. Like the hero of my favorite TV show, which came on right after the hockey game. Over a second bowl of popcorn, it was "Wanted Dead Or Alive."

Title music: "Da-DAAA, da-da-da-DAAAAAAAH!" Spurs jangle on boardwalk. Hand rips wanted poster from wall. Cowboy smirks, tombstone eyes say "Cross me, and you die."

The very first time I saw Steve McQueen bring in the bad guys for a pocketful of greenbacks, I knew what I would be when I grew up. A Bounty Hunter! Imagine my disappointment on learning from my father that police departments had marginalized the trade.

*   *   *

My fondest childhood memories are of Saturday mornings at the newspaper. I would ride the bus into the city and meet my father as he finished work, which he steadfastly wound up by noon on Saturdays. I'd follow him from his office, where a battered old Underwood held center stage, through the bright city room full of strange, threatening-looking characters in white shirts and ties (these days reporters are more colorfully dressed, though, I believe, much less colorful in character). Next it was down the long gallery where my father would have to lift me up to look through the window and down on the giant roaring presses.

Those were hot-metal days, every letter typed out by hand and formed on to plates made from molten lead, over which a river of newsprint was transformed to words and pictures before your eyes. It was a vision of power, but I'll always remember the quiet courtesy with which my father handed over the four typewritten pages of his latest editorial to the typesetters, who stood in their blue coats, stained with ink, beside the clattering machinery.

His work done, my father would slip that week's editions of *Time* and *Newsweek* into the pocket of his woolen overcoat and lead me into the street, where in winter a blizzard might be blowing snow among the tall buildings. After supper, the Rangers and the Canadiens would face off on TV, and Sunday afternoon there'd be Walter Cronkite with "The Twentieth Century."

It was a visual history book I could read from the living-room floor, and the most influential of all my early encounters with journalism. My father would watch Cronkite with me and patiently answer endless questions about Hitler and Churchill and the Second World War...and the V-2 rocket attacks that dad and my mother Aileen survived during their army years in wartime Britain. ("We didn't have any of those Patriots to knock them down, either," my mother tells me now.)

My father didn't preach journalism at times like those, and it certainly wasn't any kind of proselytization that propelled all of us into the profession. (In addition to my older brother, Peter, and me, my sister Norma is a television reporter and anchor and my eldest sister, Susan, is a literary editor. Only Adele escaped the call, though by way of a career that demanded, arguably, even more hard work and sacrifice than journalism: she became a litigation lawyer, and is now a judge of the Alberta Court of Queen's Bench.) There was a simple reason we all went on to careers in advocacy and investigation in the legal, literary and reporting fields. We argued a lot at our house. Mostly about politics. And mostly in reaction to my father's very conservative views on everything from the Vietnam War (bomb the North into submission, he said) to miniskirts (rape-suits, he called them). But we were free to express our own opinions, which each of us did, frequently and at high volume.

A lot of ideas got tossed around at our house. It was a stimulating if not always peaceful atmosphere, presided over by two people of different faiths and backgrounds who loved each other totally.

They had both been with the Canadian Army during the Second World War. My father and his platoon had been posted to Britain to help fend off a possible German invasion, and my mother, a nurse and a lieutenant, followed soon after. They were married there during the war, and that always fascinated me–that with the world exploding around them, they had the confidence to start a family together.

"Well," my mother explains with a shrug, "we had to get on with things. Couldn't let a little creep like Hitler stop us, could we." As kids we all benefited from the patience and skill and warmth my mother developed as a nurse. She has never lost her optimistic, loving outlook on life, which offered the perfect balance to my father, who was forever seeing things with the darker wit and cynicism of a seasoned journalist.

As a couple, the time of year they most looked forward to was summer. They'd pack us all into our '56 Pontiac with a big canvas tent folded up on top, and drive us into the interior of British Columbia, where we could turn off the Trans-Canada Highway and find a place like Christina Lake, teeming with trout and surrounded by forest. Peter, ten years older than I, was the first to leave home. He ran away and joined the navy, where he promptly got his lights put out trying to be a boxer. Somehow, though, he always emerged as a kind of hero for his buddies (who called him Pee-Wee) and for me, on whom he never laid a rough hand. Peter tried the army, too, before tripping by accident into radio at CJOR in Vancouver. He was a natural; soon he was back in Calgary and up there on our own TV screen, reporting from the CFCN studios on the hill above our neighborhood.

Then Vietnam. In 1967 Peter went there for CFCN News, and suddenly I had a brother in the war. As he was filming his own reports on the other side of the world, flying with American fighter-bombers over the jungle, I sensed those first few delicious tingles of road-fever. I was fourteen, and reporting was right there in front of me—along with girls and my new black Honda 65. Steve McQueen had long since jumped the barbed wire on a stolen motorcycle in *The Great Escape*, trying to shake German soldiers off his tail. Now my own brother, McQueen's double, was appearing on our TV set in the infamous Living Room War.

Even in the peaceful suburbs of that most peaceful of cow-towns, Calgary, I sensed that war was real, not just the game with plastic guns that filled so many of my childhood days.

* * *

At school, all the Kent kids had drilled for The Bomb. Sirens blared and we walked home quickly, trying to take cover in the strongest corner of the basement within twenty minutes of the alert. I was fascinated more than scared by old films of mushroom clouds and by talk of radiation sickness. And I wondered how those strange long-bodied Russian bombers could ever make it all the way to the eastern slopes of the Rocky Mountains.

Rockets were more likely, we were told. There would probably be short-falls, warheads launched towards California that would come down instead on the grounds of the Calgary Exhibition and Stampede, wiping out not only "The Greatest Outdoor Show on Earth" but the entire city too.

For a kid, I guess, I had a pretty good understanding of why the Russians and Americans kept each other covered with atomic bombsights. Walter Cronkite and my father had filled me in. And the basic concept of death in war had personal meaning for me because of a cache of pictures and personal effects I kept in a drawer in the basement.

I had found the photograph of Uncle Clyde and his letters home in the old cedar chest, which was stuffed with family keepsakes. Clyde was my father's older brother. He died at the age of nineteen in a German artillery barrage at Passchendaele in Belgium, the climax of the third battle of Ypres, one of the most horrible battles in the history of human warfare.

The picture is in good condition, and I always had a hard time believing it was taken in 1915, just after Clyde's seventeenth birthday, when he left the family farm in Lacombe, Alberta, for the war in Europe. The letters, along with family lore about his death, made him a very real presence to me. My father recalled for me the night in November 1917 when Clyde's dog got spooked for no apparent reason, howling ominously and pacing around the farmhouse. My father and his parents, Jim and Isabel, couldn't figure out what was wrong with him, though Isabel had been awakened earlier the same night by a disturbing dream. She'd dreamt of being in the fields on a summer day. Clyde was calling out to her, over and over, but though she searched feverishly, she couldn't find him.

Weeks later, my father came home from school to find his dad, Jim, sitting in the corner with his head in his hands, weeping. A letter from the War Ministry was spread out on the table. His elder son had been killed in action, just about the time of Isabel's dream and the dog's distress.

As I approached my own teenage years, I found it inconceivable that anyone so young could die in battle. And unthinkable that it was happening still–the TV pictures from Vietnam showed me that war was far from obsolete. At no time did I go looking for war, but even at that age I felt certain I would see and experience something of it for myself one day.

Books and great storytelling began to fuel my imagination as I reached high school. Jules Verne's *20,000 Leagues under the Sea* and *The War of the Worlds* by H.G. Wells opened my mind to wild new possibilities, and I was held spellbound by the dark wonders of Edgar Allan Poe. Then one day at the corner drugstore I saw the book with the golden girl on the cover. Ian Fleming's *Goldfinger* swept me into the world of popular fiction. I read all the James Bond books, and thought that spying, with all the cars and casinos and fast women, would make a pretty decent substitute for Josh Randal's bounty hunter.

But then came *Animal Farm*. And *Lord of the Flies*. And *A Clockwork Orange*. If James Bond had inspired me to action, the works of writers like Orwell and Golding and Burgess challenged me to think about people and the powers that guide our lives—political beliefs, religion, magic and myths.

Not that I could articulate any of this. George Arthur Kent was the most stultifyingly average of students, invisible in the classroom and missing from the honor rolls. But I learned how to observe and listen. And then one day, when I was seventeen, I took the first real career decision of my life. I would try to become a reporter.

My father and my brother didn't push me into journalism; in fact, I don't remember discussing the idea with either of them more than once or twice. But it seemed like a good way to travel and confront some of the mysteries my books had revealed to me. (Besides, my part-time job at the local aquarium feeding tropical fish and taking care of Charlie the alligator taught me that manual labor wasn't my bag.)

But would higher education suit me any better? When I went east to Carleton University in Ottawa, I realized I had just squeaked into the place by the narrowest of margins. I had a lowly 60 per cent grade-point average. My most illustrious achievements in school up to that point had been rebelling against my third-grade teacher—shouting out loud in class that the pulling of ears was cruel and unusual punishment—and then, in eighth grade, setting the gymnasium on fire with a smoke bomb.

The difference at university, I told myself, was that I was now working towards a real *trade* and *profession*. My schooling, I convinced myself, was now *practical* and *relevant*. But despite the efforts of the best professors at the school of journalism, I ended the year as I had started it—60 per cent. I seemed destined to be the sixty-forty kid, not the gunslinger of a reporter I wanted to be.

Still, my teachers and my father encouraged me. Dad had retired from the newspaper by that time, and his colleagues decided to give me a break with a summer job. I got a shirt and tie and one of my brother's old sportsjackets and showed up for work at the *Herald*, circulation 110,000–every single copy of which, I was certain, would soon represent a reader with whom I would establish profound reportorial contact.

* * *

The day after I got my first byline (on a story that had to be extensively rewritten), one of my father's more liberal-minded colleagues slapped a file of Canada Grade A, small "c" conservative Parker Kent clippings on to my desk.

"Read these," he advised. "Your father is a good writer. An *irritatingly* good writer."

I tried to pick up some of his technique that first summer of my career. But in the end, I scraped through not by virtue of any inherited talent for writing (which I'm sure my disappointed editors believed would never manifest itself) but because of the instincts I had observed in my father's work and had tried to emulate. He was a skeptical person, and while he always favored the forces of law and order over those who called for civil disobedience, deep down he harbored a visceral distrust for all political organizations, government agencies and big businesses.

These, he felt, were either corrupt or incompetent, and any individual who blindly placed his trust in politicians, bureaucrats or ambitious businessmen was exposing himself to great danger. "Be your own boss," he frequently advised me, "and be your own man."

So stories about a citizen's quest for justice, or a good fight against city hall, invariably caught my interest. I loved to chase down tales of official neglect or chicanery and to use the victims' own words to turn the tables on the villains of bureaucracy or business.

One day a homeowner phoned to complain that a city cleaning contractor had filled her kitchen with great dunes of grit while sandblasting a bridge beside her property. She'd phoned the city works department. They told her to call the contractor. He hung up in her ear. The contractor did the same to me after snarling, "Write what you like–call me Donald Duck if you want to."

The night editor liked that line. "Donald Duck, eh?" he said cheerfully, pointing to a typewriter. "Go get 'em, kid."

And we did. The story was tight and tough and it went on the front page of the city section with the wiseguy contractor getting the "Donald Duck" label he'd asked for in big bold type, right in the headline. Next day, the city agreed to pay for cleaning up the house, presumably from the fee once destined for the quacking sandblaster.

That autumn I returned to university in Ottawa. My writing had improved, according to my professors. Feeling slightly more sure of myself, I landed a part-time job at the city's leading TV station, CJOH. The news director there, Max Keeping, was a friend of my brother's.

"You got your foot in the door," Max told me. "Now show me if you're anywhere near as good as Peter." Once again I went after stories of the little guy in the squeeze. Small-town newspaper publishers who were losing their newsprint supplies because the big mills deemed it was "uneconomic" to continue producing special stock for them. Personal stories, like that of an Inuit girl living and studying far from the Arctic, in a city that didn't seem to care for her. Or tenants thrown out of their apartments by greedy landlords.

Late one afternoon the station receptionist put a call through to me. A blind man was on the line complaining that a restaurant owner had refused to let him bring his seeing-eye guide-dog into the restaurant.

"That's terrible," I said, barely interested.

"Yeah," he said, "especially since there's a city by-law that says I can take my guide-dog into any restaurant I like."

I grabbed for a pen and said, "Where can I meet you, sir?"

Within an hour I was following man and dog back into the restaurant that had turned him away. I had a tape recorder in my briefcase, and my cameraman, Dominic Lacasse, was set up on the sidewalk, filming us as we walked into the place. As before, the restaurant owner turned the pair away.

"But isn't there some kind of law..." I asked him.

"I don't care about the city by-law," he said. "This is my place and there's no dogs allowed."

"But maybe you could..."

"And if you don't like it," he told me, "then you can get out too."

I got it all on tape and film, and called the mayor to make sure he watched our story on the late news. He wasn't pleased with what he saw. He sent a health inspector around to the restaurant the next day. The inspector found a few "hygiene problems" in the kitchen, ones that might mean closing the place indefinitely. Unless, of course, the owner showed some respect for the law. All the laws. Including those written to protect people with disabilities.

Suddenly, the owner was not only inviting the blind man and his dog back for a meal, but he offered to host the entire guide-dog users' convention, scheduled for the following weekend. Two hundred people, two hundred dogs and beefsteak on the house for all of them. I was feeling pretty pleased with myself when Max, my news director, called me into his office.

"That restaurant owner," he said coldly. "He's got a big fat advertising contract with our station." My face turned bright red. That was a big fat reason why I'd probably be looking for a new job.

"I just had a long meeting with the man next door," Max continued. He was pointing to the station's executive offices. I was sweating now. "Our general manager has told the guy to go ahead and fuck off if he wants to pull the account. But the guy's staying. THAT is why what you did was good reporting. You got him cold. He had no choice. Neither did we. We had to back you up."

I was relieved. But not for long.

"Now what have you got to top it for tonight?" Max asked me, and the hunt for a story began all over again. It would be many years before I would work for an editor as good and as uncompromisingly fair as Max Keeping.

It was a hectic life being a reporter and a student at the same time, but the learning and the seasoning came all that much faster. At work I was riding with homicide detectives, chasing errant federal Cabinet ministers and making clandestine appraisals of the latest strip acts down at Pandora's Box on Bank Street (all in the line of duty on the community-standards beat, of course). Experienced reporters and commentators at CJOH were criticizing my stories each day—heavy-weights like Charles Lynch, Douglas Fisher and Bruce Phillips. They were approachable and frank, and my contact with these prominent Canadian journalists got me wondering how long it would be until I encountered my heroes south of the border: Cronkite, Eric Sevareid, Mike Wallace and Charles Kuralt; Chet Huntley and David Brinkley.

At school, meanwhile, I was being steeped in theory and higher principles. My professors provided a microscopic survey of the industry, an investigation from a vantage-point high above the front lines of the business. It was a view that exposed many of the shortcomings and prejudices of the journalistic establishment, as well as its best achievements. Most important of all, the university environment encouraged me to read books.

To me, books—not just journalism texts, but all books—are the best way to explore the hidden meanings and complexity of society, to understand the need to consider all issues and conflicts from more than just one or two sides of a debate. My professors influenced my reading a lot, but my sister Susan became my most trusted guide to literature and good journalism. Through her I discovered Gore Vidal's novels, those masterpieces of historical journalism. And the delights of satire, from Voltaire's *Candide* to Hunter Thompson's *Fear and Loathing in Las Vegas*. If journalism is a craft of the street, these works proved that writing and storytelling could also reach for the sky.

* * *

Astounding all who knew me, I graduated in 1975 with first-class honors, tied with two other students at the top of the class. My first full-time gig came from Max at CJOH, and a year later I was off to CBC in Toronto, where my brother was about to become anchor of the evening newscast, "The National." My work was becoming strong enough to overcome the skeptics, even those who held the mistaken belief that Peter had helped me to secure my next posting as "The National's" correspondent for Alberta.

I was an aggressive and imaginative twenty-two-year-old newshound when I moved to Edmonton in 1977. The horizons of my hunting-ground had broadened. But the same indignation came back to me time and time again. The players in my stories got bigger, the victims more numerous, and the injustices more outrageous. Slowly, I worked at putting a sharper edge on my reporting.

Just before Christmas 1978 an American-owned oil giant, Amoco, put a brightly wrapped present of a story under my tree. One of Amoco's oil wells had blown out of control, threatening the environment of a massive area. My cameraman Mike Hunchak and I drove out to investigate. For "safety reasons" we were denied access to the well-site. Any information on the blowout, we were told, had to be obtained from Amoco's Canadian head office in Calgary. That office was about 250 miles from the well-site, and while that was far too great a distance for faithful observation and reporting, some of the hydrogen sulfide gas from the oil plume had made the trip easily. The rotten-eggs stench breezing through Calgary convinced a lot of people that the disaster was much worse than either the oil company or the government was letting on. We kept pressing hard for a visit to the well-site, and Amoco finally took us in.

It was an incredible sight–a 175-foot howling geyser of oil that was blanketing the surrounding forestland with a sickly yellow condensate of sulfur and other substances. Mike and I filmed the scene, and watched workers preparing the damaged well-head for a capping attempt by the legendary well-control expert from Texas, Red Adair.

But Amoco's public affairs officers severely restricted our movements. There could be no interviews with Red, they said, or any members of his team. And once we got that first story on the air, the company closed reporters and cameramen out completely. They cited safety concerns and convinced the Alberta provincial government's oil authorities–who were themselves worried about environmental and political fallout from the incident–to create a nine-mile exclusion zone around the well. Now the company and the government would decide what the public would know and when they'd know it.

We tried to reason with Amoco. If capping the blowout was as routine an operation as they claimed, and if, as the company's experts insisted, the environmental damage was not as bad as it appeared, then why hide the crisis behind a curtain of restrictions? Hell, we *knew* what was going on from Red Adair himself. He was staying outside the exclusion zone in the only hotel in the area; Mike and I had rooms there, too, and a table in the bar where Red and his boys threw back shots of Chivas Regal with us every night.

Amoco, however, stonewalled us. And so, armed with Red Adair's description of the well-site and tips on how to avoid the poisonous hydrogen sulfide gas, Mike and I set off on snow-mobiles with a couple of guides. Twenty frostbitten, bone-jarring miles later, we reached the well. The oily yellow condensate covered a much larger area than the company claimed. We filmed the mess, and cleared out before Amoco's hired PR guns could put the collar on us.

The company was furious. A major public-relations disaster was looming for them, and the wild well too was causing new problems. The blowout had caught fire and would now take longer to bring under control. A warning was soon issued by the government: anyone caught within the exclusion zone would be arrested by the Mounties and charged with trespassing.

Against all this, Red told us over a glass of whisky, "Don't give up yet, the best is yet to come." "The best" was the snuffing of the well. A steel drum packed with dynamite would be placed next to the flame and detonated. Starved of oxygen by the blast, the flame would be extinguished and the well-head could be capped.

At the hotel's New Year's Eve party, Red tipped us that the attempt would be made the following day. Mike and I slipped away in our four-by-four just before dawn and set up on a hillside overlooking the burning well. With bedsheets from the hotel, we made a tent for the camera that we hoped would blend in with the snow. Our camouflage attempt failed, however, and a Mounted Police helicopter dropped in on us just minutes before the flame was scheduled to be blasted. They told us to leave the area or face arrest.

"But I can see you've got a lot of gear here," one of the officers added, "so we'll understand if it takes you an hour or two to pack up and get out." Incredibly, they smiled and tipped their fur hats, and walked away. I could have sung the theme tune to "Sergeant Preston." The Mounties had issued their warning; they'd followed orders. But they clearly weren't too pleased about being used by an oil company to frustrate reasonable news coverage. Five minutes later, Mike got the shot we were after: the flash of the explosion, and the brilliant high candle of the well turning to smoke.

"That was a *terrific* shot!" Red yelled as he watched our story on the barroom TV that night. "Good goin' boys."

Across the room, three glum-faced Amoco officials sat staring at the screen. They were not pleased.

It was a great night to be a reporter.

CHAPTER THREE

Reporting the War on the Roof of the World

Arthur was closer to the problem side...more trouble all the time than no trouble.

—Testimony of Steve Friedman, former Executive Producer,
"NBC Nightly News"

I think Arthur's debates came as a result, again, of his passion to tell the best possible story he could.

—Testimony of John Stack, Foreign Assignment Editor,
"NBC Nightly News"

THE UNTAMED NATION of Afghanistan, in the heart of Asia, is about as far as a kid from Calgary can stray from home on this planet. Check it out on a globe, as I still do from time to time, some seventeen years after my first assignment there. It's located exactly on the far side of the world from the province of Alberta, Canada. And its terrain and people are from another space and time. That's what I loved about Afghanistan the first time I saw it–and survived it. Then, during my thirty or so subsequent visits there, stronger ties grew.

I first traveled to Afghanistan just after the December 1979 Soviet invasion. With backing from some stockbroker friends in Calgary, I was determined to film and produce my own independent documentary of the conflict.

I had left my comfortable posting as a network news correspondent at the Canadian Broadcasting Corporation to realize one of my dad's great ambitions. I was my own boss. And I was definitely going in at the deep and deadly end of the pool. At first things seemed pretty clear-cut to the greenhorn foreign correspondent: the Russians wore the black hats, while the Afghan resistance fighters, the mujahideen, were turbaned Hopalong Cassidys or Robin Hoods, noble warriors defending

23

their families from outside aggression.

As I returned year after year through the 1980s, the Russians were still up to no good (though at least they showed enough sense to get their forces out of Afghanistan in 1989). But the mujahideen came to appear more and more like their communist enemies in Kabul: corrupt and incompetent warlords interested only in power. Things got so bad that individual soldiers and guerrillas fought only for personal survival–the war eventually had no meaning beyond the struggle to see the next sunrise. Meanwhile, at least 15 million civilians were captives of foreign refugee camps or crowded towns or hideouts in the Afghan wilderness.

When I hitched my first ride on a camel train carrying rockets to guerrilla groups inside Afghanistan, I thought I had arrived on another planet. The people looked and dressed like something out of the adventure films I'd loved so much as a kid. But then I found out they were just like me. They needed their families, their homes. And the kind of peace I had always known. It fascinated and disturbed me that people could be forced to go to war to win something I'd had passed to me as a birthright. To continue financing return trips, I glued together several contracts with different companies, chiefly the *Observer*, my former employers at the CBC, and one of the big U.S. network news divisions that most aspiring young reporters regarded as an ultimate career goal: NBC News.

There's a lot they don't teach you in journalism school, and a war like this one reveals the missing lessons in a hurry. It's not just the little things, like how to recognize a camel that will bite you or a spy who will compromise you. It's the larger challenges, like how to scrounge food in a devastated countryside. How to distinguish incoming fire from outgoing. And how to deal with a desk editor half a world away whose morning paper tells him a story, based on second-hand information, considerably different from the one you've just lost forty pounds off your scarecrow-thin body to walk to and witness with your own eyes. My working battlefield was now the Hindu Kush, just as the Rockies had been my playground as a boy.

One rainy afternoon the mujahideen group I was traveling with was challenged by hidden sentries of a rival guerrilla faction.

A shot rang out, and we took cover. Armed only with rifles and shivering in the cold rain, our young commander wisely decided that we couldn't risk a firefight on hostile ground with night coming on. So we kept to the trees and crossed the valley well above the village our reception committee was guarding.

We had planned to take a much-needed rest there; instead, we now had to move on for the next 15,000-foot pass. That meant climbing through the night to reach the summit before dawn, since the morning sun would warm the snowpack at the top and increase the avalanche hazard for unwary travelers. In the quickening rain we climbed a rocky gorge, hoping to find shelter in a cave or one of the one-room teahouses that serve as way-stations in the lost wilderness of the Hindu Kush.

Darkness was falling three hours later as we emerged from the canyon. Above us, two steep ravines reached upward to the right and left, disappearing in thick, boiling cloud. The black sky pulsed with bolts of lightning; a sudden torrent of rain lashed down at us. There was panic among the guerrillas. They began to run up the slope between the ravines. One of them grabbed my arm and yelled something in my ear, but I too could now sense the danger; a strange deep rumbling sound, more threatening than thunder, was coming down at us from above.

I began scrambling for the high ground too. Luckily, a rock ledge appeared before us and we sheltered there as the roar of cascading water came at us from both sides. It was a flash-flood—the combined force of all the rains drenching the peaks and slopes above us. The flood-wash tumbled from the clouds and into view with explosive force, tossing tree-trunks and boulders on foaming crests that charged down the ravines on either side of us. These twin black rivers crashed together and surged down the canyon we had just climbed. At first awestruck and silent, the guerrillas then began to laugh.

"Our friends below," the commander said of the riflemen in the valley, "let's hope they were following us." He was laughing hoarsely, but his lips, like my knees, were quivering with fear.

All the same, we enjoyed an enchanting morning at the pass the next day. Rainbows arched over broad glistening snowfields, and under a clearing sky we could look down through granite walls at the lush green valley waiting for us below. The landscape that had nearly swept us to our deaths had now parted its black veil, rewarding us with a glimpse of its beauty. And in less than six hours our descent would lead us from the glacial cold of the peaks to the near-tropical warmth of the valley bottom.

Life in this wartime mountain world required a special kind of rhythm in your step, both physically as you crossed rock falls and footbridges, and mentally, as you crossed paths with people of a world unlike anything your comfortable Western culture had prepared you for. Walking for twelve continuous days across the roof of the world (the Hindu Kush is sister to the Karakoram and Himalayan ranges) is as rewarding as it is punishing: one morning you fall to your knees on a rocky pass, losing control of your lungs and your mind with the first symptoms of altitude sickness; hours later you are recovering on a meadow of soft, sweet-smelling grass while a shepherd and his son prepare for you a life-saving bowl of fresh yogurt. You know in your soul and in every aching joint how Marco Polo felt when he explored the same terrain.

* * *

In the valleys of the northeast in the summer of 1986, the war against Soviet occupation forces was on full boil, but somewhere between one-fifth and one-half of the population remained in the region rather than escaping down the refugee trail to Pakistan. This was a living, working community at war. For the horsemen who coaxed long trains of pack animals over the high passes, carrying semi-precious lapis lazuli stones mined in the north to market in the south, the possibility of being mistaken for a guerrilla arms caravan and strafed by Soviet warplanes was just another hazard to contend with. The farmers I met in the valleys had a lot of practice scooping up the kids who were playing in the fields and ducking into the nearest cave or dugout to wait out the bombing.

That I happened to be a foreigner and a journalist made life slightly easier for me. Mullahs and village headmen and local guerrilla commanders saw me as a prestigious dinner guest, and the country cooking was delicious—usually fresh vegetables and rice with roast or boiled lamb. Someone might offer to find me a porter or a horse to get my camera gear over the next pass, and I was always welcome to sleep in the mosque or in the home or bunker of some leading mujahed. But the rest was up to me; I had to figure out how to get into just enough trouble to shoot some good video without getting killed in the process.

I'm sure the Afghans got more than a few laughs out of me in this respect, though they were usually too polite to do it to my face. Ahmed Shah Massoud, the man I'd travelled so far to see, probably remembers me as the impatient foreigner who was always eager to photograph Russian planes bombing civilians but who couldn't keep his clothes clean in the wilderness. (I had room for only one change of clothes in a backpack stuffed with camera batteries and tapes, and never seemed to find the time to hand-wash anything in a stream but my underwear and socks.)

Unlike me, Massoud's men were the cleanest-looking mountain men you could meet, and aside from sharing the occasional pipeful of hashish, they were clean living, too. Their leader had become a living legend of the Afghan war. Some called Ahmed Shah the "Lion of the Panjshir" after his native Panjshir Valley—one of the loveliest in pre-war Afghanistan—and this soft-spoken man had in fact scored many successes against repeated offensives by the Soviet army. But my main interest in tracking him down was to profile his work as a grass-roots organizer, a mujahideen leader who earned the trust and support of his people by putting their interests before his own.

Making my way through his network of back-country bases, I finally met the Afghan the Russians called "enemy number one," and discovered a well-mannered man with striking features and a lively, almost inspirational gleam in his eye. His *nom-de-guerre* was "Massoud," Persian for "joy," and it said a lot about his whole approach to the war: tough work, but work that you might as well enjoy.

Hiding out in the wilderness with Enemy Number One put life on a different footing. As a boy I had always wondered what it would have been like to be on the run with Jesse James or Ernesto "Che" Guevara. Now I was finding out. When Massoud and his men weren't ambushing convoys or attacking army positions, he liked to structure the day: morning prayer at five; breakfast at eight; weapons drill and training planned around a one o'clock lunch; dinner promptly at eight.

Unfortunately, Red Army strategists had their own agenda,

and they were passionate believers in the element of surprise. The second morning I woke in Massoud's camp, we were enjoying mid-morning tea by the riverbank. The commander sat with a handful of his men round a rug someone had salvaged from a bombed-out house nearby; I leaned against the foam-padded plywood box that protected my camera.

I was listening to an Afghan student friend of mine, Kalir, translating the conversation when an evil rush of wind suddenly sounded through the treetops concealing us. In an instant the Russian jets were closing in, the dreaded roar of their engines echoing through the canyon.

The first explosion–a thousand-pound bomb hitting the other side of the river less than fifty yards away–caught me bending head-first into the hole in the ground some of the men used as a bunker. A gust of hot air seared across my backside and pitched me into the darkness. Landing on my head, I choked on a bitter taste in my mouth, like earth shot through a blast furnace.

I turned over, felt others crawling in around me. The dust cleared and twenty other pairs of frightened eyes gleamed in the darkness. I was scared. This was no movie, not like some chapter out of Conrad about testing my inner self against crisis and danger. The next page could be about the crushing of my body, the tearing of my flesh by shrapnel and rock and debris.

There was much coughing, and then the scream of the jets once again, getting closer, louder and louder, until it seemed one of the warplanes would fly right into the small breathing hole above us that spilled daylight into the cave. Then another deafening blast, sudden darkness, and rocks clattering off the face of the mountain. No one cried out, but the slight, whimsical mujahed named Kayoom was frowning now and shaking his head side to side, and two of Massoud's bravest fighters, Panah and Sayed Yaher, were hunkering down low and covering their heads–preparing, it seemed, to have the mountain collapse on top of us.

I felt I had to do something to keep myself from screaming out loud with fear. So I worked the camera. I focused the lens on the breathing hole and recorded the sound of a couple of the final bomb-runs. Soon our invisible attackers ran out of things to drop on us, and the rush of the river was all we could hear through the ringing in our ears.

The Soviet pilots often employed a devilishly effective trick at that point in an attack: they'd fly away for a while, then swoop back in again for one last unexpected strike. So the guerrillas gave themselves another half-hour in the shelter before we crawled out, squinting into the sunlight. Massoud appeared, strolling down from his own refuge somewhere upstream, and seeing me with my camera, he smiled and called out to me in the broken French he'd learned while studying architecture in Kabul:

"As-tu vu des rockets? Blancs et rouge—tres jolie, n'est-ce pas?"

I had to laugh—no one had been hurt, and that was reason enough for joy in Massoud's mind. Personally, I found photographing the aftermath of the bombing less reassuring: the two great kettles that had been boiling lunch for forty men had been blown over; shrapnel and dust and fallen leaves littered the earth all around; and my student friend Ammanullah was picking at one end of my camera case, which only an hour earlier had served as my backrest for tea. Two chunks of cruelly shaped bomb metal had sliced through the fabric and plywood of the box. The silver shards were still warm to the touch as Ammanullah presented them to me like trophies.

"Will you break camp and move?" I asked Massoud.

"No," he said. He picked up a stick and tapped it in his palm like a swagger-stick. "Mujahideen," he called to the men. "Forget the enemy for now. It's time for exercise, time for a swim. You too, Canadian. It will calm your nerves."

And off they went like boy scouts earning merit badges. It was foolhardy—there was always the chance of a second flight of jets coming down on us—but Massoud's cavalier spirit was infectious. The men leapt into the current, laughed at one another, and howled at the foreigner who was nearly swept away in the undertow. Massoud was right—the swim eased my tattered nerves. And it accentuated the sheer thrill of survival. I, too, had cheated the jets' high-tech assault. And next time, I'd know what to expect; I could be cooler and function better when it mattered most. That was the theory, anyway—chalk it all up to experience.

* * *

By 1988 more than one million Afghan civilians had been killed, mainly at the hands of the Soviet occupation forces. As I witnessed in Massoud's native Panjshir Valley, when the young pilots of the Russian air force grew tired of pounding heavily fortified guerrilla positions, they would turn their sights to easier prey–the farm families who fed and clothed the mujahideen.

On this landscape of destruction lived some of the most buoyant, purposeful people I have ever encountered. I was greeted with the magical warmth you'd expect in the lost kingdom the Panjshir Valley so much resembled, not the battlefield it really was. Open, smiling faces are my most vivid memory of the place, helping me feel at home and breaking through the barriers of language, religion and culture. Physically, I was becoming much like my Afghan cohorts: I'd lost weight, and I was as fit as I've ever been in my life. I could charge down a trail like a bobcat and keep pace with the strongest of the guerrillas. And I slept easier knowing I could carry my own camera in a headlong rush up a mountain slope.

The Panjshir, with its intoxicating beauty, drew me closer day by day. The war here had reached stalemate by that summer, with Soviet forces holding the lower half of the valley while civilians loyal to Massoud worked their crops along its upper reaches. Since the commander was concentrating his attacks in provinces to the north, resident guerrillas were doing little more than harrassing Soviet positions downstream, and the Soviets, busy fighting else-where in Afghanistan, countered with a limited but unpredictable bombing campaign. Red Army strategists wanted to suppress the native resistance groups and their families, and terrorized them into keeping their distance.

Journalists had seen much evidence after the fact of the ruth-less targeting of non-combatants by the Kremlin's military, but few of us had captured the Soviets on film with the smoking gun in their hand. I wanted to get the bombing of civilians on tape.

My chance came as I dozed in the mid-day heat in the guerrilla base at Safedshir ("White Lion" in Dari, the Afghan form of Persian). These riverside cave-dwellings were the headquarters of Gulzar Khan, a quiet but powerful-looking commander who was said to be married to the most beautiful woman in the valley. On July 30, 1986, we had returned exhausted from a week-long journey photographing Russian positions downriver. At noon Gulzar woke me in the cool depths of his cave; to everyone's amazement, I had been sleeping through the first ten minutes of a savage bombardment.

Stumbling outside, squinting in the harsh sunlight, I found the guerrillas pointing urgently at the sky. Two Soviet SU-25 ground-attack planes were flying in what appeared to be slow-motion directly overhead.

Massoud's men had not yet taken delivery of their first U.S.-made Stinger missiles, so only a single heavy machine-gun hammered away at the jets. It had no effect. The stubby, blade-like wings of the planes threw out bright crimson rocket trails, and explosions echoed throughout the canyon.

"They're hitting the mechanic's base," Gulzar shouted. "We'll be next."

My camera was now rolling, and I was awake and functioning, but I cursed myself for not taking my nap at the vantage point I'd chosen for just this kind of attack, an open rock ledge on the other side of the river. Over there, I'd have awakened at the jets' first howl.

But suddenly I had them in my lens—another pair of SU-25s, NATO code-name "Frogfoot"—and like glistening airborne sharks they wheeled down at our position. The mujahideen scrambled in panic for the "soufs" or cave-shelters. We were barely inside when two thousand-pounders hit just outside. I cursed again; the families out on the fields would be cowering now in their own shelters. That was the shot I needed to show viewers the reality of this war. (I seldom overcame this infuriating problem: either the bombing was too far away to photograph or it was right on top of us, forcing me underground.) For more than an hour we played chicken with the jets, ducking outside for a quick look, diving back in the cave when they roared in on us again. Thankfully, we all survived.

As we dusted ourselves off, I couldn't help feeling disappointed that I'd missed a chance to record the terror of the civilians. Then word came that more than ten people had been killed or wounded in the farm villages on the high plateau. Gulzar was reluctant to let me go there, since it would be a two-hour climb and there was no guarantee the warplanes wouldn't come back for more. But I told him there was no choice. The villagers, in keeping with Islamic custom, would bury their dead by sunset. I argued that if there was to be any kind of a meaning-ful record of the attack, the funerals had to be put on tape.

Gulzar gave in. He had two horses saddled, and he took me up the steep valley wall himself. As I urged my horse up the trail, the camera balanced across the saddle in front of me, I recalled the news report we'd heard on the short-wave the night before: Mikhail Gorbachev had announced that seven thousand Soviet troops would be withdrawn from Afghanistan–the first signal that Moscow had given up hope of taming this country and intended to pull out.

But as Gulzar and I reached the first bombed-out farm dwellings, a very different message from Moscow was displayed before us. The pilots had ravaged the place. This was not the result of a few misplaced bombs; the jets had systematically tar-geted farmhouse after farmhouse. So much for the public postur-ing of a retreating superpower.

A farmer named Mahman Najim was already salvaging blan-kets and pots from beneath the rubble. Covered head to foot in dust, he told us he'd been able to get his wife and four children clear of the house before it had been blown apart. We rode on, passing four more shattered homes, four more families reeling in shock. Then, on the highest plateau, walled in by the granite peaks, we caught sight of a gathering at the graveyard. The burials were already underway.

What little strength my horse had left took me at a gallop to the edge of the remote little cemetery. I slid from the saddle, and with a few gestures of respect to the fifty or so men and boys who were assembled around the grave, I went to work. I will never forget the expressions on their faces. There was great dignity in their grief, but shock and confusion were etched there too–why this vicious attack, and who was the foreigner falling upon them now, aiming his strange camera into their faces?

Gulzar arrived to reassure them. I kept shooting, aware that I was intruding but with no time for apologies. I was losing my light, and this tragic scene was crying out to be reported. Sorrow was deepest in the wide, watery eyes of a ten-year-old boy kneel-ing beside a fresh grave, his face freshly scarred by shrapnel. The earth had just received young Khushal's eight-year-old cousin, Khanaka. A space-age warplane had taken the life of a peasant farmboy, and Khushal, like the rest of us, couldn't fully comprehend why. Photographing him, I had trouble focusing through the tears in the camera's eyepiece. The mullah began his sad lament. A cold breeze ruffled brightly colored burial flags as the sun set behind the peaks.

We had to leave quickly; Gulzar was a trained paramedic, and there was work to do. Shah Mustapha, the father of the dead boy, was himself near death at the family's home nearby. We got there to find Gulzar's base doctor pulling twisted shards of bomb-metal from deep within the patient's body. He was doing this with no anaesthetic, his hands guided by the dim light of two kerosene lanterns. Shah Mustapha's wounds told the story. He'd been running to gather up his son when a bomb fell behind the boy. The blast had thrown Khanaka's body into Shah Mustapha's, and an outline of the son's form had been branded with shrapnel wounds into his father's chest and stomach. The boy's body had stopped the largest pieces of bomb metal, which would have killed his father—a fate that Shah Mustapha in his agony now begged for.

Gulzar and his doctor fought for hours to save the man. At one point, after they'd probed a deep slash in Shah Mustapha's chest and found a chunk of shrapnel, they asked me to pull it out for them while they kept the wound open. Carefully, I gripped the black tip of the metal shard with a pair of forceps. Our patient moaned horribly as the fragment came free in my hands. Somehow, I managed to avoid getting sick. The man needed all of us.

Finally, shock stopped the bleeding, and Shah Mustapha was saved. Our sense of accomplishment strengthened the bond of friendship I'd formed with Gulzar through the horrible events of that day.

I spent that night in Gulzar's own home not far from there. His daughter, a girl of two, had forgotten the day's excitement by the time we showed up, and she played with us happily. But the normalcy of life in Gulzar's home somehow accentuated my gloom over the random violence of the war. I felt their isolation, their vulnerability as never before.

After I left the Panjshir, I often thought of that tidy home kept by the most beautiful woman in the valley for Gulzar, one of the bravest men in the Afghan resistance. The following spring Gulzar's wife was killed in a Soviet bombing raid. Heartbroken, he eventually remarried. Two baby boys were born, and the family held on inside Afghanistan. Then news came that Gulzar himself had been killed while training his men; a faulty Chinese-made grenade had blown up in his hand.

I keep a picture of my friend on the wall beside my desk, a memento of a proud family man who believed in freedom, but also a reminder that there are two more graves I must visit whenever the war lures me back to the Panjshir.

* * *

"The Soviet Army does not engage in attacks on peaceful civilians."

These are the words of Lieutenant-General Boris Gromov, commander of Soviet forces in Afghanistan. He'd been ready for a "hostile" question such as mine. Assembled before him in the ballroom of the Kabul Intercontinental Hotel were 250 journalists, mainly from Western countries, all of them searching for a story from the man who had conducted much of the abortive Soviet ground campaign and who was now, in May 1988, beginning to turn his occupation force around and send it home.

"But General Gromov," I said, "I've seen your aircraft bomb civilian homes."

The small rugged man in uniform shifted impatiently in his chair. "You talk as though you have traveled with these opposition groups," he said.

"I have. Many times. And the aircraft I saw bombing farms and villages in the countryside carried Soviet markings."

The general seemed to understand even before he heard the Russian translation. He squared his shoulders and lifted his chin. The handsome face framed with neatly groomed blond hair revealed no emotion to the crowd of reporters and cameramen, who waited in silence for a response. My heart beat faster; I didn't like the cold glare I was getting from the general's special-forces bodyguards.

"If you have visited the provinces with the Soviet military," Gromov began, "then you will have seen us helping the Afghan people. If you have gone with the opposition forces, then you have been a victim of propaganda." He quickly took another question, and the confrontation was over.

The answer, of course, was unsatisfying, but I could hardly expect Gromov to turn this, his first brush with President Gorbachev's new policy of glasnost, into a confessional. At least he had sparred with the truth, more than I would later get from Chinese and Romanian and even American generals in other "theaters of operation."

So after the news conference I offered a handshake to General Gromov, which he courteously returned. But his eyes showed that he saw the look of the enemy about me, for he knew I had lived and traveled with the fighters who had killed more than fifteen thousand of his own men.

Then, suddenly, I was the one on the hotseat. My brother Peter wasn't pleased with my performance.

"What good does it do if you try to nail the guy and wind up getting us thrown out of the country instead?"

My brother and I had come to Kabul together. On this occasion Peter was doing the reports for NBC, while I wrote for the *Observer* and assisted my brother as his field producer. It felt wonderful to team up; neither of us had ever dreamed we'd work together overseas. But things were off to a rocky start because of my charge at Gromov. From all corners of the room Russian and Afghan government security men kept us covered with hostile stares as we broke down the camera gear.

Of course Peter was right—the Gromov encounter gained us little and made us vulnerable to added scrutiny. But as one of only three reporters in that room who had ever traveled the Afghan countryside, where in several provinces virtually every village capable of sustaining the mujahideen had been leveled by the Soviet military, I felt a responsibility at least to register our own journalistic resistance to the public-relations offensive Moscow was using to disguise its retreat.

Fortunately, the Russians let us continue our coverage unhindered. Some officers welcomed the chance to turn the sentiments of pro-mujahideen Westerners. This was a radically new experience for me—covering the war from the perspectives of the Soviets and the Afghan regime and doing it with a full field-production unit. (A couple of Texans, cameraman Jim Bowen and soundman Terry Stewart, were shooting for Peter and me.)

After the sad conclusion of my journey with Massoud's Panjshiris, I had followed the mujahideen elsewhere in Afghanistan in 1986 and 1987, mainly working on contract for the *Observer* and NBC. Now I was balancing my knowledge of the guerrilla-held countryside with the Soviet side of the story, and contributing my experience to my brother's reporting. And it was a great opportunity to watch and learn from a man who is widely acknowledged to be one of the finest TV journalists working anywhere.

* * *

With a growing number of freelance assignments under my battery belt, I was becoming an NBC "regular-irregular." Phoning the desk in New York or dropping into the London bureau for equipment and cash, I was entering the network's outer orbit of information. Or gossip—the atmosphere under the network's new GE managers was clouded with nervous speculation over the conglomerate's real ambitions for the place.

Two years after GE's purchase of the network, people at NBC News were feeling the full weight of the conglomerate's corporate culture. And they were reacting with paranoia. In time, events would prove that their fears, though perhaps exaggerated, were not misplaced.

My foreign news contacts in New York explained that it was pressure from GE that had slashed the budget for "1986," the weekly NBC News program co-hosted by Roger Mudd and Connie Chung. My brother Peter had been a correspondent on the show. Roger spoke out against GE-style budget-crunching and left NBC. At the time, during my first Afghan shoot for the network, Peter hadn't said much about the affair, but by May 1988, when we traveled to Kabul together, he confirmed many of the horror stories coming out of New York.

Like the thinking of the network's GE-appointed president, Robert C. Wright.

"Wright had a great idea for boosting ratings," Peter told me. "He wanted Bill Cosby or Don Johnson to anchor news specials."

"The Cosby Show" and "Miami Vice" were two of NBC's biggest-ever hit shows, responsible for a big chunk of the network's $300 million profit in 1985, the year before the GE takeover.

But Cosby and Johnson weren't journalists. They were entertainers. The distinction appeared to be lost on Mr. Wright, a quirk that would figure, years later, in my own battle with GE-installed management.

"And he wants to form a PAC [political action committee] to take on the FCC [Federal Communications Commission] in Washington."

This concept had reached the London bureau in the form of a *New York Times* article pinned to the bulletin board. Mr. Wright had proposed forming a PAC, a pressure group, the scourge of Capitol Hill, to force the FCC to allow the U.S. networks to own and profit by a greater share of their own programming.

It was a big money issue, important to NBC's bottom line and, therefore, to job security. Mr. Wright wanted everyone at NBC, including journalists, to sign up for the PAC. "Employees who elect not to participate in a giving program of this type should question their own dedication to the Company and their expectations," read Mr. Wright's quote in the *New York Times*.

The network trembled. In the News Division, most staffers, Peter and I included, had been trained from their first day on the copy desk to recognize that becoming politically active, especially on behalf of a corporation, would compromise a journalist's ability to report accurately and freely.

But the GE hierarchy had no real experience in broadcasting or journalism. Bob Wright had great business credentials: the GE financial subsidiary he had run just before his transfer to the president's post at NBC, GE Finance, had accounted for almost half of the GE empire's assets at the time of the NBC acquisition. He combined the toughness and skill of successful corporate accountancy with the legal disciplines essential to big business.

And he did it Jack's way. Bob Wright was Jack Welch's understudy, his creature. I remember from my earliest days at NBC that whenever one of our own executives in the News Division had bad news to break to the troops, it was always framed in language about how the big tough guys on top, Jack Welch and Bob Wright, would accept nothing but the best, the meanest, the most cost-effective and profitable solution.

From budget-cutting to program-making, the GE creed was the only creed. Sadly, that creed had no cross-references with journalism. But then GE had never come into contact with the profession–except during the frequent squalls of negative publicity generated by their many other businesses. And as their appointments to News Division management clearly showed, they favored executives who talked cutbacks rather than news principles. Jack Welch and Bob Wright showed no inclination to gain a mid-life education in reporting ethics and standards.

* * *

At the same time, in those early years NBC represented a great opportunity to me. In Afghanistan I polished my reporting and technical skills. After Kabul I set up a mini-bureau in Peshawar, Pakistan–the mujahideen groups' sanctuary–to service the CBC, the *Observer* and NBC. This was more than just a room in the Pearl Continental Hotel: I hauled forty cases of equipment in from London and up the potholed GT road from Islamabad. I had everything I would need to package and transmit television footage and stills of the war.

Preparing for each trek into the Hindu Kush was almost as exhausting as the journey itself. The challenge was to fit all the lenses, tapes, batteries, cables and tools necessary for several weeks' shooting into just two backpacks, since in an emergency I might have to drag all the gear to safety on my own. There was only enough room for one change of clothes. But what I lacked in hygiene and wardrobe I made up for in safety: I had first-aid gear, wound dressings and pain-killers; eyewashes and tension bandages and food supplements for the starvation diet on the trail. I had emergency cash, letters of passage from influential guerrilla chieftains, and my custom-made ID cards printed in both Afghan languages, Dari and Pashto, a sort of plasticized pronouncement of my status as a harmless Canadian sugarfoot in need of a meal and a place to sleep.

My mountaineering buddies from Banff used to laugh at me. You prep as hard as we do for an expedition to K2, they'd tell me, but there's a little bombing and gunplay when you reach the summit. I could get frostbite and altitude sickness and fall off a cliff, and get shrapnel wounds in the bargain. Crazy, they said. But a prepared crazy, I answered–I was ready. As ready as ready could be.

Over the years, as I journeyed from one province of Afghanistan to another, the increasing pointlessness of the war became deeply dispiriting. Instead of progressing towards a decisive military or political solution, the conflict was spiraling into a deeper, bloodier abyss. Even my driver in Peshawar, Munchi, was uneasy about the dangers.

"Last night my wife say to me–maybe Kent is killed this time." Munchi is a slender five-footer with a quiet smile and a voice surprisingly deep for a man of his size. (My spine still aches from countless hours in the passenger seat of his battered old Toyota, which, mercifully, was car-napped by tribesmen in the Khyber Pass and held for a ransom Munchi couldn't afford to pay. He was forced to find a newer Toyota, and its shock absorbers proved far less damaging to my tailbone.)

"You be careful," Munchi told me whenever I returned from beyond the Northwest Frontier. "Too many Afghan people no good, no good for you."

Periodically, I would fly to Delhi, India, where you could catch an old Tupolev airliner coaxed into the sky by Afghan Ariana Airlines. A few hours later I'd be on the ground in Kabul, on the other side of the war, surrounded once again by remaining units of the Soviet army and the Ruritanian uniforms of the Afghan government forces.

When I arrived there in November 1988 the entire front-office staff of the Kabul Intercontinental Hotel greeted me at the front door. They'd got my telex from Delhi. They could hardly have missed it–only two other guests were expected. Sad times, their thin smiles told me: not only had the war chased off tourists and business people, but now even the journalists were busy somewhere else.

I had my pick of any of the 197 empty rooms, though the west-facing side wasn't recommended. Too many mujahideen rockets launched from Paghman, a town ten miles to the west, had been falling short on their trajectories into the city. I inspected the gaping hole in one of the hotel's penthouse suites and took the management's advice: third floor, facing the city and the airport. The balcony was a terrific camera platform, and a back-hander to the desk clerk got me a key to the room across the hall, just in case the rocket-duels in the west became too exciting to miss.

Here again, the brutal symmetry of the war: now civilians on both sides would endure haphazard rocket barrages. The Soviets had imported a new weapon into Afghanistan, SS-1C SCUD B missiles—crude, inaccurate devices whose two-thousand-pound explosive warheads terrorized countryside communities supporting the guerrillas.

The Soviets, of course, had no interest in demonstrating this murderous weapon for Western news cameras like mine, so I was forced to stake out their base on Kabul's western outskirts in the hope of getting a SCUD launch on tape. (Shivering in the early winter chill, I had no way of knowing that two years later I would wait in much the same way on the receiving end of SCUD missile attacks—launched by Saddam Hussein's Iraqi forces.)

Each day I concealed myself among the giant kilns of the city's brickyard, training my lens on the Russian tanks and artillery scattered on the slopes a half-mile away. But the Soviets that month were firing the occasional SCUD only at night, accentuating the weapon's capacity for terror by forcing the guerrillas and country people to face the threat of sudden death in the darkness. And since my watchers from KHAD, the Afghan secret police, ensured that I was in the hotel each night, I never managed to tape a SCUD in Kabul. But the artillery and small-bore rocket exchanges that were routine on that side of town made terrific footage, as did the many helicopter gunships that would roar suddenly into view, skimming the desert like giant killer dragonflies.

* * *

One morning, I was stirred from a deep sleep by the hotel operator, jangling the phone beside my head with urgent short bursts. The Soviet embassy was on the line. It was one of their diplomats, calling to say that a request I had made weeks earlier had finally been approved. I was going flying with General Gromov's army.

The crew on board the Mi-8 transport helicopter were polite and professional, but even after we had cleared the Russian artillery bases on Kabul's southern perimeter, they still wouldn't tell me exactly where we were going. So I checked the cockpit compass and took some bearings from the terrain. "Logar," I said, "...we're going into Logar."

The pilot, Wing Commander Alexander Chesnokov, smiled and nodded. The man behind me wore an even broader grin. Michael Eustafiev was the Kabul correspondent for TASS, the Soviet news agency. But he was also a fluent English-speaker, and I'd first met him in his former capacity as translator for the Soviet embassy in Kabul: Michael had been the intermediary for my confrontation with General Gromov the previous spring.

"Yes, Logar," he said into his headset. "Just wave if you see anyone you know."

Mike and I could joke openly about our experiences on either side of the war. He knew all about my many journeys with the guerrillas, but he was one of Gorbachev's "new thinkers." With the help of some of his liberal-minded colleagues at the other key Russian news agency with a bureau in Kabul, Novosti Press, Mike had persuaded the army to take the Canadian "mujahed" out for a little re-education. But he couldn't have known how extensively I had traveled Logar province with the mujahideen. And that Asadullah Falah, one of the most effective guerrilla leaders there (and a crack shot with a shoulder-fired, heat-seeking Stinger missile), was a close friend of mine.

The helicopter roared angrily but was reassuringly stable. Still, the ride I was seeing through the viewfinder and feeling in my legs as I stood in the open doorway was one of the wildest of my life. We were flying so low and so fast that the nose-down attitude of the chopper convinced the eye that the big machine was a split-second away from plowing into the stony terraced fields.

Mike's voice crackled through my headset: "The pilot says you must forgive him for flying so low. We have to be on guard against the Stingers."

You bet, I thought to myself—hug those hillsides, Alexi. It would be thoughtless of me to allow Asadullah to discover my remains in the wreckage of a Russian helicopter. He'd curse me for going over to the other side, however temporarily, but he'd never forgive himself for inadvertently putting my lights out for good.

Beside us flew another transport, and to the rear a pair of the infamous Mi-24 gunships. These flying battleships had flown virtually unchallenged in the early years of the war. But the gunships' battleworthiness had been severely curtailed by the guerrillas' Stingers; these pilots, unlike their predecessors, really had to risk their necks for their supper. I had a hard time sympathizing with them, though, because the once-fertile landscape passing beneath us was now a dead zone, burned dry and made empty by war.

Our mission was to drop ammunition and food at an "eagle's-nest" lookout high above guerrilla country I soon recognized to be smack in the middle of Asadullah's turf. The chopper touched down—a huge whirling dragonfly on the precipice—and I leapt out to get some shots of the helicopters from the soldier's-eye view.

Most of the young Russian commandos waiting there looked desperate enough to throw Mike and me off the mountain so they could take our places on the ride back to Kabul. But one of them took me by the arm and pointed a cautioning hand to the trench line on the ridge above us.

"He says not to go up there," Mike said. "Snipers sometimes climb up from below." This I doubted; Asadullah's men were far too practical in the pursuit of staying alive. But I was willing to take the young Russian's word for it. As we lifted off, there was no mistaking the look of abandonment on the unhappy faces of the commandos. The hostile Afghan hills seemed to swallow them up as we soared down the steep mountainside towards Kabul.

With white-hot flares spitting from the belly of his chopper to confuse the heat-seeking Stingers, Alexander tried to interest me in the plight of Soviet servicemen in the war.

"We came to help these people," he said. "We're sorry for the Afghans that have died on the other side, but many of our friends have been killed, too."

As we flew over the smoking kilns of Kabul's brickyard, though, the words of one of the workers I'd met there came back to me: "May these Russians get out of our country, and God willing, may they never return."

CHAPTER FOUR

Spotlight on Tragedy

I can just about manage to shoot the pictures, Art. But don't
make me look at them. Please.
    —*A network cameraman drinking off a day at work in Armenia*

THE PHONE WOKE me the morning after my flight with the
Red Army. Breaking news was about to put my reporting career
into overdrive.

"Arthur, have you heard about the earthquake?"

It was Frieda Morris, NBC's London bureau chief. The quake
in Armenia, in the southwestern Soviet Union, had been leading
every newscast on my short-wave for two days.

"Yeah. Sounds awful."

"You're going. We need all the help we can get."

I'd heard from the guys at NBC London that Frieda left little
room for negotiation when scrambling her correspondents and
crews to a big story. And the urgency in her voice told me the
quake, which was reported to be a big one, had registered a maxi-
mum "ten" on the TV-news scale. Since both the *Observer* and
the CBC would likely need help in Armenia too, I packed
and rushed off for the airport. Luckily the mujahideen rocket
launchers were idle that morning.

As the old Tupolev airliner corkscrewed up and out of Kabul,
I had mixed feelings about my new assignment. And not just
because of the shooting pain in my jaw, the result of breaking a
tooth the night before on a bone fragment lurking in my steak at

43

the weekly American embassy barbecue. I was worried that all the Afghan material I'd shot in the previous weeks might be eclipsed by the quake and other big foreign news stories.

Sure I was curious about the Soviet Union—the giant awakening to Gorbachev's reforms. But that was "mainline" correspondent country, hardly the place for a tramp reporter/cameraman just out of Afghanistan. I was still hoping enough network crews and correspondents would arrive to free me up for an edit deck and a dentist's chair back home.

I hadn't even cleared customs in Moscow when that dream was shaken by a different kind of tremor, one right out of NBC headquarters in New York.

"AR-toor. Please hurry!" It was Yuri, one of NBC's Moscow bureau drivers. He was pointing anxiously over his shoulder. "Your brother Pyotr is here. And BRO-kov, too." His thick eyebrows rose for emphasis as he repeated, "BRO-kov!"

Tom Brokaw, NBC's anchor, here from New York? And Peter in from his reporting base in London? The mountain of equipment cases on the sidewalk outside the airport told the rest of the story—several full camera crews had just pulled in. I had started the day as a one-man band, and now, as night fell, I was joining the network orchestra.

Frieda Morris had beat us all into Moscow. She was downtown in the cramped NBC bureau putting the game plan together, juggling three telephone conversations when I walked in. "You've got an hour to get your gear together. The foreign ministry's agreed to fly us in...don't take any more gear than you have to...no telling when you'll be back...there could be fifty thousand people dead down there."

My brother told me he had been covering the story from Moscow for several days, mostly with still pictures and footage from Soviet news agencies. The quake had devastated villages and towns north of Yerevan, the capital of Armenia, and search-and-rescue teams from around the world were struggling through the Soviet bureaucracy to get in and help. No Western reporters were there yet. We'd be the first.

Sleep didn't come easy on the flight down to Yerevan, even though we didn't get off the ground until two o'clock in the morning. I paced up and down the aisle of the big Aeroflot jetliner provided by the Soviet foreign ministry. What, I wondered, could I possibly contribute to this team?

Two of NBC's top cameramen, Richard Burr and Ken Ludlow, were among the dozen NBC staffers on the plane. Tom would do the main story, with Peter covering the companion piece. An old friend of ours, CBC Moscow correspondent Don Murray, was there for the Canadian network. It looked as though I'd be an extra hand—a third lens and, if necessary, another voice should the story become a monster, requiring broader story packaging for both networks.

"Just shoot whatever you can and stay loose," was my brother's advice. It felt great to be with him again; it helped ease the shock of winding up with the high-rollers from New York. Up to that time the only contact I'd had with Tom Brokaw and his foreign producer, Marc Kusnetz, had been over a long-distance phone line.

"Great stuff from Kabul," Tom told me that night. He had introduced a story I had fed out of the Afghan capital by satellite only a few days earlier. He and Marc were reassuringly open, and there was a mood of quiet determination aboard the plane. NBC News was leading the other two commercial network news divisions in the U.S. ratings. The flagship "Nightly News" broadcast and its anchor were at a competitive high-point. I could sense it like a warm rush—the feeling that I was bonding with the team. It's a connection the network bosses and anchors are quick to encourage in young staffers. It inspires enterprise, risk-taking. With Tom and my brother hot on the trail of the story, I wanted nothing more than to contribute, to help NBC keep its edge. But we were all acutely aware that the new owners of the network were watching their profit and loss statements closely, with their fingers on the budgetary trigger.

General Electric's tough-talking chairman, Jack Welch, had stated publicly in 1988 that he would own only those businesses that were market leaders in their respective fields. The harsh, unyielding GE management culture was contributing, in the view of many of our colleagues, to a growing sense of insecurity at NBC, irrespective of the network's dominant position. Advising us not to be too comfortable with success, Mr. Welch and his appointees injected a big dose of uncertainty into NBC, particularly into the

News Division, resulting in a devastating loss of morale. I had sensed it even down the phone line from Afghanistan. Now, among all these NBC News regular troops, I could practically taste the tension.

Ironically, our flight carried representatives of another institution plagued with confusion and uncertainty–the government of the Soviet Union. Guiding us were three staffers from the office of Soviet Foreign Ministry spokesman Gennady Gerasimov, the man who had opened the door to the quake for NBC. All three men seemed a little puzzled by the strength of our contingent and the sophisticated gear we'd brought with us. These were the early days of glasnost, and in their minds the workings of U.S. network television typified capitalism's bizarre blend of luxury and turmoil.

One of the foreign ministry men told me that dozens of networks and newspapers from the West had been telexing his office pleading for entry visas to Armenia.

"Why must ALL the American television companies rush into our country?" he asked. "Surely it would make more sense for you to supply your pictures to everyone. That way the others could work somewhere else and share with you, like a co-operative."

I looked at him long and hard to see if he might be joking. But no, he was in fact wondering why U.S. network television news couldn't be organized along the lines of a collective farm, with all the reporters and editors and managers happily discarding the industry's tradition of competitive excellence in favor of some kind of government-supervised production scheme. I wasn't surprised to hear such a suggestion from a Russian communist–there was a funny kind of totalitarian naïveté about it. But there would be no smile on my face two years later during the Gulf War, when American generals and statesmen would herd us into just this kind of news corral.

As we stepped off the plane in Yerevan, we knew we were making a remarkable foray behind the Iron Curtain. This was one of the most sensitive corners of the Soviet Union, as the communist superpower stood at that time. Western reporters had been frustrated in their attempts to cover the bloody clashes between Armenians and the people of neighboring Azerbaijan; now here we were, and with a much larger, more immediate story combining a Soviet emergency with a huge international aid effort. Trouble was, most of us hadn't slept in at least two days. There was no telling when we'd next see anything resembling a pillow and a bed. Food would be scarce, but we'd be first in line for heaping helpings of human misery and bureaucratic obstruction.

"I love this business," said Richard Burr. He wore the sardonic grin of a veteran cameraman—a weary smile of forbearance put on by most news nomads as they lurch exhausted into yet another disaster.

"Mustn't complain," chirped soundman Derrick Herincx, whose bald cranium had years earlier earned him the nickname "The Skull." "Unloading the gear will cheer us up."

As we clambered aboard an immense military helicopter, it was pretty clear that the earthquake-relief effort hadn't been as lucky: squadrons of transport aircraft sat idle on the tarmac as far as the eye could see.

"Why aren't they in the air, hauling supplies?" Brokaw asked quietly. Word had already filtered out of the area that people were dying while their would-be rescuers were delayed at customs. We braced ourselves for the worst, and that's exactly what we flew into.

The city of Leninakan looked as though a drunken giant had stumbled through town. Huge footprints of devastation scarred districts that seemed otherwise untouched. We made several low passes over apartment complexes that had fallen in on themselves. A few heavy-lift vehicles were moving among the hills of rubble, but mainly the debris was alive with the figures of human beings.

Through the lens, they looked like chain gangs: people condemned to pick through quarries of shattered brick and timber. To the east, things were worse. The town of Spitak might have been a bombed-out Afghan town passing beneath our rotor blades; practically every building had been ripped apart.

A cold, gloomy determination gripped our team as the helicopter landed at the edge of town. We'd all seen death before, but this looked like a nightmare. We would have to work fast; if we spent more than thirty minutes on the ground here, we would jeopardize the opportunity to shoot additional footage back at Leninakan, and might even miss the return flight to Moscow.

We broke into teams and fanned out on foot. Tom and one crew worked the near ground around Spitak's flour mill. The towering silos had folded in on themselves like an accordion drooping in the middle, and several search teams were climbing among the ruins. Peter took a second camera team and stalked off towards some collapsed housing, while I flagged down a passing car and climbed in the back with my camera—and with our "secret weapon" from NBC Moscow, production assistant Madeleine Lewis.

A lovely young Welsh woman with dark, arresting eyes, Madeleine added two key ingredients to our blitz on Spitak: fluent Russian and an adventurous nature. She asked the weary Armenians in the front seat to drive us into town, and never stopped asking questions on the way.

As the car crept along streets bordered by mountains of rubble, the driver told us that three-quarters of Spitak's population of 25,000 was either dead or missing. Help had been slow in coming. Foreign search-and-rescue teams had just reached town, four full days after the earthquake. Very little food and clothing had arrived yet.

"This is a city of the dead now," the driver told us. He was looking for a tractor to help clear debris from his own home. His wife was buried there, "yes, dead by now, I think." A black tear ran through the grime on his face.

We reached a three-storey apartment block that had been cracked open like an eggshell. We stopped, and I started shooting. The front half of the building lay in a heap before us, revealing the walls and ceilings and floors at the rear. Furniture dangled in mid-air from some apartments; bright pictures clinging to the walls at crazy angles spoke of everyday life before the quake. A dozen men and boys, cloaked in dust, tossed bricks aside and pulled at steel reinforcing rods.

Only one man had a tool to work with—a tablespoon. He scratched away, shifting debris a handful at a time. Both Madeleine and I were silent. The professional observer in each of us was recording the picture, noting details. But we were more than that, two human beings looking into a massive tomb and catching the scent of decaying flesh in the wintry air. We moved from house to house, asking about the people who had lived at each address, collecting a horrible anthology of tales: wife or husband missing, two of three children dead, everyone dead. Entire families were buried beneath their homes with only a few neighbors left to speak for them or dig their bodies free of the ruins.

The streets were a gallery of human despair and hopelessness. Among the recognizable remains of dwellings and schools and offices, the loss of life was more disturbing–the living had every-thing in common with the dead, with one exception. Only the mad random blow of the earthquake, impossible to predict, divided the people of the town between those lucky enough to have been outside at the time and those doomed by being at home or at work.

Several times Madeleine pointed out battered clocks in the debris, their faces frozen at the hour of sudden death–11:41 in the morning. Schools and public buildings had been full; their shoddy walls of brick and cement had cracked and tumbled within a single minute of furious upheaval. A sharp aftershock four minutes later killed or trapped scores of survivors from the initial tremor.

We came across a team of French search-and-rescue specialists standing sullenly over an immense pile of concrete blocks.

"There was a music school here," said the team leader. "Ninety children were in the class. We've found none alive."

I focused and rolled. Dogs sniffed around two craters that had been cleared into the mess, but the animals looked lost and they whined anxiously. Above them the rescue team stood in their brightly colored uniforms, ready to climb in to unearth survivors with picks and crowbars and breathing gear. The look on their faces said that wasn't going to happen. No life stirred beneath us. Panning right, my lens found a local man picking through the rubble, and I kept rolling as he grabbed something and tossed it on to a slab of concrete. I followed the object and zoomed in on it–a child's arm, still wearing the blue sleeve of a sweater.

I got the shot, then turned away, a dry horrid taste in my mouth. We looked at one another–Madeleine, me, the French searchers—all of us a bit lost about what to do next. The helicopter engine groaned to life in the distance.

"See those soldiers over there?" I asked Madeleine. Nearby, a few troops were leaning on their Kalashnikovs.

"I know," she said. "They're just standing there. I haven't seen any of them doing anything to help out."

That was part of the story that clearly needed to be told, and as Madeleine and I hurried back to the landing site, we decided to ask the others if we might stay behind in Spitak. Surprisingly, Victor had no objections, even though he could leave no one from his foreign ministry team to supervise us. We would be on our own – unheard-of freedom for Western reporters in this part of the Soviet Union.

I handed over my tape to Tom and told him what we'd shot. He was concentrating hard on the story but it was clear that he too had been appalled by what he'd seen. "Good luck," he said. "We'll get the stuff on the air." And then Madeleine and I backed off and watched them all fly away.

The drone of the helicopter faded, replaced by the sound of shovels against stone. A deathly, scraping noise echoing across the tortured landscape.

We were tired, drained both by lack of sleep and the emotional weight of the story. But we had to keep working; in only a few hours the grey daylight would give way to night. We had to get a better fix on the relief effort—identify what was most needed to help these people now, and determine where, exactly, things had broken down in the aid chain. We decided to shoot interviews and visuals of the rescue work throughout the afternoon and the following morning, then find a ride back to Yerevan, hopefully transmitting our second-night coverage from the television station there.

A warm greeting from the French rescue team did a lot to cheer us up. A captain resplendent in blue uniform and gendarme's cap offered us space in his tent for the night and the complete co-operation of his dog-handlers and recovery teams. But while I was slipping another battery and videocassette into my camera, there was a reminder of what had brought us there: a strong aftershock rippled the ground beneath our feet. We froze; the earth shifted silently. Hanging lamps swayed ominously, then became still once again.

The captain and his people went back to work. Another few bodies had been pulled from the flour mill across the road. We filmed there, then thumbed our way back into town, photographing several groups of idle Soviet soldiers along the way. A few directed traffic, while most seemed to be waiting for orders from someone, somewhere. We saw no troops that day taking the initiative to help in the searching or the digging. We were shooting the twisted remains of the post office building, where two hundred people were said to be buried, when a pudgy officer walked up and barked a question at us.

"He wants to know what we're doing here," Madeleine said.

"*He* wants to know what *we're* doing here?" I pulled the lens wide and took my eye from the viewfinder. But I kept rolling on the curious colonel. "Tell him who we are and then ask him just what in the name of Christ *he's* doing here."

The officer's full face wrinkled up around his eyes as he listened intently. He had seemed satisfied with Madeleine's explanation, but grew angry when the tables were turned on him. He growled out a few sentences, and then Madeleine moved quickly to calm him.

"We've upset him," she said. "This is still the Soviet Union, even in a disaster."

"OK. Sweet-talk him if you have to—we've got enough of his act on tape already."

The colonel looked increasingly self-important as Madeleine soothed and flattered him. Then he lectured us both while waving a chubby finger in our faces. He shuffled away, scribbling intently into his notebook, making a great show of recording our names for some implied dire official purpose.

"What'd he say?"

"He says we can stay. But he's sending a description of us to Moscow. And he said one more thing: 'Make certain you show the Soviet Army in the best, most positive way.'"

We walked down the street disgusted. "The best, most positive way." All around us civilians were scratching into the debris with bloodied hands and improvised tools.

A local man with a face streaked with tears came running to us, taking me by the arm. His clothes were torn and his eyes told

me he hadn't slept since the quake. I tried to pull away but he
held on, repeating a panicked plea over and over. Madeleine's face
fell as she figured out what he was saying. She shook her head with
an astonished little smile. But the smile, I could see, was there to
keep herself from crying.

"He thinks your camera is an X-ray machine to find people
under the rubble. He wants us to come to his house and find his
wife."

I tried to explain that we were just reporters, not miracle
workers. I could tell it was sinking in by the way his eyes gradually
stopped darting back and forth with feverish hope. His grip
loosened on my arm and he stepped back a few paces. Looking
as if I had just crushed the last particle of hope that he would
ever see his wife alive again, he mumbled a few words, then
walked away.

"Sorry," Madeleine said. "He said he was sorry to bother us."

When darkness fell we shuffled out of town for the warmth of
the captain's tent. Despite a rather deliberate show of *esprit de
corps*, the French team members seemed deeply discouraged.
They'd pulled only a handful of people alive from the rubble.

"This is just corpse recovery now," said one unhappy Parisian
fireman. The captain was cautious and diplomatic in his interview
with us. It had taken his group two full days to get into Armenia
and deploy, even with the French government pressuring Moscow
to speed their way. Though reluctant to criticize the Russian
authorities he depended upon for support, he couldn't hide his
frustration with the Soviets' long tradition of secrecy.

"Look at the maps we have to guide us. We've had to make
them ourselves as we go along–chart the entire town by hand. The
Russians say only the army has detailed maps, and they wouldn't
supply them to us."

Next day, Madeleine and I hitchhiked back to Yerevan to get
our material into NBC's second-day coverage of the quake. Tom
had anchored as planned from Moscow the previous evening,
with Peter backing him up. The show had been a stunning
scoop, and now I had been propelled into the principal on-site
correspondent's slot.

More of NBC's veteran camera crews and tape editors had
made it into Armenia. I discovered over the following days that

the news roadies follow a simple creed: sleep, eat and drink whenever possible, work like hell, and surrender wholeheartedly to one vice or another to relieve the aches and frustrations and loneliness of life on assignment. While it's probably true that our craft is plagued by drinking and drugs and broken marriages (our downtime frequently results in legendary drunks, punch-ups and romantic intrigues) it's equally the case that the hard-living men and women of the road distinguish themselves by being on top of their game when it counts most—getting the story on tape and up to the satellite.

The bartender of our hotel in Yerevan instantly sensed that our unit radiated an aura of quick and ready cash, and so it was that the rather sad little bar of the Hotel Dvin suddenly became stocked with a wide variety of alcohol: the best reserves had been called up from the basement for the thirsty foreigners. The bar became our night-time sanctuary from the horror of the earthquake. We drank to forget the sight of the bodies and the scent of death and the reeking incompetence of all levels of Soviet bureaucracy. It didn't seem to matter how much we drank, because day by day the story had a harsh, sobering effect on all of us. Our sympathy went out to the victims, but our anger was directed at communist officialdom.

While travelling up the road to Spitak with the NBC camera/sound team Ken Ludlow and John Hall, we discovered that Spitak's football stadium had been transformed into a huge mortuary, an assembly line for handling death on an unimaginable scale. Long passageways wound through stacks of coffins that might have been packing cases ready for the day's production. Victims were brought in at one end of the field, dusted off and identified if possible. Most were simply placed in coffins and set out in rows beyond the bleachers for inspection.

We positioned our camera and watched as ashen-faced townspeople, searching for relatives, walked up and down the rows, lifting the coffin lids one by one to examine the faces of the dead. One man, shaking his head and crying softly to himself, lingered a moment as he opened one of the caskets nearest us, revealing the figure of a young woman, chalk-white and still.

Though cloaked in dust, her striking features and smooth hands were unmarked by the violence of the quake. We gazed at the sleeping beauty until the man gently closed the coffin and shuffled away.

These images proved overpowering at times, even to our toughest crews. Cameraman Brian Calvert and soundman Peter Sansun at one point found themselves surrounded by so many visions of horror that there seemed "too many pictures to take." They'd come into Armenia through Turkey, ushered across the border by an unusually accommodating group of Soviet guards. Under "Purpose of Visit" on their visas, the soldiers had written, "To help the people who are suffering."

Exactly how any of us could help wasn't clear. And most of the foreign newshounds crowding the Dvin bar didn't waste scarce drinking time by preaching theories of aid-through-information. But having breached the Iron Curtain, we pounced on the issues at stake with journalistic claws bared. Our cameras couldn't locate survivors in the ruins, but we could focus on the lessons this disaster was teaching on every level.

Perhaps no one did that better than the Soviet journalists who were slashing a new frontier of open criticism with their writing and photography, which until then had been tightly controlled. They condemned everything from poor construction standards to the pathetic state of emergency services. In a region notorious for earthquakes, how, they asked, could architects and builders be allowed to erect structures that fell apart like matchboxes? And why was Soviet civil defense itself a catastrophe waiting to happen?

My own journalistic sense of indignation was eating away at me like the pain from my broken tooth. So I had no hesitation in cornering the distinguished visitor from Moscow who strolled into the lobby of the Hotel Dvin thirteen days after the quake.

"Mr. Gerasimov," I said to Gorbachev's spokesman to the outside world. "We'd like to talk to you about the relief program." The imposing figure halted and shrugged like a kind uncle. "Certainly. Can we do it now?"

Gennady Gerasimov was as quick-witted a public-relations man as they come, but his great strength in handling aggressive Western journalists was his ability to fence in the English language and take the offensive when he had to. He put off attackers with sudden candor—doses of glasnost so strong that combative reporters were frequently transformed into faithful scribes documenting the long painful battle that was perestroika.

"The foreign groups, the rescue groups," he told me, "acted as professionals. But we acted as amateurs, because we had no previous experience."

I felt a surge of adrenalin. The man's boss had been in town two weeks earlier promising the quake victims all the help the Soviet state had to offer, and now Gerasimov was admitting in a one-on-one interview that the system just couldn't perform up to world-class standards.

"We are not creating any walls against foreigners," he continued, countering suspicion that he'd come to Yerevan to tell reporters and search teams that it was now time to go home.

"Thanks for the straight talk," I told him as we shook hands after the interview. "Sometime soon I'd like to hear what you have to say about Afghanistan."

"Please," he said, "one disaster before lunch is enough, don't you think?"

Gerasimov spoke to some other reporters, then invited us all into the restaurant for something to eat. He spoke freely about the immense difficulties facing the Soviet Union, and warned us that Western countries were mistaken if they believed that Gorbachev's "new thinkers" could reform their nation all by themselves. We in the West would have to help, would have to overcome the mistrust of the Cold War years and become partners in change.

It sounded wonderful, and improbable. But then we had no way of knowing that our cameras would soon be focusing on visions of global turmoil we had never imagined possible. Ahead of us lay a year of great danger, a time of brutality giving way to great achievement, of tragedy giving way to joy, then turning back again to death and disenchantment. Some of us leaving Soviet Armenia that Christmas thought we knew what a changing world looked like.

Then we stumbled into 1989.

CHAPTER FIVE

Cold War to Old War: Return to Afghanistan

I truly believed that all the hardware we brought here was supposed to help the Afghans find peace. But I guess it was just about killing Russians.

—U.S. State Department official based in Pakistan

My blood and the blood of my friends has been spilled there. If Afghanistan should fall, this will have been for nothing.

—Soviet Army veteran returning to Moscow

These superpowers will be the death of us all.

—Afghan psychiatrist fleeing Kabul

THE YEAR BEGAN with kudos for my work in Armenia from NBC's executive offices in New York, and still more fresh images of death and turmoil. I found my way back to Afghanistan by mid-January, just in time to accompany the last front-line Soviet combat force in its withdrawal. After a disastrous nine-year military adventure, it was a historic about-face for the Soviet empire, in many ways the beginning of the end of the Soviet Union.

But there wasn't much history in the cold winter air of Kabul as I touched down that February. Just hunger and fear.

"I think you will *not* stay with us very long this time, Mr. Kent."

Mohammed Nabi Ammani had been cool but cordial towards me in the past. The communist government's foreign affairs spokesman, he was a smooth and sophisticated functionary, always smartly dressed in a Western-styled business suit. He was usually soft-spoken, particularly in French. But today he had only clipped phrases in English for me, none of them the kind of thing I wanted to hear. He hadn't liked the unique new way I had arranged my entry visa back into the capital—with the help of the Soviet foreign ministry.

Ammani refused to give me one of the regular foreign ministry guides, and I was handed over to a leering young thug, clearly a new operative in the party's secret police, the notorious KHAD. Ammani told me not even to think of trying to extend my ten-day visa. And since the ministry was busy with post-withdrawal business, there wasn't anything he could offer me in the way of interviews with regime officials.

"*Au revoir, Monsieur Kent.*"

And that was that. I chalked up his hostility to the strong-arming the Soviets had done to get me back into town. His Afghan pride had been wounded, and I was now in the darkest corner of the doghouse.

My only chance, I knew, was to renew old contacts. My friends at the hotel, who had kept my room and equipment safe while I was away, helped me track down Samad Ali, my driver. A fistful of Afghani notes persuaded my KHAD "minder" to let me drive down to the bazaar, where I bought two full cases of Russian vodka, or "KHAD-repellant," as I described it to Samad.

Next morning, I had my shadow come to my room for tea. I passed him a forty-ouncer of vodka and told him I had only a few routine errands to do that day. With him out of the way, we slipped off to army headquarters. I lucked out with the chief of propaganda, who let me spend a day with an artillery unit that was blasting away at known guerrilla transit camps on the city's outskirts.

This by itself wasn't a story, though. And interest in the Afghan war on my news desks in London, New York and Toronto was sliding.

"We're not exactly on the edge of our seats for another bread-fight from Kabul," one wisecracking bureau chief told me, referring to the bread-line sequences that had featured prominently in TV coverage before the Russian withdrawal.

Then one morning I met a pair of fourteen-year-old Afghan boys, Raz and Lal Mohammed. They had been through considerably more than a breadfight, and getting their story on tape took me on a tightrope-walk over the worst obstacles the regime—and my own editors—could devise.

One of the people I checked in with by phone each day in Kabul was Philippa Parker, head nurse at the emergency surgical hospital run by the International Committee of the Red Cross. Elegant, capable and cool as mountain snow whenever torn and bleeding bodies poured through her door, Philippa that day sounded as if the war had suddenly thrown her a few patients too many.

"You'd better get yourself over here," she told me. "We've had eight kids come in—all mine injuries. About fifteen arms and legs amputated. It's a mess."

Samad rushed me across town and soon I was dressed in gown, cap and mask, and shooting over the shoulder of an ICRC doctor. He was sawing through a young boy's thigh. Fine white dust rose from the bone; I framed the shot just above the horrible wound and thanked God the picture in the viewfinder was in black-and-white. Behind me a second team worked over another boy. He'd lost an eye, a couple of fingers, and a leg that had been torn off at the hip.

"This one probably won't make it," a doctor told me. "Mine injuries are always the worst. It's not just what the explosion tears away; it's the damage left behind. We can amputate, say, here, then sew him up and watch gangrene set in because the bone stump was shattered inside."

I kept shooting until the heat and the smell and my own weak knees sent me outside for fresh air. A fourteen-year-old boy named Jamal was sitting in a wheelchair staring at the two bandaged stumps sticking out where his legs had been. Beside him was another fourteen-year-old with injuries almost identical to Jamal's. Two Afghan nurses were trying to comfort him in his chair, but the look in his eyes poured agony into the lens.

With my fractured Dari, I got his name: Raz Mohammed. The nurses told me his cousin Lal was the boy in the operating theater, the one not expected to live. Raz insisted on telling the rest of their story himself. They had been walking together near the perimeter of an abandoned Soviet firebase on the edge of the city. They were scavenging for tools left behind by the soldiers, and stumbled on to an anti-personnel mine instead. Luckily, a local man driving by heard the blast and brought their bleeding bodies to the hospital. I backed away from Raz's chair to get a wide shot. He started crying.

"I'm going to throw myself down the stairs," he told me. "I don't want to live anymore." The nurses stroked his face and scalp, which had been scarred by fragments of the mine, and tried to silence him. "Just give me something to put me to sleep," Raz cried. "How can I live without my legs?"

Philippa came by on her rounds and quieted Raz the best way she knew how, with a firm hand on his shoulder. She wasn't asking him to be strong. She was telling him it was his only choice. Gradually, he calmed down. She showed me around the rest of the ward.

A twelve-year-old named Bakr was having a burn dressing pulled from his face. Walking in the bazaar, he had picked up an unspent flare, the kind the big Soviet Ilyushin transport planes spit from their underbellies to confuse heat-seeking missiles. The flare had gone off in Bakr's hand; his face now resembled a peeling red basketball. Even worse was a three-year-old girl, Nadia, crying in her father's arms nearby. White and red flakes of skin hung from the back of her head and her shoulders; she was an image of screaming hot pain. I didn't bother asking her father where he was from. Standing there in a hospital in Kabul, he wouldn't want to talk about home. His face, his eyes, his beard...they all said Panjshir Valley–mujahideen country.

"What was it?" I asked in Dari.

"Rocket."

"What rocket?"

"The new one."

I leaned closer. "SCUD?"

He made sure no one was watching him. "SCUD," he whispered. So he was, in fact, from the other side; his daughter's burns were bad enough to risk coming down the road into government territory. He'd made it through the army checkpoints with one excuse or another, probably passing himself off as a trader or government informer. But getting back home once his daughter was better–that was a riddle of the war he had yet to solve.

With these images on tape, I recorded a few interviews with the doctors and rushed back to the hotel. Samad Ali, at the wheel, was worried about the tears rolling down my face. He tried to talk to me about what I'd seen, but the only way I could steady myself was to think about the story. So I sat in silence and mapped out in my head a flow of pictures and sentences.

The faces of the children would speak for themselves–of that I was certain. Trouble was, it looked as though no one back home was going to see them.

"Sounds feature-ish," Marc Kusnetz, the foreign producer at "NBC Nightly News" remarked down the phone line from New York. "We'd like the story, but you'll have to ship it to us–the satellite's too expensive for a piece that won't positively go in the show tonight."

I told him there was no secure way to ship tape from Kabul. Aeroflot and Ariana were unreliable; a courier service in Afghanistan still meant caravans of camels or horses. We'd either have to feed it via satellite from Kabul TV or forget about the story until I left the country, by which time it could well stand even less chance of seeing air. But for budgetary reasons, Marc felt he had to pass.

This was too much to bear. Only two weeks earlier, editors everywhere had been crying out for stories from Afghanistan. Sure, their attention had turned elsewhere now, but to me, deeply involved in the war, these tortured kids were no less news that night than they would have been a month before. I had one last chance. I called my friend Momen at the post office and had him put through a call to Toronto.

It was long past dark in Kabul, but Nigel Gibson was just starting his daily routine as producer of CBC-TV's "The National," the newscast that aired my Afghan stories in Canada. Maybe his sales resistance was low at that time of day, but I'm sure it was more the human quality of the story that convinced him to risk several thousand dollars and go it alone on the satellite charges.

"All right, Arthur," he told me, "if you feel that strongly about it, we'll make the unilateral booking and you can feed it on up the line."

I assured him he wouldn't regret it. I was confident that once Marc saw the pictures, he'd want the story too and would order it cut and ready to air as soon as he could fit it into "Nightly News." That way CBC could lay off part of the bill on to NBC in New York, and viewers in both Canada and the States would see the kind of human meat-grinder Afghanistan had become. (We'd shown plenty of civilian casualties in the previous nine years. But timing is everything in the news business, and I sensed that the story of Raz and Lal would really hit home so soon after the flurry of attention over the Soviet withdrawal.)

Luckily for me, it worked. I fed the pictures and my voice track out of Kabul's TV station the following night, and even with bad sound quality due to a faulty relay through Moscow, the tape editors in London loved the stuff. Yves Pelletier cut the piece for CBC, Mark Ludlow for NBC. When the story was broadcast in Canada, stockbrokers were among the viewers who called CBC's Toronto switchboard wanting to donate money to the hospital.

"Stockbrokers!" Nigel told me over the phone the following night. "Wanting to *give* money! I think we touched a nerve with that one, Arthur. Keep 'em coming."

I told him I fully intended to. But soon it was clear I wouldn't be doing it from Kabul. The day after my transmission to London, I was summoned to Mr. Ammani's office. He was about twice as unhappy as he'd been on my arrival a week earlier.

"Mr. Kent," he said in the stiff English that signaled trouble, "I have another visa for you. An *exit* visa. You will leave on tomorrow's flight to Delhi. Your time here is over."

Try as I might to shuffle around him, Mr. Ammani was in no mood for a little soft-shoe from the likes of me. He wouldn't come right out and say that he was throwing me out of town because of the references in my child-casualty story to "Soviet mines" and "Afghan government SCUD missiles," but by that point in my career I knew what an editorial "difference of opinion" felt like, and we were having a barn-burner. All our feeds out of Kabul TV were monitored by the government, and my story had been about as negative as they come—hospitals in the regime's capital treating civilians wounded by the regime's own weaponry. I had no choice but to pack up and go. Ivanyenko, my Soviet foreign ministry contact, wasn't happy to hear that I'd blamed the mine that crippled Raz and Lal on his side. I told him, sure, the mujahideen had planted plenty of their own mines, but in this case the evidence pointed squarely at the Red Army, and he'd better just shut up and take the vodka I was offering him because I'd be damned if I was going to leave it with my KHAD spook.

"Where are you going now?" he asked me.

I looked at him without speaking. It didn't take him more than a few seconds to figure it out. He shook his head, but managed a smile. The professor, the investigator, the Afghan specialist in him spoke next.

"In a way, I wish I could go with you."

Not likely. The mujahideen guerrillas were not in the habit of inviting Russians to join them in the field. Particularly for what was about to happen next—the biggest and longest set-piece battle of the Afghan war.

* * *

It felt strange to switch horses to the other side of the war so swiftly. And now, sitting in Pakistan with one of my closest guerrilla contacts, it felt a little unnerving, too.

"How very interesting, Kent, that you should come back to see us just now." Mohammed Ishaq was always quick with a smile. He had to be, as media spokesman, interpreter—and frequently apologist—for the ramshackle Hizbe Islami mujahideen party led by Younis Khales.

Sitting in his office in Peshawar only two days after my expulsion from Kabul, I sensed a strange, unsettling quality in Ishaq's grin.

"You must forgive me," he said, "but it's not every day that I have a Russian spy in my office."

I guess my mouth hung open stupidly, because the two teenage guerrillas who slouched in their chairs opposite us with AK-47s on their laps chuckled at my reaction.

"Didn't you know?" Ishaq continued. "You've been brainwashed by Najib and the Russians. You're working for THEM now. Just a moment, I'll show you."

He went into the next room and came back with a single sheet of paper. It was a photocopy of one of my stories in the *Observer*—a piece I'd filed from Kabul two weeks earlier contrasting President Najib's effectiveness with the guerrillas' ineptitude. Not a good calling card among the hard-line mujahideen.

"Where'd you get this?" I asked. Ishaq mentioned two names. They belonged to a pair of right-wing political hucksters from the States who had been in Peshawar for years dreaming up refugee-aid and reporting scams that would make them rich in a hurry. They were failures, but dangerous failures.

"They've circulated copies among all the party offices," Ishaq said. "Everyone will want to have you shot. But since you came to us first, I hope you'll let our firing squad have the honor."

I was happy to laugh with Ishaq—relieved that he could see through this cheap trick and that he still trusted me. I needed his help to get to Jalalabad in a hurry. A major battle between regime and mujahideen forces was in its fourth day in the Afghan city, which was only about a three hours' drive from Peshawar, over the Khyber Pass. A big government outpost had surrendered to the guerrillas about the time I had been transiting through Delhi airport from Kabul, and now fighting was raging all around the city.

"Don't worry," Ishaq said. "We know you've been fair to us in the past, and that's all we ask now. God willing, you will be in Jalalabad tonight."

And I was. Jalalabad was another Afghan shooting gallery, but with both sides unleashing their largest, most powerful arsenals ever. I was spellbound by what I found there. Great sweeping arcs of fire described the flight of rocket rounds over what appeared to be a black tossing sea. The waves of the sea were treetops, leaning in the evening breeze; or were they bending from the shooting red jets of machine-gun fire that criss-crossed the thundering plain? Crazed patterns of light bolted in and out of the city, which was hidden by foliage in the distance.

Marveling at this insanity, I had to wonder what, exactly, had brought me there, both to that lethal orchard and to one of the most desperate and exposed crossroads of my own life and career. Strangely, I knew that I belonged right where I was at that moment: in deep trouble, trying my best to get out of it all with a decent story. But the guerrillas I wound up with weren't in the mood for deep reflection. In fact, the deadly significance of the battle seemed lost on Kahar Badshah and his men. A sleepy-eyed twenty-three-year-old son of Jalalabad's farming suburbs, Badshah was now master of a small hard-scrabble hill just outside the perimeter of Jalalabad's airport. A deserted, battle-scarred cluster of farmhouses served as a base for him and his twenty-five mujahideen—and for the newly arrived TV correspondent.

I was deposited along with my gear on Kahar Badshah's doorstep, and I spent a sleepless night in his "command" farmhouse, listening to his men snoring loudly beneath the sound of army artillery shells. Too often, the rounds strayed from the distant focus of the fighting to our own little hamlet among the fields. As the projectiles scraped the air overhead and thumped down close enough to rattle our windows, my new companions snored on vigorously, oblivious of all the racket. I lay awake perspiring until the persistence of their snoring coaxed me to sleep too.

Only when morning came did I discover that the side of the hill facing the airport was, in fact, a cemetery. The graveyard looked as though it had been receiving the dearly departed of the village right up until this battle started. And it had plenty of room left for newcomers—fortunate, since the line between the living and the dead at Jalalabad was a thin one. The rockets and artillery had been silent for a few hours, and more mujahideen strolled in from the surrounding area to gather on the hill.

Luckily, Kahar Badshah's second-in-command, Ishaq, spoke broken English, and soon this thin red-haired farmboy was briefing me on the day's plan. Nearby was a government outpost that protected approaches to both the airport and the city. Haji Qadir, the overall commander, would pound the hilltop position with his long-range rockets, forcing the soldiers to take cover in their bunkers and enabling a swarm of mujahideen riflemen—our group among them—to storm the post.

Only one company, perhaps a hundred soldiers, would be defending. But until this position and others like it were taken, the main government force of eight thousand men could hold off the guerrilla offensive even if the various mujahideen parties could do what they had never done before—co-operate and combine to outnumber the army man for man. Our attack was set for late afternoon. It would take that long to position the ten mujahideen groups that would storm the hill. If things went badly, darkness would cover our retreat. And things went badly at Jalalabad often. I got my first taste of this around noon, when a flight of government jets swooped down on guerrilla groups advancing on another objective across the valley.

The pilots made daring low-level bombing runs, dropping cluster bombs and big thousand-pounders from altitudes well within machine-gun range, to say nothing of their near-suicidal exposure to the guerrillas' U.S.-supplied Stinger missiles. The government was desperate to hold Jalalabad, and its pilots flew with great courage and determination.

I tracked one Soviet-built Sukhoi ground-attack plane with my camera as it rocketed by less than five hundred feet from the ground, and captured on tape the bright white trail of a Stinger as it narrowly missed the aircraft's exhaust. This was a sequence every cameraman in Afghanistan hungered for, but there was suddenly too much happening around us to waste time congratulating myself. The government's ammo dump at the airport had been hit, and a chain of explosions reignited the fighting all over the valley. Ishaq and Kahar Badshah hurried their men into position for the assault on the firebase, while I scrambled up a hill behind a distinguished-looking guerrilla I had met only moments earlier. Habib, as he called himself, turned out to be a former army artillery officer. He had deserted from the Jalalabad garrison a few months earlier and was now directing rocket attacks on to it for the guerrillas.

His observation post was a deserted army bunker on a hilltop neighboring the objective—a stone hut so close to the firebase and so exposed to the army's guns that no attacker in his right mind would ever think of concealing himself there. Habib's strategy was working. The soldiers were firing cannon rounds from their post at other likely points of attack far beyond the little hut, which went unhit. I scrambled into the cramped stone-walled room beside Habib, praying that I hadn't been seen. Holding my breath as I focused my camera through a crack in the wall, I could easily make out the figures of soldiers on the sandy ridge less than a hundred yards opposite us. Should any of them spot us, a couple of quick rounds from their heavy guns would leave one less bunker and two fewer human beings on Jalalabad's smoking landscape.

The howl of incoming 120-mm rocket rounds signaled the start of the attack. Brilliant flashes erupted along the trench-line; the soldiers scrambled and disappeared as shrapnel peppered the earth around them. Habib the spotter shouted into his walkie-talkie, and another salvo rained down. But this time the rockets threw up their billowing towers of smoke and dust far wide of the target.

Below us, the lead group of mujahideen riflemen were hesitating behind a ruined farmhouse, waiting for the order to rush up the slope and into the trenches. Amazingly, between salvos, the soldiers came out of their bunkers and stood defiantly in the open, daring the guerrillas to charge. Then, hearing the rocket launchers firing again in the distance, they would dive for cover, only to emerge unscathed as the rounds continued to fall wide.

This display of madness under fire appalled me; just how brutalized by warfare, how accustomed to the threat of sudden death were these men? Gradually, they became even bolder, and opened up a crossfire on the luckless mujahideen from machine-gun nests at either end of the trench-line, firing even while the rocket barrage continued around them.

Habib cursed at my side; the guerrilla launchers were too far to the rear and from that range would never hit the target with any regularity. The battle was lost. As darkness fell, the mujahideen pulled back, ducking and running beneath the crimson tracers from the government guns. One of their fighters was dead, a second wounded.

From their firebases at the airport and in the city, the army that night mounted a long and intense artillery barrage, as if celebrating the feat of holding Jalalabad against the odds for one more day. Kahar Badshah and his band of farmboys returned to their quarters on cemetery hill, where I was assured that morning would come with a new plan of attack from Qadir.

That plan didn't arrive, but the government jets did. Wing upon wing of them, all day long, with groups of four planes bombing for fifteen minutes or so every hour. Through most of this, Ishaq and Kahar Badshah reclined in a farmhouse bedroom listening to the BBC's Pashto-language service on my pocket short-wave. Danger, to them, was manageable—as long as you ignored it. Two of the other men cooked fried potatoes on an open fire in the yard. The earth rocked and giant columns of smoke and debris rose into the air within a hundred yards of the house; meanwhile, the most delicious, sizzling hot chips you could ask for came off the mujahed broiler.

I photographed this phenomenon, having nothing better to do, since the only avenue of escape—the highway—was being liberally strafed by the jets. As the day wore on, the old urge to get the best possible bombing footage got the better of me. I wanted to show viewers the terror of the government counter-strike and the stubborn response of the guerrillas. If Jalalabad signaled anything, it was that the fever of warfare in Afghanistan would continue to rise, not fall, with Soviet forces out of the picture.

Two Stinger operators were on the graveyard hill scanning the sky for attacking planes, and I positioned myself between them, ready to shoot a missile launch. But the clear blue sky hid the jets well, and the pilots that morning were dropping their bombs from a higher altitude than usual. When a bombardment was coming dangerously close, the scream of the jet engines would rise suddenly–terrifyingly–and only the sound of the aircraft passing unseen would signal the release of its bombs. At this point, the Stinger operators and I would hit the deck, praying that the bombs would fall somewhere other than the graveyard.

I got some stunning footage of near misses, but two days of this pounding and the absence of a new initiative by the guerrillas convinced me to withdraw to Peshawar and get my story on the air.

* * *

I arrived to discover that NBC's producers and executives in New York had lost whatever transitory interest they'd had in Afghanistan. Other stories were breaking, and with the Soviets no longer in the equation, Washington's strategic interests–and therefore the viewing habits of the American public–had to move on. But I stuck with the Afghan story, since the people at CBC Toronto and the *Observer* couldn't seem to get enough of it. This was, after all, the visible aftermath of the longest, bloodiest confrontation of the Cold War.

"Not often do we see real action and a great political drama being played out at the same time," Adrian Hamilton, deputy editor of the *Observer*, told me on the phone. "Keep on it." It wasn't the first time a few gentle words of encouragement from Adrian had lifted me out of despair on the road, and thankfully, it wouldn't be the last. In the following weeks it became clear that if Afghanistan was the war that wouldn't end, Jalalabad was the battle that couldn't be won.

The four principal mujahideen parties fighting there could not communicate effectively, and their political bosses in Peshawar failed to agree on common goals and objectives.

Against them, the army hung on unexpectedly well, not because of loyalty to the Najib regime but because each individual soldier had come to understand that he was fighting for his life. So although my first shoot at the front showed the mujahideen stubbornly trying to press home their advantage, my next journey revealed the futility of the guerrillas' strategy of mounting one abortive offensive after another.

It sickened me to watch Kahar Badshah's spirited, if misguided group of fighters whittled down one by one as the bombers improved their aim with each passing day. It made me think of a war long before, one between Christian armies, in which my own Uncle Clyde had lost his life. Jalalabad and Passchendaele, of course, had nothing in common in terms of tactics or weapons or even objectives. But the mindless waste that claimed my uncle, I reasoned, must have been similar to what was all around me now. Clyde had been, like most of the Afghans, just a nineteen-year-old farmboy fighting for a few hundred meters of bomb-tossed mud and debris. He had suffocated when a cannon shell exploded nearby, toppling the walls of his foxhole and burying him alive. How many of the young Afghans were going to finish like my uncle? Would I die, too?

My mujahideen abandoned the graveyard hill only when it took a direct hit from a thousand-pound bomb. No one was killed in the attack, but four men suffered serious shrapnel wounds. The commander, his sidekick Ishaq and I had taken cover with some newcomers to the battle, one of whom turned on me even before the smoke had cleared.

"Who are you?" an Arabic-looking stranger in guerrilla clothing demanded. I recognized the zealot's gleam in his eye–he was an Islamic radical, an Arab, one of thousands of foreign Muslims who had leeched on to the cause of the Afghan mujahideen.

"A reporter," I told him.

"Are you Muslim?"

"Christian."

"Then you are with the enemy!" He spun round in the bomb shelter, drawing the attention of Kahar Badshah and the others. Our ears were still ringing from the bomb blast, but the man wanted to make a speech.

"Who is this stranger among you?" he asked them. He

pointed an accusing finger at my camera. "What is this strange instrument he brings to your camp? If he is not a Muslim, then he is on the side of the Russians and their stooges."

Ishaq sidled up to me and assured me I had no cause for concern. "A Wahabi," he murmured. "He cannot harm you here."

The Wahabis are an arch-conservative sect from Saudi Arabia, and hundreds of their young hotheads attached themselves to the guerrilla leadership in Peshawar to "Islamicize" the cause. I had met quite a few of them on the trail over the years, and to me they rated a distant second to the Afghans in both courage and purity of faith. But this particular Wahabi was waving a loaded Kalashnikov in my face. I was armed with a Sony Betacam.

Kahar Badshah finally stepped between us, but all the young commander could do was to ask the Saudi to leave his smoking ruin of a base. From that moment on, I realized, wherever I went on the battlefield, I could count on there being a trigger-happy Wahabi nearby looking to even the score.

In a strange way that brought me closer to the average mujahed, the dogface of the Afghan trenches, because they too had to keep one eye peeled for treachery from their "allies" among the mujahideen alliance. Many of the parties could be relied upon to appear only to loot captured army positions. As this malaise spread, many decent resistance fighters sensed the odds rising against their own survival. More and more of them drifted off to Peshawar and never came back. Group commanders became particularly unreliable, disappearing for days to "discuss strategy" with their higher-ups while rank-and-file guerrillas endured daily bombardment.

Afghan journalist Naim Majrooh, whose father Burhannudin was murdered by mujahideen hard-liners for advocating political responsibility and restraint among the resistance, told me that Jalalabad proved that the guerrilla leadership had lost its way. "What the people of Afghanistan need now is a plan for rebuilding their towns and cities. If the mujahideen wish to hold the support of the civilians, they must demonstrate that they can restore power and water and administer the country wisely, not just tear it apart with constant warfare." But within the seven-party Alliance of Afghan Mujahideen, the disaster at Jalalabad created only more infighting and disagreement. In the absence of any real political initiative, half-hearted military operations continued.

The Soviet withdrawal was to have ushered the Afghan people back into their country. Instead, at least 80,000 more refugees had fled to Pakistan. And they were the lucky ones. Inside Jalalabad city, 60,000 civilians were held in an especially perverse kind of captivity. Government forces hoped to use the families as a human shield against an all-out guerrilla attack. Meanwhile the mujahideen ambushed truck caravans trying to escape to Kabul, trapping any civilians lucky enough to bribe their way out of the city. To Afghans seeking peace, the proud cause of resistance had now become a national disgrace.

CHAPTER SIX

Death and Democracy

What we have here is a counter-revolutionary rebellion. All of you must leave Tiananmen Square immediately. The martial law force will use whatever methods are necessary to clear the area. We cannot be held responsible for what will happen to you if you do not go now.

> —*Chinese authorities over loudspeaker, June 4, 1989*

I have had the privilege in the past to work with brave and dedicated professionals. But I have never seen bravery and professionalism exhibited to such a degree as these gentlemen exhibited last night.

> —*Bud Pratt, NBC's Beijing bureau chief, writing about News staffers who covered the Tiananmen Square massacre*

WHILE I WAS tramping across the Afghan wilderness in 1988, big changes were happening on the other side of the world at NBC headquarters in New York. The president of the News Division, Larry Grossman, had fallen out of favor with the new GE management team. And, it was rumored, with Tom Brokaw, anchor of "Nightly News." Tom was said to feel threatened by Grossman's suggestion that he accept Diane Sawyer, the rising star at CBS, as his co-anchor.

I was in NBC's London bureau preparing my gear for another foray into Afghanistan when news came of Grossman's replacement. The new president of NBC News was Michael G. Gartner, a man from a newspaper background with credentials as long as a broadsheet. He was on the Pulitzer Prize board. And Tom Brokaw had been among the people who had suggested him to the top people at GE as Grossman's replacement. But staffers at NBC News in London and New York were on edge over the appointment. "Let's see how he handles the hatchet men," my contact on the foreign desk told me.

This would be, in fact, the litmus test of Gartner's news and management savvy. Long before his appointment, GE executives had hired a business consultant, McKinsey & Company, to study

71

NBC News and explain it to them. News was by far the most difficult, byzantine division in their corporate dominion. The McKinsey report did little to cheer them. It projected huge losses for NBC News (which hadn't earned a profit since the late seventies), and worse, forecast no traces of new revenue.

Enter Mr. Gartner. Stories began to surface of his management record in newspapers. In 1974 he was named executive director of the *Des Moines Register* in Iowa. He was said to have walked away with a huge personal profit when the Gannett chain bought the paper in 1986. Then he joined Gannett to help them with two struggling midwest newspapers. He amalgamated the papers, and Gannett sold the new daily off for a big profit. It became clear to us that the columns in Mr. Gartner's head had less to do with journalism, more with profit and loss statements. That brought a chill of foreboding: this was a GE man in the making.

In March 1989 I was back in London for a little R and R–burned out after Jalalabad, and realizing that I needed to rethink a few things. For instance, my relationships with the trio of news companies I had been servicing. I was living and working on battlefields for them, but just how committed were they towards me? Was any of them interested in strengthening the bonds that held me to its organization–not least, of course, the financial bonds that supported my field operations?

The answer came as I arrived at NBC's cramped little bureau above the central London YMCA. A short, grey-faced man wearing striped suspenders and a bow-tie dashed across my path as I walked in the door. Evidently he hadn't seen me–or anyone else in the room for that matter. His brow was furrowed, his lips tight, his stride purposeful. He might have been rushing off to consult the chairman of the World Bank. This, I soon learned, was the new president of NBC News. And he wanted to see me–although Frieda Morris, the London bureau chief, didn't make that sound like a very inviting prospect. Frieda was facing the hard facts of Mr. Gartner's new budgetary regime: she was having to fire people, and she didn't like that.

"You're what the new NBC News is all about," Michael Gartner told me, shaking my hand. He sat down on a couch littered with notepads and papers. All I could make out were numbers. Was this the future of NBC News, scattered about in front of the man in bow-tie and suspenders?

"Your stuff from Armenia was fantastic," he told me. "And Afghanistan! Really fine reporting."

I thanked him for that, and for the written tributes he'd placed in the weekly management newsletter, the *Friday Report* file in the NBC News computer system.

"You know," he continued, "when I got here last summer things weren't looking so good. News was taking nearly 20 per cent of NBC's expenses but brought in only 10 per cent of revenue." I frowned and shook my head; even a reporter could figure that arithmetic. "Fifty *million* dollars in losses," Michael said, arching his forehead, and letting his mouth gape open in exasperation. "That couldn't go on."

He told me of big changes underway, "right-sizing," he called it—a euphemism my father would have laughed at: "Beware of strangers bearing doubletalk." Michael said he wanted to hire me, make me a staff correspondent at NBC News. I admit, I was flattered. The job would put me into a higher league, both in income and in terms of getting my stories on the air more regularly. But I felt I had to explain myself and my fieldcraft, just in case Mr. Gartner mistook me for some kind of new breed of cost-cutter. The camera work, I told him, was something I did for safety and speed. I would never advocate what was becoming known as "one-man-band" TV news reporting. Shooting, I told him, takes time. In daily news, especially at the network level, a correspondent needs a full crew: camera, sound, producer, tape editor. Minimum.

"Sure," he told me. "But changes are coming. Anyway, we'll see. Have you got an agent? Have him call us. We want you."

I left walking on air. Soon, I'd be crossing paths with network correspondents I admired—great writers and reporters like Bob Simon at CBS, NBC's Garrick Utley—and, of course, Peter Kent. I called my brother, who graciously put me on to his business agent, Stu Witt. Stu began negotiating a contract for me with NBC's attorneys in New York. I decided to make the most of this new opportunity, meanwhile tucking away as much NBC income as possible—just in case the company continued to change for the worse, and I felt the need to bail out somewhere down the line. It was one, two, three: climb on to the big network bus, report up a storm, and save for a rainy day. What risk could there be in that?

* * *

In late May I was back on the Northwest Frontier counting bodies and refugees pouring out of Jalalabad. Then I got another midnight call from Frieda Morris in London.

"China," she said. "We need you there as soon as possible. Things are getting out of hand. The place could explode at any moment."

Pro-democracy marches had been going on in Beijing for a couple of weeks at that point. A leader I'd never heard of, Premier Li Peng, had imposed a state of martial law, which had drawn even more international attention to a colorful band of dissident students who marched and chanted and starved themselves in the name of democracy.

Dramatic stuff, and the story was drawing an even larger NBC News contingent than the one I'd been part of in Armenia. The idea of joining the circus again for a while appealed to me, but I still had the blues for Afghanistan.

"China?" I groaned down the phone line to Frieda. "I don't know a damned thing about China."

"You know how to explore and how to take care of yourself if there's trouble. That's what we need. Meet us in Hong Kong. Hurry."

By morning it didn't seem like such a bad idea after all. It'd be like a holiday from the war, I told myself. No bombs, no rockets, no suffering in the rising tide of blood and excrement at Jalalabad. And the Chinese students were on a high. There was a picture of them in Peshawar's *Frontier Post* demonstrating under the famous portrait of Mao Tsetung that hangs at the symbolic heart of communist China–a place called Tiananmen Square.

Now I too was on my way to Tiananmen Square, leaving behind the danger and the waste of Afghanistan for a strange, ancient land that was on the verge of a bold new beginning. Sure, Tiananmen. I needed a bold new beginning of my own. I packed and scrambled for the airport.

After sneaking myself and my camera through Chinese customs with "Sports Consultant" scribbled on my visa for cover, I rejoined the NBC circus in Beijing. The operation had out-grown the network's tiny bureau in the diplomatic quarter and was now based on the fifteenth floor of a luxury hotel, the Palace.

This glittering skyscraper seemed to me totally out of place among the surrounding buildings, especially with the graceful Oriental rooftops of the Forbidden City only a few blocks away. Our own newsroom and edit suites were an even bigger surprise, fitted out with marble tables and broadloom and room service. A long way from the shattered farmhouses of Jalalabad.

I quickly sensed that all was not well within the team. The brass in New York, my colleagues told me, had short-staffed the China story to save money. While that may have made a certain kind of budgetary sense to NBC's cost-conscious overseers at GE, it had turned out to be a major mistake in terms of news economics.

Beijing had been vaulted into headline status by the rapid growth of the pro-democracy movement. Every newspaper and network and news agency wanted the story. Our competition at CBS and CNN had wisely chosen to staff China heavily, and quickly outgunned us on the air. Two NBC correspondents, Keith Miller from Hong Kong and George Lewis from Los Angeles, were left to pick up the slack on their own. They had done well but were working around the clock to do it.

Now, late in the game, NBC management was flying in rein-forcements. London-based correspondent Rick Davis had arrived a day before me with Frieda Morris, who was taking control of the operation. Keith Morrison, a correspondent-anchor from Los Angeles, was on his way, and the operation was strengthened with the best producers, tape editors, camera crews and engineers in the News Division.

But expansion was happening fast, and unlike the smooth growth I had witnessed during the Armenian quake assignment, petty power-plays and squabbles broke out among senior staffers from the London and Los Angeles bureaus. Fortunately, I was teamed up with a fiery Chinese-American freelance producer, Annie Pong. We happily turned our backs on bureau politics and hit the street to get some fresh angles on the pro-democracy movement.

Tiananmen Square that last week of May was like a country fair crossed with a music festival. Colorful flags and banners streamed over a crowded tent-city that pulsed with loudspeakers playing old rock anthems like Procul Harem's "A Whiter Shade of Pale" and inspirational classics like the Radetzky March. Shrill young voices called out political diatribes on megaphones. Democracy was needed in China immediately, they said. But beyond the blaze of color and noise, the serene presence of Mao Tsetung appeared unmoved by the specter of young people enduring long hunger strikes to press their demands. A huge portrait of the father of Chinese communism hung solidly on the wall of the Forbidden City. No one dared deface Mao's image, and to many outsiders his unchanging gaze was a reminder of the violent, unpredictable nature of Chinese communism. Some of the students laughed at this painted face. But Mao gave me the creeps.

Annie and I soon wound up on the wrong side of martial law. My camera was impounded by the police when we were caught shooting a People's Liberation Army base in the south of the city. But after a scolding, our passports and gear were returned to us, and we took the advice of Gordon Manning, NBC News vice-president of special projects, to get out of Beijing for a few days until the whole mess blew over. We headed for Xian, ancient capital of the Qin dynasty.

Remembering our shakedown in Beijing, we tried to keep one step ahead of the police while shooting Xian's pro-democracy movement. The city had been a major focus of protest during the country-wide demonstrations. Many students from the city's big Northwest University campus had joined the Beijing rallies, and thousands more had clashed with Xian's police and army—on one occasion the demonstrators had all but pushed the security forces off the street.

The city was quiet but uneasy by the time we got there, and the police took an immediate interest in the foreigner with the sophisticated camera. In fact a policeman armed with a camera of his own started clicking away at me while I was taping citizens reading pro-democracy posters on the wall of an ancient monument in the city's main square. As we interviewed students working at a makeshift information center nearby, plainclothes cops eased into the crowd of onlookers to listen in.

It's doubtful the presence of a foreign news camera had anything to do with what happened in the small hours of the following morning. A showdown had been threatening long before Annie and I showed up. Still, the coincidence sent a chill through both of us: sometime after dark, just hours after we photographed the square, Xian's political and military bosses sent in several companies of troops. By dawn, every last poster had been stripped from the monument. Annie and I had happened along on the last afternoon of open political debate in Xian.

As we stood on the street corner surveying this political vanishing act, I felt an eerie sense of foreboding. The crowds of onlookers were gone. The students were nowhere to be seen; an empty sidewalk lay where their tents and broadcast booth had been only a day before. I photographed the bare walls of the monument and the deserted street corner to give our story the now-you-see-it, now-you-don't feel of the scene.

At the university campus we found the students unbowed by the authorities' show of force. One of the protest organizers smuggled us past the gate of the main residence complex, and soon we were taping a strategy session in one of the tiny dormitories.

"To tell you the truth, I'm not really interested in politics," one physics major told me. "But what I've done is necessary—it's what I should do and what all the people of China should do."

A crowd of people was gathering outside. Excited, angry voices crackled through megaphones. The protesters would not risk leaving campus, we were assured, but it was becoming clear that some kind of showdown between China's civilian demonstrators and the authorities was now unavoidable. In their tiny dormitory cell the students listened intently to Chinese-language broadcasts of the BBC and the Voice of America. These foreign services were their only source of news about what was happening in Beijing and, more importantly, the main source of hope that the movement for democratic reform would triumph.

"The world is watching us, supporting us," one organizer told me. "We will succeed—the free world will never desert us." It was Wednesday, May 31.

We returned to Beijing to find that the students had erected a Statue of Liberty look-alike in Tiananmen Square. The

"Goddess of Democracy" stood face to face with Mao's portrait. By Friday afternoon the eerie duel was getting on our nerves. I shared a cool beer on the steps of the Heroes' Monument at the center of the square with cameraman Tony Wasserman and his soundman, Maurice O'Dello. One of NBC's top crews, these seasoned South Africans had done weeks of shiftwork in the day and night deathwatch on the demonstration.

"This can't go on forever, mate," Tony said. "The shit's gonna fly, and soon. Just you watch."

It was five o'clock Friday afternoon. The inhabitants of the tent village shifted slowly around the square, or just slept in the afternoon heat. Banners and flags dangled lazily in the suffocating breeze; loudspeakers droned the inevitable "Whiter Shade of Pale." Wuer Kai Chi, a student protest leader, was barking out a speech over a megaphone.

The Goddess of Democracy stood with her back to us. Mao gazed back placidly, looking right through her.

* * *

By Saturday, the show was on. We could all feel it. There were huge crowds in the streets, protesting a failed attempt by unarmed police to retake the square the previous night. All along the perimeter of the city, troop columns were on the move. The forces of Chinese history were set to collide once again.

At NBC's newsroom at the Palace, Bud Pratt had just returned to the assignment desk from a break at his bureau in Hong Kong, and was calmly and methodically preparing his troops for action. Bud, I sensed instantly, is a professional's professional. He had all the gear and people he'd need to run a smooth, safe operation. Walkie-talkies, street maps of the city, stacks of background information in the office so that all staffers, from office boys up, could brief themselves on emergency procedures. There were translators and guides and transport available at a moment's notice, as well as food and first-aid gear. As well, Bud was holding open a phone line to New York—our lifeline should the unthinkable happen and the office be raided by the authorities.

Bud had fielded every available camera unit and was tracking all of them on a blackboard. By then, everyone was either on the street, keeping the office updated by radio on movements of troops and protesters, or on stand-by in the hotel for immediate scramble should the confrontation erupt in violence.

The only NBC correspondents on the story were me (still a freelancer shooting and reporting for CBC and the *Observer* as well) and Keith Morrison, who had just arrived from Los Angeles. Both George Lewis and Keith Miller had left China the previous day for a break in Hong Kong, and although New York had ordered them to turn around and fly back immediately, they wouldn't arrive until the following day, Sunday.

By nightfall Saturday tape was coming in from all over the city; everywhere, troop units were visible but stationary, holding their positions. At eight o'clock Bud radioed our car and sent producer Denise Baker and me east along the same road we'd photographed that afternoon. A much larger convoy had returned and was bogged down by barricades and crowds. Tension between the soldiers and the protesters had risen beyond anything we had witnessed to that point.

Then, around ten o'clock, as Denise and I were pulling up to the Palace, Bud's voice came over our walkie-talkie.

"Art, we've got word of some gunshots in the west of the city, near the TV station."

We went up to the newsroom to drop off our tape and to confer. The shooting report had been first-hand: Bud had sent his most seasoned Beijing-watcher, Eric Baculinao, on a drive along the city's outer ring road, where he'd seen a massive armored column rolling in from the west. Eric had been forced to take cover in a hospital when the shooting started, and had called in word that the soldiers had fired directly into the building as they'd passed by.

I huddled over a map with Bud. He had Tiananmen Square well covered: Tony and Maurice were roaming the south side, while Ken Ludlow from London and veteran Hong Kong cameraman Gary Fairman had the overhead shots from the balcony of the Beijing Hotel to the north. Bud was holding cameraman Brian Calvert and soundman John Hall in reserve—both men had a lot of experience with riot and battlefield conditions and could move quickly to flashpoints as they developed later on. I was the only "floating" camera, so the assignment to the west was mine.

"See what you can find out," Bud told us, "but be sure you've got a place to hide if it gets too hot out there. We don't want anyone to get hurt."

As we rushed back downstairs, the student translator who had been helping us that day ran behind me: "I'm coming with you."

"You can come until the first sign of trouble," I told the young man, who asked us to call him by his English name, Frank. "Then you're outta there and back to the hotel. Got it?"

"Yes. Got it."

Our driver picked his way through the crowds, getting us as far as the Great Hall of the People at the northeast entrance of Tiananmen. Denise, Frank and I started walking. I carried only my Betacam and a small "quick-run" bag with batteries and tapes. We tried to laugh about the irony of our route—directly up Chang An, the Avenue of Eternal Peace—but there was already a sense of grave danger around us. Students ran ahead of us with sticks and the odd Molotov cocktail. They shouted excitedly; something quite apart from Eternal Peace was going on farther up the avenue.

We walked past the ornate Oriental gate of Communist Party headquarters. A row of tough-looking PLA soldiers stood stiffly shoulder to shoulder across the entrance. The honor guard had been posted since the start of the Tiananmen demonstrations—rifles gripped in white-gloved hands, emotionless eyes fixed forward, expressions never flinching even when protesters tried to stare the troops down nose to nose or shouted in their faces.

"Tough mothers with a score to settle," I told Denise. "Watch out for them if things go badly and we have to come back this way."

We passed several intersections barricaded with buses, and then through the darkness up ahead there were a few sharp cracks of gunfire. We tried the walkie-talkie—out of range, as was the cellular phone we'd brought as a back-up. Quickly, we agreed Denise would take cover in the Minzu Hotel just ahead. But as we approached, a crowd of students and civilians exploded through the front doors and out on to the street, waving pikes and sticks and chair legs above their heads. Frank spoke with a few bystanders.

"Soldiers have been shooting a lot of people up at Mu Xi Di bridge. The students caught two policemen here–they say they were spying for the army."

In almost total darkness I held my camera over the heads of the crowd and taped the beating of the two policemen, presumably to their deaths–no one could have survived that mass bludgeoning. Suddenly a few club-wielding youths turned on me, shouting. Frank pulled me back as one took a swing at me; other people in the crowd grabbed my attackers and screamed at me to leave.

"They think you'll show their faces to the police," Frank said.

I turned to Denise. We agreed she had to find sanctuary in the hotel and make contact with the office. Then a peel of gunfire sounded nearby, and as the crowd surged I lost sight of her. I wheeled around and ran with some students towards the gunfire.

"Get out of here, Frank," I yelled over my shoulder. "If they catch you here, they'll think you're a demonstrator. Get back to the Palace and tell Bud what's going on now!"

I heard Frank say "OK" as I knelt down and steadied my camera on an upturned paving stone. Students near me were hurling rocks and shouting abuse up the street. Others were throwing up makeshift barricades of signposts and wrought-iron fencing and anything else they could unearth from the roadside. I focused through my lens into the empty darkness up the avenue, but I saw nothing. Then my heart rose up into my throat and my mouth went dry. An undulating black wave seemed to be washing down towards us–I made out the glistening black riot helmets and then the shields of the advancing troops. I was photographing the main assault force of the People's Liberation Army.

A flash of sparks and a loud bang erupted in the foreground, then another and another–crowd-dispersal munitions, just noisemakers basically, but terrifying. Then came the crackle of rifle fire and the unmistakable whistle of bullets knifing the air. I was up and running, my camera still rolling, the students falling back in despair all around me.

A young Chinese voice shouted the obvious at me in English. "It's *dangerous!*"

I caught sight of Frank running off my shoulder and yelled at him to get a move on. I spun around and dropped to the pavement, focusing up the street again. A student was cycling forward and throwing a stone in the foreground. I saw rifles flashing; the army had closed the gap. I was up and running again.

"Take care," another student yelled at me, "take care of yourself!"

The protesters seemed to be running too slowly, the army too quickly, and the gunfire was louder now. I taped a clutch of students hauling a dead comrade down the sidewalk, and I thought of Denise and Frank and prayed they were safe. Then I was at a barricade of buses, several of which were blazing now, and civilians were throwing anything they could into the intersection to block the army's progress.

An old woman dragged a flaming rug into frame; a student took it from her and tossed it into one of the buses. A bicycle was heaved in after it, but the faces I was shooting now revealed shock and the first signs of hopelessness–what chance did a rabble of protesters have against an armed offensive by the PLA?

I balanced my camera on a handrail and worked the lens to get the widest view of the street. I pressed the record button. I focused on the bright search-beams flooding towards us. Engines roared–armored vehicles were heading our way. The assault force intended to steam-roller anything and anyone in their path. A loud cry of protest went up from the crowd. A couple of spinning points of fire described the arcs of Molotov cocktails hurtling towards the armored personnel carriers. Then gunfire, lots of it, and a strong grip on my shoulder from behind.

"We must go!" It was Frank again. I began to scold him. He shouted back, "They will kill you too. I will *stay*!"

We both ducked low and ran for our lives, my camera still rolling. Passing the barricades at the next intersection, we found the crowd had captured an armored personnel carrier that had somehow wandered on to the avenue from a side-street ahead of the main advance. The students clambered all over the vehicle, pounding it with tire irons and steel rods, but the crew hatches were buttoned up tight. I pushed in closer, saw fires burning under the APC. Then a soldier bolted out the rear escape door. Instantly, the crowd was on him.

"Don't beat him, stop beating him," someone in the mob pleaded, but it was much too late. Hook-shaped rods and steel bars thrashed at the body on the pavement. A sick feeling came over me as Frank dragged me off once more–someone else was threatening to smash my camera if I kept shooting. We fell back towards the square. I breathed deeply, collected my thoughts. Then I told Frank to run up ahead and find the driver we had left at the Great Hall, and get the engine running.

"You will come?" Frank asked.

I nodded, and he ran on ahead.

We were only a few minutes from the square, at Communist Party headquarters. I stopped and looked a moment at the motionless guards standing at the gate. Heavy gunfire and revving engines spoke of the clearing of another barricade; the troops were on their way now–relief for these beleaguered pickets. Exhausted and wounded students were retreating past them towards the square. As I raised my camera, one of the guards took an aggressive step forward. I froze, held out an open palm and moved on–the balance of terror had been tipped back in the army's favor. Another limp body went by, dangling by wrists and ankles clutched by the victim's friends. I ran beside them, holding my camera at street level to record their flight. My lens only inches from the dying boy's head, I saw blood oozing from a hole in his temple. "Hold his head, hold his head," his friend cried. "We're almost there. I can't carry him any longer...who'll take my place?" I pulled up at the Great Hall and let the group pass out of frame.

When I reached our car, I was relieved to find that Frank was waiting. Our driver was trembling with fear, and his eyes were bulging. I opened a rear door, and Frank climbed into the front passenger seat. I stepped back out, slammed the door behind me and shouted at the driver to get the hell out of there and return to the hotel.

The car rushed away, tires squealing. Nothing could stop that driver now, I thought–both he and Frank were out of reach of the soldiers. I put a hand to my face and felt the sweat pouring from my body. Then the gunshots began again, and a big running crowd of protesters spilled out of Chang An and into Tiananmen Square. Barricades were erected. Soon armored vehicles arrived with troops marching alongside, brandishing rifles and light machine-guns.

"We are the Beijing martial law authority," announced an army loudspeaker in Chinese. "What we have in Beijing now is a counter-revolutionary rebellion. We can see this because we are attacked by ruffians."

Some students stepped in front of the camera and hurled rocks at the approaching APCs and trucks. Flames danced behind the silhouettes of the soldiers.

"The ruffians set fire to military vehicles, and they put barricades on the road and kidnaped the People's Liberation Army soldiers."

The crowd jeered the voice on the loudspeaker, and the soldiers answered with gunfire. I turned my back, running, with my camera still rolling. I held my breath and stooped low, tightening every muscle in my body, bracing myself–I was certain I would be shot. Gasps and shouts nearby told me others were being hit and were falling. I dove for cover behind a tree.

"We cannot protect you if you are in the square," the disembodied voice barked. "You must take responsibility for the consequences."

It didn't matter to me that I couldn't understand a word of this or hope to have it translated on the spot. The message from the soldiers' rifles was clear enough. I crawled away, once more bracing myself for what my Afghan friends had described to me as the smashing, burning sensation of a bullet striking the body. But the rounds whistled wide of me, and I ducked towards the center of Tiananmen Square, not far from the Goddess of Democracy.

"You've kidnaped our soldiers," the loudspeaker barked. "And you are trying to overthrow the socialist system." Another peel of gunfire. I held my camera low and ran backwards, photographing on the go, recording what was going on around me. I felt a combination of exhilaration mixed with fear; I realized that I was pushing the outer limits of safety, but there was a thrill in performing there, both physically and mentally. I had to keep going, keep pushing myself as long as I had tape in the camera, as long as these images surrounded me.

"Quick quick!" a voice pleaded. "Run quickly!" A young girl and what appeared to be her mother ran by me. I brought my camera to my shoulder, still rolling, and focused on some activity near the first line of tents on the square. I walked in among a group of students dressed in white, stooping over figures stretched out on the ground. It was the protesters' clinic, now turned into a battlefield hospital.

A victim's blood-soaked chest lay before me and came into camera frame. I stepped around him, panned to another man being given heart massage and mouth-to-mouth resuscitation. It seemed of little use–a head wound, glistening red, indicated a bullet direct to the brain.

"Quick, look here!" someone told me. "There's someone else hurt," a voice cried to the young medics. "Work faster!"

I followed a stretcher-borne patient to a bus standing nearby. The students struggled to get the wounded through the doors and on board while the APCs and troops came closer.

"The martial law force will use whatever methods are necessary to clear Tiananmen Square." Around me now were faces full of disbelief, of confusion, of hopelessness.

"We were just asking for dialogue," one man said somewhere near me, "and now look what happens." "They've shot so many people!" another cried. "They just rolled over people! It just doesn't make sense..."

But now the PLA's strategy was becoming all too clear. Having consolidated the northeast corner at Chang An, and with units pressing in from the south and the west, another troop of soldiers was marching along the front of the Forbidden City wall, right beneath the cold steady smile of Mao Tsetung's portrait.

"Now the square is being destroyed," the army announcer called out. "We must clear it. We don't want it occupied by those of the small minority of counter-revolutionaries, so we have to take action!"

Within the soldiers' ranks I made out the portable light of what appeared to be another TV crew freely photographing the army advance. I climbed a barricade and approached them across the open road, wondering whether it would be safe for me to photograph that close as well. It was a Chinese crew, of course; the regime was covering the story its own way. I pulled back just in time and managed to scramble back among the protesters without getting shot.

Now my thoughts turned to my colleagues. Was Denise safe at the Minzu? Or had the army raided the place, taking captives? And what about Calvert and Hall, and Tony and Maurice? There was shooting coming from all directions. My walkie-talkie was with Denise; I couldn't reach the office. I fell back to weigh my options: stay for the final assault on the square, or get out now with the video I'd already recorded.

Some of the troops marched over the Pearl Bridge and into the Tiananmen gate of the Forbidden City. The main body of the protesters who had occupied the square all those weeks were now filtering back into their tent city, and as I approached the Heroes' Monument I found a sea of faces of disillusionment and sorrow. A sense of tragedy gripped my own heart too, and if I hadn't felt a duty to document what I saw, I'm sure that I too would have sat down and wept.

A boy stood up and waved a bloodstained jacket in front of me. "Look!" he cried in Chinese. "His brains are all over the jacket. Not only his blood, but his brains, too. He was beaten—they smashed his head open!" No one reacted. Resignation was written on every face. Someone seeing my camera managed to raise a hand with a "V" sign. Everyone became silent and still; the army's engines and loudspeakers sounded all around us.

On the top step of the monument I came across a teenage couple, two beautiful kids sitting there, waiting; the girl's face tilted on her lover's shoulder. To me, they were the very image of the hope that had been crushed out of China's youth that night. Their expressions said everything that needed to be said: young people had been fenced in once again by ideology, their futures foreshortened by ruthless old autocrats with brute force on their side. I lowered my camera and nodded to them, a gesture of respect. There was a good chance they would soon be dead.

Suddenly the protest leaders were addressing the crowd on their megaphones. "Put down your sticks. We'll face the armed soldiers. We'll continue to sit here peacefully. That is what we always did. We always agreed we must sit here peacefully without violence to protest the government's fascism."

I taped the banners and flags one last time as they flew against a night sky pierced by the army's searchlights. I could see a huge rank of soldiers running four abreast from the northeast end of the square. The PLA were going to surround the square, then move in. I scanned the southeast corner and saw the last open gap, the only way out of Tiananmen Square. The soldiers were chanting aggressively now, and quick-stepping down the east side to close that gap. I started running, at first slowly, then faster and faster in an effort to beat the troops to the southeast corner. The story wasn't over; there would likely be a final massacre on the monument, but staying to photograph it could be fatal, and most certainly futile if I couldn't get the footage safely back to base and on to New York.

The chanting of the soldiers became louder and louder, but I outran their maneuver and sprinted on to a side-street as they closed the square behind me. My next immediate challenge would be to get to the Palace Hotel without running into the army or the police. I walked swiftly, keeping to the shadows on the tree-lined side-streets. Every few minutes a burst of rifle fire would sound in the direction of the square, followed by a roar of condemnation from the protesters.

I caught sight of the Beijing Hotel. Maybe I could find sanctuary there, tie up with Ken and Gary. I ran towards it, only to have a group of plainclothes policemen swarm into my path— the authorities had evidently regained the hotel entrance from the crowd. I backed away in time and ran for it. An old man on a peddle-rickshaw appeared before me; I waved a fifty-dollar bill in front of him and jumped in the back.

Sinking low into the seat, concealing my camera, I tried to concentrate. Had the police grabbed everyone with a camera, every foreigner on the street? Were all the hotels in the hands of the authorities? What would I do and where would I go if the army had raided the NBC office and shut us down?

My spirits plunged as we pulled up outside the Palace. Buses were drawn up, sealing the place off, and a dozen dark figures with peaked hats stood guard at the front doorway. A long burst of gunfire somewhere nearby told me I had to get off the street. Praying that I'd be safe inside, I tucked my camera under my arm and did an end-run through the shadows, around the buses and the guards. Suddenly I was through the doors and inside the reception hall, blazing with light and eerily silent. Someone had followed me. I turned, ready to duck. It was a hotel security guard. The men outside hadn't been the People's Armed Police after all.

I ran for an elevator and was still trembling when I reached the NBC office. At last I saw a familiar face, a friend–videotape editor Leon Ferguson. Watching me sprint down the hallway, he looked as if he'd just seen a ghost.

"They're slaughtering them," I said, grabbing his arm. Leon took my videotapes.

"We've been scared shitless," he said. "We thought they got you."

Then Frank appeared from one of the rooms and threw his arms around me. "You're safe!" he cried. "Safe."

* * *

There was relief–and surprise–that all our crews had made it through the night. Brian Calvert and John Hall had found themselves in the line of fire of the same assault group I had been covering on Chang An, with Brian photographing several students being shot directly in front of him. Brian had experienced a lot of close calls over the years, but he later told me that out on that square he really expected to be killed.

Like me, Brian and John had nothing but praise for our young Chinese colleagues. "Even when bodies were dropping around us," John said, "they stayed right with us, and then ran the tape back to the office." NBC couldn't have done its job without them. Yet ongoing repression in China prevents me, even now, from using their Chinese names.

Tony Wasserman and Maurice O'Dello meanwhile had been on the square from the start of the attack, and been trapped by the army's advance in the south. Like me, they had finally faced imminent capture and found a "safe house" in which to hide themselves. They later walked back to our hotel, having concealed their camera gear in the home of a friendly citizen for recovery later on. (The next day Tony would photograph the enduring image of the disaster–a man, unarmed, standing in the path of a PLA tank trying to leave the square.)

At the Beijing Hotel, Ken Ludlow and Gary Fairman had manned a high-shot position from a room on the twelfth floor.

They were fired at regularly from the street below but never left their post, and were the first to send tape back to the office. With them, Annie Pong had been on the phone to New York describing the scene during live network cut-ins.

Some colleagues from other networks and news agencies covering the disaster had not been as fortunate. The soldiers had smashed every camera they'd got their hands on, and a few reporters and camera crews were taken prisoner for a time. I had been lucky enough to evade the Chinese authorities when it counted most, but my colleague and friend Jonathan Mirsky of the *Observer* hadn't been as fortunate. Soldiers and policemen seized him near the Forbidden City. "Kill Kill Kill," they had screamed at him. "Kill the motherfucking foreign journalist!" Badly beaten, with injuries to his head and back and legs, Jonathan was eventually released and made his way to the airport and back home to London.

In the aftermath of the massacre foreign journalists had only one means of striking back at the hard-liners—with graphic, truthful reporting of what had happened. The minute our editors got their hands on our field cassettes, they began isolating and dubbing our best shots. The highlight tapes were then run upstairs to engineers Jim Carroll and Chris McCarthy, who fed still-frame images through a long-distance phone line to New York using a Pixelator. Our viewers in the United States saw pictures of the massacre immediately after it had begun. Meanwhile, composite tapes of the best action footage were assembled, copies of which were carried by "pigeons" on commercial airline flights to Hong Kong and Tokyo by mid-morning Sunday, June 5th. (Later in the week, I had my own field tapes transcribed: every ultimatum from the army, every cry for help from the students was translated into English. Still now, I pore over that transcript from time to time, in part to remind myself, I suppose, to what extremes some ruling elites will go in order to crush the free will of the people they claim to govern.)

For China and the Chinese, the aftermath of the massacre was a plunge backwards into repression. Nowhere was that more evident than in Yanzhen, a tiny village I had profiled a few days before the crackdown. Back then, while the pro-democracy demonstrations in China's cities were continuing, the workers in the rice-fields had been surprisingly open and welcoming. But a sudden chill had descended by the time I revisited the commune several weeks later.

"What do you think happened at Tiananmen Square?" I asked a laborer.

"Whatever the Party says—that's what happened."

"But you must have your own ideas..."

"Of course I do. But I keep them to myself."

As we spoke, the village leader approached. The laborer suddenly turned on me. Caught talking with a foreigner, he panicked.

"Make him show you his travel permit," he urged the leader. "He's been asking all sorts of questions about the unrest."

The leader was not happy to see us: even before the crackdown, the bureaucrat in the Mao jacket had been wary of my camera. He hustled my translator and me into his office. A dozen or so sloe-eyed Oriental beauties gazed down at me from the many calendars lining the room. An army officer joined us. He and the village leader scolded us and lectured us for about an hour. But they seemed too lazy to go through the procedure of having us arrested. Just in case, I asked to visit the leader's outdoor john, where I slipped the recorded video-cassette out of my camera and into my jeans—not a comfortable fit, but at least I'd get the "after" portion of the Yanzhen transformation story back to base.

"You know," the leader told us, "the ruffians plotted to kill 457 Party members." I managed not to grin at this supposedly damning statistic. "And they desecrated Tiananmen Square."

So that was it: the students got what they deserved; the official truth is the only truth. The calendar girls on the leader's office walls smiled obligingly from beneath their parasols. Life and law were once again sweet for regime loyalists, big and small. And as we left Yanzhen, the village loudspeaker was barking out a tribute to the brave defenders of Tiananmen Square, the People's Liberation Army.

CHAPTER SEVEN

Live and in Color:
the Death of Communism

There was a written order from Honecker for a Chinese solution.
It could have been worse than Beijing.
> *–Markus Wolf, former head of East Germany's spy agencies, on his*
> *President's response to pro-democracy demonstrators*
> (New York Times, *November 17, 1989*)

THE BERLIN WALL was an imposing backdrop for a foreign correspondent in a trenchcoat, especially when an evening rain had left the concrete barrier glistening under the spotlights with a suitable Cold War chill.

"OK–*Achtung!*"

I had to smile, taking my cue from Joe Oexle, a veteran news cameraman for NBC in Germany and one of the company's longest-serving employees anywhere in the world. How many dozen other fresh-faced young correspondents had stood before his lens during his forty-plus years shooting for NBC?

"How many?" He shrugged, unable to think: his eye was still glued to the viewfinder. "I don't remember. We are still rolling..."

Heinrich Walling, Joe's soundman, assured me, "Don't worry, he has the number somewhere in his head. He's a walking history book."

Indeed he is. And there I was, talking authoritatively about events on the other side of the infamous Berlin Wall only two hours after having laid eyes on the divided city for the first time in my life. Yet even after more than forty years of this–after shooting Brinkley and Chancellor and Utley and Brokaw and all the rest–Joe had taken great care in framing me for my "stand-up." This was the closing thought of my story, the part of a TV news story in which every reporter needs to look and sound as though he knows what he's talking about.

"Excellent," Joe pronounced. "Just like your brother Peter."

A huge compliment, especially from Joe, but as I gazed at the Wall and sensed the dark history there, I knew I had a lot to learn before I could truly join ranks with my brother, before I would genuinely deserve the position I had just taken up—that of staff correspondent for NBC News.

"Come with me, Arthur," Joe said in his heavily accented English. "I want to show you something."

It was October 1989. Two months after my departure from China, I was traveling Europe from my new home base at NBC Rome. I had taken Michael Gartner's offer, closed down my Afghan operation and returned my beloved Betacam to the Canadian Broadcasting Corporation. The days of shooting my own stories were over, for now at least. I would team up with a full NBC production unit everywhere I went.

That change would take some getting used to. For one thing, I hadn't had a staff job since I'd left the CBC way back in 1979. What's more, the company I was joining was slouching deeper into confusion and dismay. Rumors of large-scale restructuring were coming out of New York, and people in NBC's foreign bureaus felt certain that major staff cuts were on the way.

Having just been added to the payroll, I didn't catch the same scent of danger troubling many of my colleagues, but morale was low, and that concerned me. Now that I was really on the team, I wanted to see us all on the offensive. But it's not easy to be a hard-charger when you fear that you and your family could soon be out of a paycheck. NBC's executives tried to reassure everyone that the company would survive. But it was common knowledge that the News Division was in the red and that GE's management team were under pressure to find some radical ways of turning the financial picture around.

It wasn't a happy background on which to plan news strategy, especially if your turf, your coverage zone, was trembling with the first hints of sweeping political change. Which was exactly what was going on in Eastern Europe, just across the Berlin Wall, where Joe Oexle and I were standing now.

"That's where the tanks came at us." Joe and I had climbed on to a viewing platform, and he was pointing into the no-man's-land between the inner and outer barriers of the Wall. "The crowd scattered—it was terrible," he said. "That was 1953."

Joe had been filming on that same spot for NBC News before I was born. During the 1953 uprising that was the first major challenge to Communist control of East Germany, Soviet tanks had crushed the people's quest for freedom; the question now was how the hard-line East German government would respond to this current season of unrest, some thirty-six years later.

Tens of thousands of East Germans had fled to West Germany since late summer 1989 by crossing through Hungary, where links to the East Bloc were being cut and bridges to the West were opening up. The flood of refugees threatened to trigger a violent crackdown from the totalitarian regime under Communist Party leader Erich Honecker. At least 178 East Germans had been shot trying to escape over the Wall since its construction in 1961, and there was no evidence that the aging Honecker and his cronies planned to ease existing restrictions.

Standing by Joe's side, looking into Honecker's prison-state, I remembered all the old newsreels I'd watched on TV: Cronkite's voice describing Hitler's defeat, the Berlin airlift and the start of the Cold War. The Wall had been a grotesque monument to division and represented danger to me even as a child, when my father would watch with me and tell me more about the things Cronkite was reporting, about the threat of nuclear war that the world lived with every minute of every day. The possibility of world war was a constant menace, just like the patrols of the East German border guards, the Volkspolizei, with their license to kill any of their countrymen who tried to scale the Wall.

"Another bloody revolution, Joe? You think it's possible?"

"I hope not. But they are crazy people, the ones in control over there."

This was no overstatement: the Honecker regime had sent a message congratulating Li Peng for showing firmness against the crowds at Tiananmen. And in East Germany's rigidly controlled official media, use of the words "perestroika" and "glasnost" was forbidden. There was to be no Gorbachev-style reform in Honecker's socialist fantasyland.

* * *

I teamed up with producer Michelle Neubert for NBC's first big scoop that autumn in East Germany. We were the only U.S. network team in the country the day Erich Honecker was finally dumped as East German leader by his Politburo colleagues. Within days Joe Alicastro joined us from Italy, and the NBC Rome team was officially under way on its first story—which, in the evolution of Eastern Europe, meant shuttling back and forth between collapsing communist strongholds.

Continuing police crackdowns in Czechoslovakia sent me scrambling to Prague, where the story of public unrest gave way to a sudden swing in the East German crisis. Honecker's replacement as Communist leader in East Berlin, Egon Krenz, announced in late October 1989 that the border with Czechoslovakia was open. This meant that East Germans trying to flee to the West could reach a halfway point in Prague by car or train without fear of being shot in the back. Producer David Page convinced me to hang around a while in Prague to see if, in his words, "this refugee thing turns into anything." By noon that same day, both of us were fairly confident it would.

It started with a trickle of East German families and students arriving on the morning train, asking for directions to the West German embassy. By noon hundreds of them were pulling into town; by nightfall thousands converged on the embassy compound. They were looking for two things: somewhere to spend the night, and advice on how to complete their journey to West Germany.

Michael Steiner, the West German embassy's spokesman, was awestruck by this new wave of escapees. As he welcomed group after group of tired people with yearning in their eyes, his cool, businesslike manner began to brighten noticeably. He was excited. The German in him—the bond of culture and nationality that he shared with the refugees—was telling him that something decisive was happening.

For us, it was story time. David and I put a piece on tape with our camera team Tim Ortman and Max Matteoli and fed it by satellite to New York. But the guys at "Nightly News" did not share our enthusiasm.

"East Germans have been coming to the West since September," they said. "It's nothing new."

According to a friend of mine in New York who was present at the editorial session that turned thumbs down on the story, one of our editors went so far as to say, "We can go back to the story any time if we want to–it's never going to amount to anything."

We were horrified. The other networks had been asleep at the switch in Prague–they hadn't even fed a story that night. We'd been way out front. Now we were out in the cold. David took a triple dose of his favorite brandy and went to bed groaning while the rest of us kept drinking. It was around noon the next day that New York finally woke up to what was going on. Now they *had* to have a piece from us. We were pleased, until we found out why they'd changed their minds: the *New York Times* had spread the East-Germans-hit-Prague story all over the front page that morning, above the fold. Our editors had been afraid to be first, and now they'd pay for it by having the story a day late, like all the other networks. But our spirits were soon on the upswing: the unbridled glee among the refugees was infectious. Newcomers were so impatient to find sanctuary in the crowded West German embassy that they began bypassing the front door to climb over the back fence instead. The compound became a campground, filled to overflowing, and all talk was of heading West. No one had time for the repackaged regime in East Berlin.

"The Communists will never give up power," a machinist named Hans Sander told me. "I want to be free now; I don't want to wait ten years."

Beside me, on the outside of the compound, another East German, Jorg Sielisch, disagreed. He was in Prague on vacation and was amazed to see his countrymen taking flight while the process of change back home was just beginning. "East Germany needs you," he shouted at Sander: "You're destroying what few advantages we have."

Sander grabbed the fence and shouted back at him: "The politicians always talk of fighting today for something tomorrow. I'm not interested in the future–I want to live today."

The exodus filled the streets of central Prague with deserted cars, mostly Trebants, frail plastic vehicles with two-stroke engines. I approached one young couple who were leaving their

"Trebi" in front of a church.

"We'll have no use for it in West Germany," they said. "Here, catch." They threw me the keys. I gave them back, reluctantly. The Trebant was a classic East European artifact, a true collector's item, complete with a sticker on the dashboard celebrating Gorbachev. But if things went wrong for the couple, they'd need their wheels to get home.

Remarkably, on November 4, Communist Party boss Egon Krenz announced in Berlin that any East Germans who wanted to settle in the West were free to travel through Czechoslovakia. They would no longer need a visa to leave East Germany and would not have to renounce their citizenship to enter the West. The Communist Party was giving the people a little bit of freedom, hoping that this gesture would slow down the exodus. Instead, the flow of refugees accelerated.

We went to the railway station as soon as we heard the news. Special trains were already filling up for the journey west. One East German leaned out an open window as the first train pulled away.

"This is for you, Herr Egon Krenz," he called out as he threw a handful of East German money on to the platform. Many others copied him; we had a shower of coins and notes falling into the camera lens.

As journalists, we all felt the earth moving. East Germans couldn't yet climb over the Berlin Wall, but they could now ride a train around it.

The next day we were ordered back to Berlin. East Germany was changing by the hour. The government's Council of Ministers had resigned, followed by the Politburo. Krenz was hanging on, but Dresden's reform-minded mayor, Hans Modrow, had ascended to a place on the new, smaller Politburo. Even Party members were demonstrating for a clean sweep of the old guard.

NBC was all over the story. Mike Boettcher, our Frankfurt correspondent, had been following events in Berlin with Michelle Neubert and bureau chief Suzette Knittl while David and I were in Prague. When we returned, we were part of a full-scale invasion by the network News Division. Tom Brokaw had arrived with Marc Kusnetz and a team from New York. Joe

Alicastro was still with us, and London had sent camera crews, tape editors and engineers. It was a potent force, and an expensive one.

Suzette and Michelle had put together an office at the Schweizerhof Hotel in West Berlin, and we all crowded into it for a strategy session. We were ready for anything–but would "anything" really happen? The whole operation was a huge gamble. We had to ask ourselves: would the political situation in the East develop quickly enough to justify the cost of our invasion? It wasn't until the afternoon of Thursday, November 9, four days after the team began to assemble, that we realized not only that the answer to that question would be an emphatic "yes" but that all of us–from the president of the company down to the grunts on the street–were about to look like geniuses and heroes.

Michelle had set up an interview for Tom that day with Gunter Schabowski, East Berlin's Party secretary. Before taping could begin, Tom and Michelle, together with Marc and Joe Alicastro, had to endure a seemingly endless news conference. But as Schabowski wound up the briefing ("Just as we were all about to fall asleep," Joe tells me), the Party official mentioned that a new travel law would give East Germans access to the West through any border crossing.

Tom jumped on this in his interview. Schabowski acknowledged that the Wall would no longer be an impervious barrier. New York was alerted, and within minutes we were cutting into network programming with the news–Tom reporting from the phone in the car, which was by then speeding him back to the West, and I and others from telephones in the Schweizerhof.

There was no immediate reaction from West Germans to the news; in fact, producer Linda Ellman had to run down to the bar to tell people what Schabowski had said, and get their reactions. The barroom consensus seemed to be "Great news, but let's see if anything really comes of it." Disbelief and shock had put some of our own staffers into a tailspin, especially some of the American student-translators who figured they knew the German persona as well as they knew their language.

"This doesn't mean people are going to start pouring through the Wall overnight!" one of them exclaimed.

"But what if they surprise us?" I asked him. "What if they do start pouring through and we're not there ready to record it?"

Suzette was taking no chances. She fielded all her camera crews while the rest of us went to work on the phones, checking contacts and sources all over the city to discover whether East Berliners were, in fact, going to test the newly announced travel law.

Meanwhile the issue of how to produce "Nightly News" was being decided in the back of a Mercedes. Marc suggested taping Tom at various crossing points and building the show from these recorded segments. "No, you've gotta go live," Joe told him. "You've got to put Tom next to the Wall and anchor the show live from there." This idea won out in the end, not only because it would give the show a sense of immediacy but because it would give us the chance to update the story even while we were on the air.

It was less than two hours before show time when we discovered what a wonderfully fateful decision that would turn out to be. That's when Peter Sansun, his face flushed red, came sprinting into the office with a freshly shot videocassette in his hand. Normally a soundman teamed with cameraman Brian Calvert, Peter had been out patrolling the Wall that evening with a camera of his own. His eyes were wide with excitement.

"They're coming," he said breathlessly. "Everywhere..."

The rest of us, in unison, gasped a well-worn expletive. There was a chill of expectation in that room none of us will ever forget. Suzette scrambled her forces. All at once everyone jolted into motion. Brian Calvert picked up his camera and with soundman Tony Cooper at his side met me by the front door.

"Shall we have a look?" he asked me.

"I think we'd better." A surge of adrenalin took us out of the building even faster than Peter had entered it. Traffic was already choking the streets of West Berlin. Horns were blaring, and we had our first taste of the carnival atmosphere that was sweeping the city. Our driver sped us over sidewalks and boulevards and occasionally by road towards the crossing point at Bornholmer Bridge. But we had to pull up several blocks short. There were just too many jubilant people in the way.

"Good Jesus Christ Almighty," Brian gasped. "Look at that ... "

I don't think Brian or Tony or I said anything that made much sense after that. We just grabbed the camera and the lights and waded into the flow of humanity coming at us from the East. Old people, young people pushing baby carriages, Trebants filled to overflowing with cheering students. There were champagne corks popping, horns and whistles sounding. East German citizens reached out to West German border guards, who took them in their arms and embraced them.

The images and the noise and the overwhelming warmth of emotion all but paralyzed us with wonder. We performed our functions almost mechanically; we shot, asked questions, recorded answers. But it was too much to absorb. We were used to wars and disasters–long years on the foreign news trail had led us to believe in death, not miracles. At one point when Brian had the camera off his shoulder, I saw a tear rolling down his cheek. Our shields were down; the cynicism journalists use to distance themselves from scenes of turmoil had completely fallen away. This was pure happiness, a hot blast of joy catching us all full in the face.

I think the three of us would have stood there blubbering in the street if we hadn't had the show to think about. It was only twenty-five minutes to air time, and we were at least a mile from the feed point. Luckily, a West Berlin police officer listened sympathetically as I explained our predicament. He put me, grasping our tape cassette, into the front seat of a SWAT van with two of his best men while Brian and Tony went back to continue shooting. The police hit their lights and siren, and somehow got me through the traffic and crowds to our transmission platform near the historic Brandenburg Gate.

The show was already on the air, with Tom ad-libbing straight into the camera, telling our viewers about the incredible scenes all around us. He never missed a beat–it was a masterful performance, a pleasure for all of us to watch. Jeff Riggins from the Frankfurt bureau was manning the camera. He winked playfully at us during a commercial break and panned the lens side to side, showing us he had a terrific shot in almost every direction.

A huge crowd of West Berliners had gathered around the platform, and in the background, just over Tom's shoulder, young people from the East had scaled the Wall and were celebrating wildly. With hammers and picks, they chipped away at the Wall. We were thrilled to be witnessing it, but I couldn't help wishing I was back on the receiving end of the broadcast, where I knew the program would look magical. Confirmation of that was soon hanging on our office wall in the form of a telex congratulating us all for a triumphant piece of television news reporting. It was sent to us by the president of the News Division. Not our News Division, though. The hero-gram was signed by Roone Arledge of ABC News.

"Guys," Suzette said, "I think we did good tonight." But the night wasn't over. We had a special to do at an ungodly hour of the morning.

I hit the streets again with cameraman Howard Smith and Fred Richter, his soundman, to check on one of the most infamous stretches of the Wall, Bernauerstrasse. Construction of the Wall in 1961 had carved right through the heart of this residential neighborhood. At one time or another almost everyone has seen newsreel footage on television of the families here who were divided by the armed East German border guards, or "Vopos." Many other infamous scenes were filmed here, including those showing people leaping for freedom from the windows of tall buildings that initially formed part of the Wall.

Not surprisingly, residents on both sides of Bernauerstrasse started smashing away at the concrete barrier as soon as word of the new travel law swept the streets.

"Look!" a man cried at us as Howard set up the camera. "We've punched a hole through it–the monster is coming down!"

West German firefighters were forcing the cheering crowd back so that their crane could swing its iron ball to knock a breach in the wall without hitting anyone. Curious young Vopos were peering over from the other side, some of them clearly frightened by the prospect of the neighborhood being reunified. But it was the Wall, not the Vopos, that the people wished to crush.

"As long as that cruel thing is still standing," one resident told us with tears in his eyes, "there can be no future for Germany."

The Bernauerstrasse story made strong television, and it played well on our special later that night. Tom anchored the

show against a backdrop that improved as the night went on—
the crowd on top of the Wall was getting bigger and noisier as
the hours ticked away towards dawn. Then it was my turn on the
camera platform, reporting live to NBC's affiliated stations across
the U.S. It was a terrific feeling. And as each station signed on
with us and established contact, we got a sense of how many people were watching and listening to Berlin's freedom celebration.
At one point a voice crackled into my earpiece with an oddly
familiar drawl. But it wasn't North Carolina calling me; it was
Sydney, Australia. The whole world was watching us.

Jerry Lamprecht, NBC's long-time foreign news chief, had
been on the platform all night. His verdict, as we shut down at 6
a.m., was simple: in the foreign news game, we won Germany.
But our victory was small compared to the one the German
people were looking for, namely a lasting victory over the social
and economic trials of forty years of separation.

This was particularly true in East Germany, whose people
seemed to us to be the orphans of the Cold War. Joe Alicastro
and I teamed up again to investigate the effect of the Wall's collapse on East Germany's quest for political reform. Four days
after the floodgates had opened in Berlin, we drove down to
Leipzig, the industrial city in the south that had been dubbed
"The City of Heroes" for its role in sparking the popular movement for change. Monday night services at Leipzig's Nicolai
Church had been a springboard for reform rallies, one of which,
just a month earlier, was to have been put down by force on the
orders of Erich Honecker. Those orders had been withdrawn at
the last minute, and the city's reputation for courageous dissent
had been assured.

When Joe and I got there on Monday, November 13, we found
that the Krenz regime's opening of the border had only served
to deepen the people's desire for reform. "Thanks for the trip," one
protester's sign read, "but we want more." A huge crowd chanted
for the Communist Party's resignation from government.

Among the speakers waiting to address the crowd was a well-
dressed man with an official air about him—a local Communist
official who was getting the crowd's message.

"Listen to this," Dr. Ewe Fischer told me as the chanting
welled up all around us. "The cries of the people—that is the

reality." He admitted that the Party had no choice but to surrender power and make way for free elections. "My party has a chance to fight for its own existence," he said, "not more."

It was a hot story, one that reignited speculation about the complete downfall of what had been the most secure of Eastern Europe's Communist dictatorships. We jumped into the car and crept through a dense fog before finally finding the highway to Berlin. With Jimi Hendrix peeling away at his guitar on the car stereo, I wrote the script for what would become the lead story on that evening's "Nightly News."

We had a distinguished visitor in the edit room when we reached the office. Michael Gartner, the News Division's president, had come in to observe the operation. He watched Joe and Leon Ferguson edit our story. It was the first time I'd seen him since signing my contract, but more importantly it was the very first time since his appointment a year earlier that he had witnessed one of his foreign teams putting a spot together under pressure in the field. He seemed impressed.

Many of us thanked him for helping to make the decision more than a week earlier to go big on the Berlin story; it had assured us of being fully up to speed when the Wall started to crumble. But Michael was clearly staggered by the sheer size of the operation. There were at least fifty of us when you took drivers and translators into the count. Gartner seemed overwhelmed by that. Later, one of our senior business affairs people confirmed to me in the hallway that this had literally been a million-dollar story. Hotel bills, airfares, satellite transmission charges, the cost of support staff and cars—all of it added up to one hell of a lot of money. And despite our unquestioned success in nailing the story on the head, we had not managed, as things turned out, to cause a huge swing in the ratings. That was the all-important numbers game that showed advertisers how many people were watching NBC rather than the competition, which in turn determined how much money the network could earn selling commercial time. The reality of life at NBC under General Electric was dawning on us. We could beat the world on a story, but if it cost money, it would probably cost some of us our jobs down the line.

CHAPTER EIGHT

Christmas with the Anti-Christ

How can you do this to me? I've been like a mother to all of you.
*—Elena Ceauşescu, on trial for treason and crimes against
the people of Romania*

AS WE ARRIVED at the Rome bureau three days before
Christmas 1989, we knew why the phone was ringing. Joe
Alicastro and I had heard the news on the car radio as we were
pulling into the courtyard. Nicolae Ceauşescu had fled Bucharest.
After twenty-four years as supreme dictator of the people of
Romania this monstrous figure had been swept from power, forced
to run for his life after two weeks of violent demonstrations.
Once again NBC's Rome bureau was getting its marching
orders—and just days after our return from Bulgaria, which had
followed Czechoslovakia and East Germany in that exhausting
train of turmoil that was the collapse of East European communism. Except this one felt different, right from the start.

"Learjet..." Joe told me as he listened to instructions from
the desk in New York. His eyes widened. He hung up. "*Two*
Learjets if we need it. You, me, Max and Stefano and all the
gear—straight to Bucharest. No visas."

"Shit," I said quietly: a four-alarm scramble.

It was only our second project together as a team.
Massimiliano "Max" Matteoli, a quiet, intense soundman, had
graduated to the bureau's cameraman slot after Tim Ortman had
moved back to Chicago. Stefano Generali was Max's soundman;

an upbeat, wiry forty-one-year-old with a Pancho Villa-style moustache. Both of the guys were supposed to be starting their Christmas holidays that night. Neither thought for an instant of turning the assignment down.

Like thousands of other reporters, we had been trying to get access to the Romanian story for nearly two weeks. But Ceauşescu's Iron Curtain administration had been holding against both the uprising and the growing appeals for civility from the outside world, and no visas for journalists had been issued. Now all that had changed. Chaos and bloodshed appeared to be offering us all a chance to crash right through, any way we could.

We lifted off from Rome at dusk, the four of us packed into the tiny Learjet cabin with all the camera gear and suitcases we could squeeze in.

"In about eighty-five, ninety minutes, we'll be speaking with Bucharest Control," said Captain Cesare Plantuni. "Then we find out if we have permission to land." He smiled jauntily, and turned back to the controls.

I wondered: does this guy really understand what we've asked him to do? Did *any* of us really understand? Looking around the cabin, we might have been flying off to some political convention, not a hot-blooded revolution in full swing. Max and Stefano were munching on panini, casually running through a verbal check-list of the gear they'd managed to get on board and of the excess baggage that was to follow on the second plane a couple of hours behind us.

Joe was frowning; the wire copy we'd scooped up on our way out the bureau door was not encouraging. Ceauşescu had fled by helicopter, and a lot of regular army units had apparently joined the public revolt. But a die-hard gang of secret policemen, known as the Securitate, were holding out for their dictator's return. This private army of trained gunmen was sniping at civilians and soldiers all over town.

"War," Joe said. "Urban warfare."

The seventy-one-year-old Ceauşescu had subjected the Romanian people to outrageous policies, such as his "systemization" plan to bulldoze fifteen thousand villages and resettle residents in concrete tower blocks. (The block-houses made surveillance easier for the estimated one-in-five Romanians who worked for Ceauşescu's security apparatus, spying on their fellow citizens.) The regime's cruelty, combined with the onset of another cold winter without heat or food, triggered the uprising. Ceauşescu's iron fist came down hard on the people, but on this occasion his violent reaction provoked wider protests. Now it was shaping up to be a fight to the finish—either the end of Ceauşescu, or of any hope for freedom in Romania.

I thought of Tiananmen. Of Afghanistan. The prospect of another violent uprising didn't cheer me. At least I felt good about the people I was with, our new team from Rome. The four of us had grown pretty close in the three months we'd been together. Part of the glue that held us together was our shared disappointment with the small amount of air-time we'd received from "Nightly News" during the ten-day assignment in Bulgaria from which we'd just returned. That Communist stronghold too was opening up, but New York was weary of chanting crowds and waving banners; East Germany and Czechoslovakia had pushed the Eastern Europe story past the saturation point.

Our superiors at NBC News were more distracted than ever from the pursuit of good journalism. Chronic financial woes combined with an on-air identity crisis were dragging morale even lower. The "Today Show" was continuing its steep slide in the ratings. We just couldn't seem to do anything right—a farcical suggestion, since NBC News teams, particularly in foreign operations, were, I think, the brightest and most capable in the business. But the unforgiving GE corporate culture laid a heavy hand across our accomplishments, particularly with its doctrine of questioning success and berating every small failure. And the constant warnings that we had to make the news pay for itself "or else" had taken a firm grip on the company, from the news desk in New York right down to the dogfaces out in the field. With this kind of gloom hanging over the News Division, it's not surprising that it took the explosive shock of the Romanian uprising to put the East European story back on the map.

We knew that at least two other NBC teams had been scrambled from other directions. But none of us felt like guessing whether an advance group had made it into Bucharest. We all fell silent. There was just the hush of the engines around us now.

"We've got permission to land," the captain shouted suddenly.

Joe pointed out a spot of bright red light. "What the hell is that?"

It was a fire, a large one, right in the center of the darkened mass of buildings beneath us. We had reached our destination, and it wasn't just the Lear's descent that put a sinking feeling into my stomach.

"I wonder who's got control of the airport."

"The good guys, I hope."

"How do we know the good guys from the bad guys?"

"The good guys'll probably arrest us. The bad ones will just shoot us on sight."

Captain Plantuni and his co-pilot positioned us in front of the sinister blacked-out hulk of the terminal building. A power failure, we wondered, or was the airport about to be attacked? Our captain opened the hatch. A man in uniform, an officer, stepped out of the darkness. I saw a helmeted soldier standing off a ways– a threatening shadow clutching an AK-47.

The officer stuck his head into the plane. His right hand went up in salute; there was a yellow and red ribbon tied around his arm.

"Welcome to Romania," he said in English.

We unloaded the planes, and with a gaggle of journalists that had been accumulating at the airport all day we squeezed into a couple of creaking old buses and got to within a few miles of the city center. I left the guys at a hotel there–they would pull our gear together while I continued on foot to Bucharest's TV station. I made it, but too late to feed even a voice report to "Nightly News" in New York, so I went off into the night in search of the Intercontinental–the hotel we'd targeted for a base. I'd been told it was near Royal Palace Square, where the worst fighting had taken place.

Soon I saw street lights up ahead. I reached a broad plaza. Tanks were poised on all sides, their gun turrets showing the emblem of the uprising–the Romanian tricolor with a hole in the middle where Ceauşescu's Communist emblem had been cut out. The soldiers seemed pretty relaxed, so I approached one of the tanks. A civilian standing with them spoke English.

"You come all the way from Italy?" he asked. He took our

interest as proof that the revolution had succeeded. "Thank you for coming, thank you, thank you."

He was a rugged-looking man of about thirty in a cloth coat. A woolen toque was pulled down over his head. His eyes had an unusual staring quality, but then all the people I'd met that night seemed strangely agitated. It didn't take long to get a sense of the profound anxiety of the Romanian people. You had to wonder what kind of life had led them to this.

"What's your name?" I asked him.

"Socrates."

"What?"

"That's right—just like the great man of Greece!"

The philosopher's namesake looked trustworthy, and I hired him on the spot. We shook on it, and he led me to the Intercontinental, which was a bullet-scarred, blacked-out tombstone of a building that looked to me to be trembling under the fire-red sky.

We walked into the front lobby. Empty. Dark.

"Get down please!"

The voice came from behind the front desk. Socrates and I walked over, looked down. Three men were crouched on the floor.

"Please—we have had some, er, problems here tonight." And then, without missing a beat: "Do you have a reservation?"

BLAM! BLAM! BLAM!

I ducked. Socrates chuckled. "Don't be worried, Kent. It's in the square. Almost half a mile away."

A phone rang.

"Does anyone here want to speak to Vancouver in Canada?"

Vancouver? The lobby was filling up with other journalists now, and I had to get information to the news desk somehow. I asked how long it would take me to get through to New York. By morning, they told me, if I was lucky. So I took the phone. Sure enough, it was Vancouver—radio station CKNW to be exact. Vancouver—summer vacation land for my Mom and Dad and all the Kent kids. And this time of year, there'd be skiing in the mountains, and sailing in the Georgia Straits down below...

"Can you tell us what's happening?" the radio announcer on the other side of the world asked me. "We're recording."

"Yeah, I'll be pleased to tell you what's happening. Just get this message to NBC News in New York."

So on CKNW's tape I gave the New York desk a "fill" on the situation. Gave them the hotel telex number. And I asked them to phone our families and tell them we were, for the moment, all right.

Then I felt a hand squeezing my arm. A tall guy with a French accent said, "Are you talking with the outside? With London, Paris, perhaps?" He was shock-white. Bleached. "I am a cameraman for Le Cinq," he said. "My journalist has just been killed by a tank."

Now CKNW was taping a message for TV-5 in Paris. I put all the details down the phone line. Jean-Louis Calderon, correspondent. Crushed by a tank. Crew requests that Paris newsroom inform his family before breaking the news on the air. Hell, I thought. Guys are dying, and Joe and Max and Stefano are on their own on the other side of town.

The French cameraman went sort of blank after he'd seen that we'd got a message out. He went over to a couch in the lobby, brushed some broken glass from it, and sat down. Socrates and I went outside.

Trucks loaded with shouting civilians were racing up and down the streets—chaos and the flag of the revolt came at us from all directions. It was 4 a.m. There were no taxis to move Joe and the boys up to some of the fifteen rooms I had block-booked in the Intercontinental for NBC.

"We try hitch-hiking," Socrates said, and a minute later we were almost run down by a truckload of cheering young rebels. I pulled out a hundred-dollar bill, a crisp one, and held it up in the beam of a streetlight. Within five minutes we heard some tires squealing, and an old white Mercedes truck, something like a small moving van, pulled to a halt before us. Perfect, I thought. We piled in beside the driver, a red-eyed character with a mad grin who had several ribbons tied around his arm.

"He takes food to the soldiers," Socrates said. "A butcher."

We had rented a meat-wagon.

"But he knows where all the snipers have been! We'll be pretty safe."

The butcher rocketed up the avenue, standing on the accelerator at suspect-looking intersections. He would sit as far back from the wheel as possible, cringing in case a bullet came whizzing through at us, and Socrates and I tried our best to "get small" with him in the cramped, exposed cab.

We reached the hotel on the outskirts where Joe, Max and Stefano were holed up. The clerk told me they were upstairs waiting for me, and I was relieved they hadn't moved out on their own. Maybe they'd even got a few hours' sleep–there wouldn't be much of that in the days ahead. The clerk handed me a message. It was from Max. "Call us as soon as you arrive," it said, and, "P.S.: DON'T DRINK THE WATER!" (I laughed at the time, but the boys later told me that a rumor had swept the hotel that some Securitate agents had poisoned the city's water supply.)

At 5 a.m. we were slinging boxes into the back of the meat-wagon for the run back to the Intercontinental. We could hear gunfights, see tracers in the sky.

"Guys," I said. "Maybe this isn't such a good idea." We talked it over, considered the risk. We decided to go ahead: if the driver thinks he can get us through, we reasoned, then we must have a good chance. Besides, there was nothing that looked like a story where we were standing now. Max and Stef and Joe clambered in on top of the gear and gave us a grin as we closed the door on them. The floor of the truck's box was slick with beef and blood, and someone made a wisecrack about forgetting to load the bureau barbecue.

"Socrates, tell the driver to be careful. Imagine his mother's in there with the boys. And if there's trouble, he has to stay at the wheel until the backside of this truck is out of the line of fire. Got it?"

Socrates translated. "Yes, Kent. Got it. He says it's time for all of us to go to bed now, time to sleep."

Terrific. Snug and safe in bed. Just one last gauntlet to run through a city at war.

* * *

The first blushes of an ominous grey dawn found us on the street, camera rolling. We had made it to the hotel without getting shot, stashed our gear in our rooms by 6 a.m., and now, with no sleep, we were huddled with a crowd of excited Romanians, watching bullets flash off the pavement not thirty yards away.

"*There*! Up there!" a voice cried. "*Se-cur-i-taaaa-taaaaa...*"

A half-dozen soldiers just in front of Max's lens swung their rifles up and unleashed a torrent of fire directly overhead. Stefano looked as though a freight train was driving through his ears – he dipped his boom microphone, tipped his headphones off one ear and cranked back on the mixer. I heard some choice Italian oaths between the rifle bursts.

"Where are you from? Do you know where is Ceauşescu?"

The man's English wasn't flawless, but it was smooth. I answered him. As the pace of gunfire slackened, the crowd closed in on us. Their faces were taut, anxious – a hundred pairs of eyes red with lack of sleep.

"Yesterday," the man told me, "I saw that bastard fly away from the rooftop, by helicopter, right over there."

Max and Stef had the guy on camera now; Socrates was holding back the crush, giving them room to shoot. Gunfire echoed through the narrow streets near Royal Palace Square.

"You think Ceauşescu's gone forever?" I asked.

"Yes–we will *win*!" His voice was breaking. "We're going to have free speech! Free elections!" The crowd hummed its approval. "We're going to be *free*," he shouted, "*free!*"

A burst of automatic rifle fire hammered out a shower of sparks and bits of cobblestone.

Suddenly the curious were running scared, and we ducked with the civilians into a restaurant doorway and jostled for cover with some soldiers. We were fifty yards from the entrance of the Palace Square, not far from the Central Committee Building. The day before, just after Ceauşescu's dramatic rooftop escape, the army had moved in to support the massive crowd of protesters in the square. But then the Securitate gunmen had opened fire, sniping from buildings on all sides, then disappearing into a network of secret underground passageways and hideouts. Now the army was trying to flush the Ceauşescu loyalists into the open.

"There, that window up there!"

A white flag was dangling from the window of a fifth-floor apartment half a block away. A platoon of soldiers dashed by us and took careful aim. Not one of them paused to see if the signal of surrender was genuine. They just emptied their Kalashnikovs into the window. Enough bullets smashed into plaster, wood and glass that small flames licked up into the window frame where the flag had flown a moment before. The crowd applauded.

Max and Stef turned and looked at me. We were a long way from happy Berlin and peaceful Prague. This wasn't Wenceslas Square, where just breathing the air of the Czechs' "Velvet Revolution" filled you with exhilaration. This was Tiananmen, but with guns on both sides.

We shot for two hours and then pulled back to the Intercontinental. Joe had scrounged a car and driver, an enterprising young man named Radu who was making good money dashing customers back and forth through the sniper-traps. Except when his tiny Czech-made Skoda sedan was commandeered by the army or some civilians to carry a body to the morgue, at which times he donated his services free of charge.

"I try clean blood from seats, OK?" he said as we piled into the back seat. It smelled like the back of the butcher's truck.

We took off for the TV station. We wanted to feed our pictures and voice track by noon if possible—eleven hours before Saturday evening news-time in New York—because we couldn't be sure how long the army could protect the TV building and keep the satellite working. The place had become the new focus of popular rule in Romania. A group of intellectuals and rebels from the former government called the National Salvation Front had set up shop in the studios and was trying to broadcast its way towards legitimate control of the country. That made the station the Securitate's prime target.

Our car made it to within a mile of our destination when Radu started looking nervous and pulled over. Shots rang out up ahead.

"I wait for you," Radu said. "I go no farther."

And so we started walking, lugging not only the camera gear but a heavy videotape playback machine and cables we'd need at the station. Soon we came across a couple of hundred people gathered at an intersection. Most were on their tiptoes and craning their necks to see the gunfight across the street. On the other side of the empty crossroads—a no-man's land presumably in the snipers' field of fire—another crowd looked on from the relative safety of a bus-barricade. Occasionally, a few civilians would dash across the open ground to change vantage points. A dozen or so soldiers, ignoring the crowd, scanned the top floors of a sterile-looking office block towering above this little urban battlefield.

"Well?" I asked the boys.

"Let's cross," Max said.

We waited, got a feel for the pace of the exchange of fire. Then we started across, one by one. I walked swiftly into the open and ducked behind a car sitting abandoned in the middle of the crossroads. I noticed two clean punch-holes in the rooftop. Max dashed by me, then Stefano. They made it safely to the other side–the fire from the building was being directed somewhere else. Joe darted out and joined me.

"This is bad," he said.

"Yeah. We've gotta keep going."

I ran the rest of the way and joined Max and Stef. Then it started–a hail of bullets flashed off the pavement between us and Joe. Some soldiers came out of nowhere and ran in beside him, returning fire on the building. Joe ducked low; he had good cover. He signaled to us to go on to the feedpoint–he'd get back and wait with Radu at the hotel. I didn't like leaving him, but we had no choice. On our side of the sniper trap, the only way out was straight ahead.

We reached the TV station just after the army had caught a few Securitate infiltrators out in the open. A bullet-riddled car oozed blood into the street. A house just opposite the station office tower was in flames. Civilians picked through the debris while soldiers reloaded their weapons and stayed under cover.

Mike, the technician I'd met the night before, came outside and got us past the guards. Every interior passageway on the two main floors of the studio annex was covered by fireposts made of upturned tables and sandbags. There'd been running gunfights in the hallways. Mike told us that the Securitate were like moles trying to chew into the would-be government cloistered in the studio next door.

We went into the control room and hooked up. Because of the less than ideal operating conditions, we couldn't talk by phone or through the satellite hook-up with NBC control in London or New York. We could feed our videotape and my voice track to the outside world, but we'd be doing it blind; there was no way to confirm that our signal was clean, or even if anyone at NBC's London bureau was recording us.

Again, we had little choice. I called out my name and an NBC identifier over the control room microphone. Then we played our videotape. I read my script, the story of the battle for Bucharest. It was like a Hail Mary pass into space; we could only hope the satellite was reaching a friendly video deck somewhere in our system. When we were finished, Max and Stef stashed our feed machine in a corner of the control room. We'd be back after dark, I told Mike.

"Be careful after dark," he told me. "This isn't over yet. They will attack us again, you can be certain."

Exhausted, the three of us returned to the street. We needed our beds. Instead, we went to work at the death house.

"That one. He is one of them." The nurse scowled as she pointed out the form of a man under a soiled hospital bedsheet.

Only one thing set this patient apart from the fifty or so other wounded people in the ward—his right forearm was fastened to the bedframe with a pair of handcuffs.

"He and his friends are shooting us down like animals," cursed the bandaged woman next to the Securitate man. "We will never forgive them. Never!"

This one was past forgiveness. Mouth gaping, eyelids not quite closed over the lifeless grey orbs beneath, he looked about twenty years old, powerfully built with thick, curly hair.

"I'll treat him last, if at all," the nurse hissed. Her dark eyes pierced the dying man with hatred.

Max and Stef got a few pictures, but there would be no interview with patient 52.

"We're covered for wounded," I told the guys. "But we gotta get the morgue. You guys ready, or do you want to get some fresh air first?"

"No," Max said. "Let's get it over with."

The putrid atmosphere of the operating theaters had done little to prepare us for the horror of the hospital mortuary, which was filled to overflowing with the civilian dead of the past two days of fighting. The hallway leading to the main coldroom was choked with bodies laid out side by side. People searching out missing relatives stepped clumsily among the tangle of limbs, scanning the faces of the dead.

"My son hasn't been home since yesterday morning," one man wept. "I thought I would find him here, but no, no..."

We walked down the line of bodies. I looked at the victims, old people, children in tiny shoes, a woman in a red raincoat whose face seemed frozen in the act of gasping for breath. The wounds were terrible. The place was like a gallery showing off the effects of high-velocity bullets on human flesh and bone.

Some of the victims had been shot full in the face. Gaping wounds in thighs and arms revealed bones fractured by the force of .762-mm Kalashnikov rounds fired at optimum range. Multiple bullet wounds, closely spaced, indicated that painstaking marksmanship, not wild or random bursts of fire, had led most of these people to the place they now lay.

"Look at my son, look," cried Steriana Alexandrina, a woman in her late thirties. "They shot him in the head just because he marched against Ceauşescu!"

Max and Stef recorded my interview with her. As I turned away, my hand came up against the touch of cold leather. It was the bare foot of an old woman laid out on a slab. I closed my eyes, and we walked out of there. But I knew those scenes would remain with me always. Battlefield casualties are bad enough, but looking down on those people—gunned down in their own neighborhoods—made me think of our own home towns.

Many of us who try to keep experiences like Bucharest in neat, isolated little boxes labeled "somewhere far, far away" eventually learn that the human capacity for brutality recognizes no border. The Romanian disaster could be duplicated anywhere that political extremism is allowed to flourish. Too often I think that people back home who watch our stories view them as a diversion, a kind of sideshow. But they should be taken as lessons, too, that nobody's system of social order is immune from breakdown, not even our own.

In Bucharest and across Romania that weekend, however, there wasn't much time to reflect on higher truths. Journalists were paying a high price for covering the story, too many of them with their lives. In addition to Jean-Louis Calderon, who had been crushed by a tank, a Belgian TV correspondent, Danny

Huwe, was shot to death by the Securitate in Bucharest. And Ian Parry, a twenty-four-year-old photographer with Britain's *Sunday Times*, died in the crash of a Romanian transport aircraft–he'd been trying to get his pictures out of Bucharest.

Four other journalists were shot and wounded in the city of Timisoara, far to the west, where the Romanian uprising had begun: John Tagliabue of the *New York Times*, John Daniszewski of the Associated Press, Jacques Langevin of Sygma and Pasquale Modica of AGF. Given the short time-frame–just a few days– these casualties made Romania one of the bloodiest news stories of our careers.

On that Saturday night, December 23, every member of our team counted himself lucky to be unharmed. The boys and I got back to the Intercontinental to find Joe alive and well. He'd been pinned down for a while after we'd left him on the way to the TV station but had slipped away during a lull in the fighting. He'd got a call through to New York and found out that reinforcements were on the way. Producer David Page and correspondent George Lewis had made it into Timisoara. Another unit led by correspondent Tom Aspell was on the way from Belgrade in Yugoslavia. And we were relieved to know that Michelle Neubert was marshaling still more support through Bulgaria.

We would be on our own for at least another full day, which would make three days without a break. But then who could sleep? Ceauşescu was rumored to be in detention by the army, but fighting raged in cities all across the country. The battle was far from over.

That night the gunfire was so heavy that we couldn't reach the TV station. We ventured near, and we tried every approach. But the bleeding bodies carried towards us out of the darkness meant that it was too risky to continue. Dejected at what appeared to be a second straight night of defeat, we trudged back to the hotel and opened a few beers. Eventually, we decided to phone our story to New York, and miraculously the hotel operator got our call through within minutes.

Dennis Sullivan, who was producing "Nightly News" that Saturday, tried to cheer us up. David and George, he told me, were going to get a satellite report out of Timisoara–a truly magnificent accomplishment since the fighting was horrible there too.

And Tom Aspell and his crew had survived the bizarre circumstance of having made a flight into Bucharest airport earlier that day, only to be forced to fly back out again when yet another battle broke out around the terminal. But they had managed to tape the action and had transmitted the story from Yugoslavia. Our story would be number three from Romania.

Garrick Utley in New York interviewed me over the phone. My answers were recorded and subsequently illustrated by the pictures we had transmitted that afternoon.

All that remained for the four of us, pinned down in Bucharest, was to say good night and hang up. We were in agony, cursing our luck at not having been able to feed our own updated story. We were sitting on some compelling footage, including the hospital material. Disappointment gripped us all.

Then the phone rang. The operator wanted to tell me the charge for the forty-minute call to New York: "Are you knowing how expensive is the foreign telephone calls from Romania?" she asked.

"No," I told her. "But now that you mention it, I can't stand the suspense. So tell me—How-Expensive-Is-the-Foreign-Telephone Calls-from-Romania?"

"For this call you must be paying to the hotel eight-thousand-six-hundred-and-twenty-four dollars. Thanking you and good night."

We had no way of knowing how well our story had played into the mix at "Nightly News" that evening. Our phoner, with its raw, immediate tone, ran more than four minutes on the show. New York was ecstatic, and NBC later won an Emmy Award for the program.

* * *

Next day, back at the TV station, the hallway around Mike's control room looked like the last stand at the Alamo. Barricades had doubled in size and number overnight. The soldiers there now manned a pair of PK light machine-guns, which I hadn't seen since Afghanistan. The long gunbarrels were sighted straight down the hallway. Mike locked the studio door behind us. "Seven people were killed inside the building last night," he told me. "Not by shots from outside. By knives and pistols. We don't know who is who in here, who hides inside the uniform of the army, or in the clothing of civilians."

We established contact with NBC London, and the feed went smoothly. We put enough picture and voice track through the satellite to serve all the day's shows, from "Sunday Today" to "Nightly News." When we had finished, Joe motioned to one of the station monitors. A pretty girl with a guitar was playing and singing on Romanian TV. I recognized her: she'd been just ahead of us as we dashed in single-file through the sniper trap outside the building. It seemed odd to hear the sound of music after the commotion of the previous few days, but it was a wonderful sound, clear and soothing. It was a signal that the TV station that had been Ceauşescu's personal organ of propaganda was now in the hands of the people, and they were holding on.

On our way past the sentries, a British reporter suggested that we stay in the studio, as his team was doing, to avoid being shut out again. That seemed like an odd suggestion to us, since the story was on the outside. But within minutes of leaving the building, we were wondering if we'd pushed our luck too far.

A squad of soldiers escorted the four of us into the surrounding neighborhood. The troops were nervous; they had their fingers on their triggers as they scanned the windows of the surrounding homes. The place was menacingly quiet now. I looked over my shoulder—the troops back at the station were watching us intently down their gunbarrels. No one believed the party was over.

"Max," Joe called in a low voice. "Come on, keep moving."

Max and Stefano had paused at the previous intersection to photograph a soldier peering into a window. But it was the house just across the street from Joe and me that caught my attention. The shutters of an upstairs window flew open. Joe and I had time to duck behind a tree before the shooting started.

The soldiers with us started blazing away in all directions. We lost sight of Max and Stef. For five terrible minutes I truly thought we'd lost them. Then the exchange was over, and they came jogging up the street with their hair-trigger escorts close behind. Stefano was shaking his head and laughing, but his eyes told me what the videotape later confirmed: we had all come far too close to getting hurt. Max and Stef had hit the deck, camera rolling, as soldiers fired directly over their heads at the fleeting shapes of snipers. The pair of them had acted with the highest degree of professionalism and courage, and their footage was frighteningly good.

Our reward for holding out that day was the arrival of rein-forcements. George Lewis and David Page made it into town with their crew after driving across country from Timisoara. The rest of our forces began trickling in from Bulgaria, where Michelle Neubert had set up what amounted to an emergency relief operation to get us the trucks, cars and food that we were lacking in Bucharest. All this brought with it the prospect of a full night's sleep for the first time in four days.

On December 25 we were at something resembling fighting strength when the uprising threw its most mind-numbing events at us. Things began peacefully enough. The fighting had ebbed in Royal Palace Square. Churches around the capital were cele-brating Romania's first freely observed Christmas in more than forty years. It was late evening when the real news of the day broke on Romanian TV.

"Good news for Christmas," the announcer said. "The Anti-Christ is dead."

Then came one of the most bizarre public-service broadcasts in the history of television. Romanians watched silent pictures of what they were told was a military tribunal sitting in judgment over their former tyrant, Nicolae Ceauşescu, and his wife, Elena. The pair had been found guilty, said the announcer, of charges including genocide, theft of state funds and trying to flee the country. The verdict was guilty; the sentence, death.

At first the Romanian student I had taken on as a translator that day sat there saying nothing. He just watched the broadcast with his mouth hanging open. His eyes, bulging with disbelief, were only inches from the glowing bright images on the TV. Finally he leaned forward, closed his eyes and rested his forehead on the screen.

"Oh my Christ," he sighed, "this is wonderful."

A chill ran down my spine. Dracula had been dispatched with a stake through the heart, but Romania's torment would continue.

CHAPTER NINE

All Roads Lead to NBC Rome (But Don't Stop There)

We who are about to die salute you.
—*Gladiators' customary oath to the Emperor before fighting to the death*

I don't care how tired you think you are, get on that plane tonight!
—*An NBC News assignment editor*

ROME. THE ETERNAL CITY. And our eternal heartache was ever being forced to leave this incomparable place for the hell-holes where foreign news was breaking. In my first four months as NBC's man in Rome, I spent a grand total of nineteen days there. But what days.

My Roman lair was the top floor of a building dating from the fifteenth century. The neighbors say that Roman soldiers crucified St. Peter on the hilltop that overlooks the broad red-tiled patio. Today the district is one of fragrant kitchens and tables covered in fine white cloth set out along the sidewalks and cobblestone passageways. This is the Rome of pasta and wine and vines tumbling down through the lamplight and dangling lazily in the night breeze. But apart from putting together periodic reports on organized crime or the unraveling of Italy's corrupt political system, our bureau team saw Rome as a mirage; one that became visible only between journeys to the torn scorched edges of the world. Such as Afghanistan.

* * *

Early in 1990 Joe Alicastro and I decided to capitalize on the kudos we had earned in Romania by proposing an ambitious two-pronged assault on the Afghan story. The news desk in New

York went along with the scheme. Joe and Max Matteoli and
Stefano Generali would shoot for two weeks in Peshawar,
Pakistan, focusing on the mujahideen guerrillas and the refugee
families, while a second camera team would fly from Moscow into
Kabul to work the other side of the story with the Soviet-backed
regime. I would be the human ping-pong ball in this master-plan,
bouncing between the two units.

What I was looking for was balanced coverage. What I got was
a one-way ticket to the frozen hell of Tashkent, USSR.

"Welcome to Tashkent, Garden City of the Soviet Union."
When he spoke those words, Kevin Bishop, our Moscow-based
producer, thought he was being funny. Our rattling old Afghan
Airways Tupolev had just thumped down into a howling
February blizzard, and as we bumped along the runway towards
the terminal building, the mean grey skies gave an even more
uninviting look to what is arguably the most charmless city in all
of Asia.

"A right shit-hole if ever I saw one, mate." Howard Smith,
our cameraman, was in pain. His lanky six-foot-two frame was
compressed into a narrow window seat beside Tony Cooper, the
soundman who had been with Kevin and me for the final Soviet
withdrawal from Afghanistan one year earlier. Thank God it was
only a stopover. The four of us were exhausted. We had checked
in at the airport in Moscow at four in the morning. We'd done
that the day before, too: our original flight had been canceled
without explanation. We had to load up all the gear, go back
into Moscow, stash everything in another hotel, then get up in
the middle of the night and start all over again. We'd been without sleep two nights running and we still had another two-hour
flight to Kabul. And I had warmed up for all this abuse with
a forty-eight-hour triathlon from Pakistan–Peshawar to
Islamabad by road, then a plane to London, where I slouched on
to my connecting flight to Moscow like a zombie on downers.

But now, the *pièce de résistance* of bad news! The Tashkent
ground agent of Afghan Ariana Airways even had the gall to
smile as he gave it to us straight, right between our bleary eyes:
"Kabul is under heavy snowfall, so you will stay in Tashkent for
some time."

"Some time?" Howard said. Panic surged among the team.

"What does he mean by *some*-fucking-time?"

Three days, as things turned out. Three entire, full-length twenty-four-hour days of tortuous monotony—with nights thrown in too—waiting for the skies to clear over Kabul, so we could get to the civil war down there and really start to have a good time.

Ariana, being among the poorest of Third World airlines, couldn't swing enough weight within the horribly corrupt Tashkent bureaucracy to get us into the official Intourist hotel (a grim place in its own right). So all of us on the Kabul flight— the grubby pseudo-hippie tourists headed for India on the cheap tickets they bought in London, the Indian families who had been unwise enough to choose the same inexpensive way to get home, the Afghan secret agents on their way back from KGB training in Moscow, and the four-man Western TV crew—all of us were packed on to a rattling old bus and chugged across town to the Hotel Mockba, which looked like a condemned skyscraper from the outside and a combination zoo/asylum within.

There were no lights in the unheated lobby. When the solitary little desk clerk saw us all coming she ran into the back room and locked the door behind her.

"Let's check out the bar," Howard said, falling back on the first and last survival instinct of the London crews.

But none of us had ever seen anything quite like the Mockba Bar before. Strange creatures in overcoats huddled round small tables cluttered with strange-colored drinks. The humanoids were all staring at the television set, which probed the Chernobyl-like haze with a warm red glow. It radiated frantic images that looked for all the world like a Bruce Lee karate film.

"It is a Bruce Lee movie," Kevin said. None of us found humor in any of this. There were too many rough faces staring at us—Uzbeks, most of them, and evil-looking characters who eyed Howard's camera covetously, and sized us up like butchers deciding which limb of the carcass to hack off first. In a place like Tashkent, first impressions can, in fact, tell you everything you need to know.

In our three days of confinement we learned that it wasn't just the bar that was thick with black marketeers, smugglers, thieves and prostitutes. Every one of the hotel's eighteen floors was populated with the same clientele. The low point of this debacle came when I was closeted in my cockroach-infested room shouting at New York through a terrible phone connection. Howard and Kevin and Tony were across town boozing at the Intourist, and I was nervous about what they might do to me if they came back drunk to find I hadn't yet found some way to get us all out of this trap. Fortunately, New York sympathized with our plight.

"YES - YOU - MAY - ABORT. RETURN - TO - MOSCOW..." John Stack had been my principal foreign assignment contact since I'd first picked up a camera for NBC. He knew I wouldn't request a turn-around unless the situation was desperate. John bellowed each word down the phone line from Manhattan; still, my ear was straining to make out the small, crackling phrases leaking into Tashkent.

I shouted back at him: "I - WILL - TRY - BUT - AIRLINE - HAS - GEAR - LOCKED - IN - PLANE - AND - THE - BAS-TARDS - REFUSE - TO - UNLOAD - UNTIL - WE - REACH - KABUL!"

The door to my room banged loudly. I stretched out an arm and opened it quickly: it had taken me two days to get the call through to Stack in New York and I didn't want to lose the line.

"Good eeev-en-ing, boychik." A fat blonde woman stood in the doorway cooing to me through her ruby-red lips. "You vont zom good *fawn*, beeyootiful one?"

I shook my head and reached out again to close the door, but it was too late; she was already inside and Stack was yelling at me again on the phone.

"DO - WHAT - YOU - THINK - BEST..."

The hooker had quite a young and pretty face, but the body beneath the sparkling blue synthetic-knit dress wouldn't have looked out of place on a Sumo wrestler. Except for the giant white breasts, of course, which the bulky beauty was proudly displaying for me while making fish lips and laughing provocatively.

With the worst of timing, the line chose that moment to break. Stack in New York was gone. I was alone with...Ludmilla. I put down the receiver and pushed her towards the door. She looked hurt. I gave her ten roubles and pointed at the room Howard and Tony were sharing.

"There," I told her. "When they get back, they're all yours, gorgeous."

But she was an impatient girl and her meter was running, so she knocked on my door again five minutes later. This time she reached purposefully into that fleshy great crevasse and pulled out a condom that she kept between her breasts. It was brand spanking new and still in its made-in-the-U.S.A. wrapper.

"You vont to play safe, zis is the problem boychik?"

I was glad when the guys came back. They were blind drunk and looked almost as dangerous as the pimps downstairs in the bar. Ludmilla wisely decided to leave us all alone.

No team was ever so glad to reach Kabul. As things turned out, a blizzard in Moscow ruled out a retreat, so we had to press on with plan A. As we suspected, it hadn't been a storm that had closed the airport in the Afghan capital, just a rocket barrage. As soon as the shooting stopped for a while, we were back on our way to the war. From that point onwards, the project went smoothly: our shoot with Afghan government forces, combined with the material Joe, Max and Stef brought back from Pakistan, resulted in a strong, well-balanced series of stories. We explained that the civil war showed no prospect of resolution. The superpowers had left Afghanistan in flames, and civilians on both sides of the guerrilla-government divide were condemned to what was shaping up to be another decade of suffering.

We were back home in the Rome bureau when the stories were broadcast in the U.S. We knew we had scored a hit when we logged into the computer to read the transcript of "Nightly News" for February 23, 1990, just before the show went to air. Coming out of one of our Afghan pieces, Tom Brokaw read something special. He'd written it himself—an on-air commendation from anchorman to correspondent.

"So many NBC correspondents have been in the middle of so much action in the last year, but Arthur Kent's record is especially remarkable. He was in Tiananmen Square the night of the massacre; he was in Berlin the night the Wall came down. He was in Bucharest when Ceauşescu was executed. He's been in Czechoslovakia and Bulgaria, as well as in Afghanistan and Pakistan. He's been everywhere. Everywhere but home."

We all felt deeply satisfied: Joe, Max and Stefano, along with our new bureau tape editor Leon Ferguson, had been with me on most of those assignments. They, too, had been everywhere but home.

It was shaping up to be another great year to be a reporter.

* * *

If only things could have stayed that sweet in 1990. Unfortunately, the year quickly began to sour. First, in Eastern Europe. In Romania, a population unaccustomed to the burden of choice flunked their first test at free elections. The Romanians traded an imposed Communist dictatorship for an elected one–almost all of them voted for politicians who had served under Ceauşescu.

In Czechoslovakia, too, the velvet touch was gone, replaced by hard political realities. Vaclav Havel was immensely popular as president, but the new government was stumbling over an old ethnic split between Czechs and Slovaks. While the country's new leaders squabbled, the economy creaked ever closer to breakdown.

East Germany was even more distressing. Slick West German politicians ran away with the March elections in the East. People voted not for democracy but for Deutschmarks, turning to any candidate who would lead them to West German Chancellor Helmut Kohl's back pocket. And Herr Kohl, mindful of his own future in a united Germany, campaigned hard in the East and embraced—hell, corralled—his new electorate.

I went down to Leipzig to see how the "City of Heroes," the town that had blazed the road to democracy, was taking it all. A pre-election debate between two men in a beer garden went like this:

"You're just a Communist!"

"I was *never* a member of the Party!"

"Liar. You're a Communist *pig!*"

When they started slinging beer at each other, we took our camera out of there fast.

"Last autumn it was easy," one citizen explained. "We demonstrated for one thing–for the Wall to come down. Now there are too many voices raised, too many arguments over what we should do next."

Over at the local Stasi headquarters they knew just what to do next. The Leipzig branch of Erich Honecker's dreaded secret police were throwing a party, and pretending the Party was still alive.

They were surprisingly warm towards us. They let us stroll in and visit with all the former informers, enforcers, goons, spooks and gunmen, and all their shockingly blond-and-beautiful families. We taped them having a dance in the cafeteria, where some bright young agent had converted a couple of old surveillance cameras into disco-cams that panned around the happy assemblage and displayed the scene on a pair of monitors hanging overhead.

I was approached by a sturdy Teutonic beauty with a severe hairdo that shone like a bullet-proof shield. She lifted her pre-teenage daughter up into my face.

"She's *proud* of her Red Daddy!" the woman announced. And with that, and a contemptuous look down her long hard nose, she dismissed me.

* * *

In April of 1990 I was on my way back to Rome when NBC's high command ordered me to fly to, of all places, the United States of America. The News Division was having one of its "workout sessions," a sort of group-grumble, where bosses tell employees What's Really Going On and employees get a chance to talk back. It's a hand-me-down tradition from the network's owner, General Electric, which at that point was forcing its expensive subsidiary as never before to squeeze every dollar it could out of the News Division's budget.

When I arrived at the conference center in Princeton, New Jersey, I joined a group of about two hundred NBC News correspondents, producers, editors, writers, researchers–bright, committed people, most of whom had long histories with the company. We enjoyed a few drinks and a few laughs together and talked into the small hours. Not just about corporate politics, but about news and craftsmanship and professionalism too. It was good to be among them all because they cared about the company and wanted to find out from our president, Michael Gartner, what they could do to help save it.

Facing the troops wasn't easy for Michael. Unhappiness with his leadership had been mounting in the division. As he forced the GE concept of "right-sizing" into our collective consciousness, he was derided by staffers as the "Man from Iowa" and the "Four-Day-a-Week President," after his habit of disappearing from New York Thursday nights to spend weekends at home in Ames, Iowa. At the time many staffers, especially overseas, were routinely made to work six- or seven-day weeks. But it was more than just his style that had contributed to a steady decline in morale.

During Gartner's tenure, name correspondents like Chris Wallace, Ken Bode and Connie Chung had left NBC. John Palmer had been forced out of his anchor roles on NBC's morning shows, and Jim Bitterman had only recently jumped ship to join ABC in Paris. Most disturbing of all, not just for me but for anyone in the News Division who knew what great correspondents are all about, my brother was planning to leave as soon as his contract in London was up. Peter didn't have to explain his reasons to me. A reporter's reporter, he was tired, exhausted. But not of the road: he was fed up with the path NBC management was taking away from the business of real journalism.

While pressures had grown on all of us to travel faster and farther to report our stories with drastically reduced resources, conditions in New York seemed sloppier and stranger than ever. We were amazed, alarmed even, when Steve Friedman was parachuted into the top spot at "Nightly News." Notorious in the industry as a bombastic showman with modest news credentials, he replaced the solid and respected journalist Bill Wheatley, who had been crudely shunted from the executive producer's chair to internal exile in the Specials unit by Michael Gartner and Don Browne. True, Steve had done well in his long tenure at the "Today Show" years earlier. But he'd been fired from his previous post at the short-lived USA Today network.

One of Steve's early experiments at "Nightly News" foreshadowed his eventual undoing years later on the show. Tiny cartoon figures, anonymous little characters with no connection to anything that preceded them in the show, popped on to the screen after the closing item–a kind of Hanna-Barbera sign-off to the network's flagship news program. It was as if the executive toys, the plastic hammers and whoopee cushions that littered Steve's desk, had been animated each evening to help Tom Brokaw say good night. Though seldom inspirational from a journalistic point of view, a visit to Steve's office was always entertaining. One day I asked him why he didn't seem to make any written requests or assignments.

"Never put anything in writing," he said with a wink. "It's easier to deny later."

Meanwhile, our rivals at ABC News regularly topped the evening news ratings. Despite our big foreign news scoops of 1989, Tom Brokaw and "Nightly News" appeared to be on a slide to the bottom of the traditional big-three network race, cartoons and all.

It was a spiral of despair, aggravated by GE's corporate style. The downturn had begun back in the summer of 1987, when GE sold off NBC Radio. There was no future in the field, explained GE chief executive Jack Welch, or at least not enough of a future to meet his personal credo that all GE subsidiaries must consistently earn at least second place in their respective markets.

Mr. Welch showed no regard for the radio network's sixty-one years of history. In the golden years of RCA General David Sarnoff had founded NBC Radio as a vehicle to promote sales of his company's radio receivers. But Sarnoff also believed in a principle of public trust—the responsibility to broadcast what the audience needed, as well as wanted, to know. NBC Radio, made wealthy and powerful by names like Jack Benny, Toscanini, Milton Berle and Sid Caesar, was the mother of NBC Television. And both illustrated that good broadcasting could also be extremely profitable broadcasting.

But under GE, we asked ourselves, was TV, like radio, just another expendable corporate asset? Everything about Jack Welch said Yes. News executives who had experienced Mr. Welch in the boardrooms and corridors of 30 Rockefeller Plaza seemed unanimous on one thing. The News Division was just another spoke in the corporate wheel, and as such it would have to bear ever more weight as Mr. Welch drove GE towards his personal goal: to overtake rival giants like IBM and Exxon to become the biggest, most powerful corporation in America.

A conglomerate worth some $50 billion when it took over RCA in 1986, General Electric was a century-old empire born long before the age of electronic communications and modern media. Welch was an aggressive, upwardly mobile forty-six-year-old when he became CEO in 1981. He had pushed and pulled the mammoth organization into the eighties, instantly achieving rapid growth and, along with it, potentially damaging controversy.

In February 1989 GE agreed to a settlement with the U.S. government of $3.5 million–the largest amount ever recovered at that time–over five civil lawsuits, including contract fraud, relating to GE's military contracts. At NBC News, where many of us were already concerned at working for a big defense industry contractor, the decision confirmed much of what we had heard of our parent company's tendencies towards excess, as personified by its chief executive.

Respected by some as a radically imaginative executive, Jack Welch horrified others with his zeal, and his apparent hypocrisy regarding employees. His speeches were long on the importance of good people and the need to avoid bullying them. And yet he had earned the nickname "Neutron Jack" for his propensity to rid himself of employees from troubled divisions, much as a neutron bomb eradicates people while leaving buildings untouched. It was his abrasiveness that became instant legend within NBC, along with his constant tirades on the themes of challenge, of reaching for ever-greater heights, even if that meant questioning the value of products that were already popular with the public.

Even Michael Gartner, whose appointment to head the News Division was made ultimately by Jack Welch, would eventually complain of "a tendency up there to want to fix what isn't broken." Michael himself became deeply involved in the most disastrous of these GE-inspired experiments. In 1989 Welch and network president Bob Wright appointed a sports executive, Dick Ebersol, to oversee the "Today Show," the News Division's successful morning program. When Gartner and Ebersol jointly decided to replace Jane Pauley with Deborah Norville as co-host of the show, they triggered the most dramatic collapse of viewership and advertising revenue in the network's modern history.

Staffers like myself couldn't help wondering where this was leading. I had come into the news industry with people like David Brinkley as role models. Now, in 1990, as I began my second year as an NBC News staff correspondent, I couldn't recognize the place as ever having been home to Brinkley, who had abandoned ship for ABC in the early eighties. As the new decade progressed, how much more of NBC News and what it stood for would soon join Brinkley as just a distant memory of greatness?

As Michael Gartner stood before us in Princeton that spring of 1990, he represented not just his own management style but that of the entire GE chain of command. He had made an attempt to dress casually, in the retreat mode typical of these think-tank sessions, but his famed bow-tie and suspenders were throwbacks to the affectations of Wall Street in the eighties. He'd brought his deputy, Don Browne, to sit beside him: like a greying quarterback facing a hopeless fourth quarter, Don showed us all a mask of determined loyalty as his mentor spoke.

Michael outlined the way he had turned the News Division's overall loss curve upward towards recovery. His charts and graphs made it look as though NBC News was within striking distance of breaking even for the first time in years. He said our "credibility" with GE was at stake if we couldn't keep the savings coming.

Since he'd invited us to speak up and ask questions, I raised my hand. "How much 'credibility' can they reasonably expect, Michael?" I asked. "The numbers show that you've cut costs, but if they cut back any more, how are we going to be strong enough to compete and win and make money?"

I could tell by the look on Michael Gartner's face that he felt betrayed by my questions. Only a year earlier, he had hired me. Now I had spoken out against him in front of the others, touching the raw nerve of the company. And to make matters worse, many of the people in the room responded to my comment with applause. Our relationship, once friendly, froze over at that moment. It has never thawed.

Don Browne, Michael's vice-president and number two, spent most of the rest of the meeting trying to take the edge off his boss's stilted performance. More than once he promised that we'd get comparable correspondents to replace those who had left the company. But it never happened. The ranks thinned even more, and the pressure mounted on those of us left behind.

CHAPTER TEN

The Incredible Gulf

We here just do not have the ability to move around the front as journalists have in past wars. We're under very tight restriction, and there's no sign of that lifting yet...
—Arthur Kent speaking to Bryant Gumbel on the
"Today Show," January 24, 1991

I think we should stop whining about this censorship thing and just get on with the show.
—Steve Friedman, executive producer of "NBC Nightly News,"
echoing management sentiment on a conference call
with bureaus during the Gulf War

THE GULF WAR was not the biggest story of my career, but it was certainly one of the strangest. When Saddam Hussein's forces invaded Kuwait at the beginning of August 1990, NBC and the other networks hit the trail with more engineers, fixers, associate producers and camera crews than you could shake a boom-microphone at. We had fully integrated teams of producers and correspondents and sub-anchormen for each key field location. And satellite ground stations–the uplinks that connected us "live" with New York–were virtually falling from the sky. All this only months after management's cutbacks had affected us so badly on foreign news that Joe and I had been forced to go to Czechoslovakia to cover the Pope without a camera crew. We'd been just a couple of guys begging for pictures from agencies and other networks.

"I've heard that GE's written a blank check on this one," an NBC vice-president whispered down the phone from New York. "We've got free rein."

Out in the real world, we had to wonder about that one. All this feverish spending, we reasoned, would put NBC News heavily into the red, which would inevitably lead to more layoffs down the line. So "free rein" could turn out to be nothing more than another few miles of rope to hang ourselves with. But management lurched onwards, turning a blind eye not only to ballooning expenses but to an even more basic threat—censorship.

As soon as we hit the road, we discovered that the closer our electronic legions got to occupied Kuwait in a geographical sense, the further we strayed from the practice of free journalism. That wasn't surprising: anyone with experience working in the Middle East understood that access would be the single most important factor to successful reporting and that the price for simply getting into Iraq, Kuwait and Saudi Arabia would be high. But few of us understood the wholesale theft of rights that our companies were so unwittingly setting themselves up for. And not so much at the hands of Saddam Hussein (not exactly a champion of free expression) but by other governments—Western ones, founded on principles of freedom of speech—most notably, the government of the United States of America.

The public relations campaign surrounding the allied military deployment to the Gulf should have alerted us to what would inevitably follow. The American news media should have put up a wall of healthy skepticism and drawn its own "line in the sand" the very first time we heard that nifty catch-phrase born in the bowels of the Pentagon—Operation Desert Shield.

This vast international police action scored its first success as a slick depiction of good versus evil. The Western democracies, supporting friendly Arab nations, constituted the noble forces of light and freedom, which had been mobilized to defeat Saddam Hussein's armies of darkness. But life and death issues aren't that simple in the modern world—particularly the Islamic world—as Western nations eventually learned in the tragic and tangled aftermath of the war.

A lot of what President Bush and his men were saying just didn't ring true in my mind, particularly on August 31 in Dhahran, Saudi Arabia, when I first met a general named H. Norman Schwarzkopf. The commander-in-chief of the coalition forces was making his first front-line visit to the troops, and I was the television news reporter whose number had come up to cover the event for the soon-to-be-infamous "pool system."

You couldn't help liking the guy with the John Wayne swagger and the good-ole-boy manner. He strode out among the troops surrounded by a brace of plainclothes, rifle-wielding bodyguards who seemed more than eager to die for the man. One of them told me, "Treat him kindly, will ya–he's a good shit."

But Stormin' Norman wasn't above a gentle fib here and there to keep morale from sagging too low. In one encounter that day cameraman Gary Fairman and his soundwoman, Ann Shannon, taped the commander assuring members of the 24th Mechanized Infantry Division that he and the brass in Washington were working out a rotation schedule to limit tours of duty. He and the Pentagon already knew, however, that a large-scale rotation scheme was impossible and that few of the troops would see home again until the confrontation in the Gulf was resolved.

At a news conference a few hours later the general took the art of military and political deception to a new level. When asked about the unclear command structure between the various national forces gathering in Saudi Arabia, he said, "We know exactly how we're going to co-ordinate...co-ordination is happening at every level on the ground out there now."

In truth, as we later found out, most American units didn't have even a rudimentary understanding of where their Arab counterparts from nations like Syria and Egypt were dug in on the desert floor, and Schwarzkopf, at that time and for months afterwards, was fighting hard behind the scenes to get the kind of authority he would need over all national forces within the coalition. I raised the matter with British Brigadier-General Patrick Cordingley as he came ashore with his famed "Desert Rats" armored brigade. "I quite agree with you," he told me off-camera; "our current command set-up is geared only for defense–we have as yet no structure in place that I can see that could move this force quickly enough for offensive action."

That comment helped me fashion an analytical treatment of the issue. We got the story on the air eventually, despite luke-warm interest from the producers of "Nightly News." It would be a full five years before the true extent of the coalition's fractures would be revealed, when Britain's top commander in the Gulf, General Sir Peter de la Billière, acknowledged that his own mis-givings about the alliance's preparations and strategy caused him to refuse a request from General Schwarzkopf for British troops to advance alongside U.S. Marines in the initial thrust of the ground campaign.

Of course, with hindsight, some of General Schwarzkopf's bluster and bravado in the early days of the deployment is under-standable–he might have had to lead his patchwork army into war at a moment's notice. But his "why we fight" reasoning seemed to me to be downright phoney at the time, and still does.

"There's not one soldier out there that feels he's been sent over here to fight for oil," he told journalists, "not one that I've run into, or that I've heard about."

The truth was that many U.S. soldiers were openly questioning the whole operation. "Who are them Koo-wackies to us, anyhow?" I heard one Marine sergeant grumble as he dug a foxhole in the sand. But it was one of the Pentagon's own public affairs officers (PAOs) who put it best. He told me, off the record: "I just don't see why we have to lie about why we've come out here. If it's to protect the oil from Kuwait and our own economic interests, why not just say so?"

The answer is as old as the practice of warfare itself–political and military leaders seldom justify the huge expense and tragic waste of war for reasons of mere practical necessity. It's best if armies (and the citizens who support them) venture into battle for a cause of burning nationalism, or with some high moral purpose, however fraudulent that purpose might be. That's why Stormin' Norman went long that day on phrases like "international rape of the first order" when he referred to the Kuwaitis' suffering at the hands of their Iraqi invaders, and short on the real reasons that all of us were gathered out there sweating in hundred-and-twenty-degree heat wondering when the first rocket would fly.

Personally, I was torn on the issue of what, exactly, the invasion was all about. I had grown to despise Saddam Hussein. A few months before the invasion of Kuwait, he had executed a col-league and friend from the *Observer*, reporter Farzad Bazoft. Farzad had been accused of spying for Israel; in truth, he was a reporter out to expose Saddam's weapons program. Following his conviction in a kangaroo court, Farzad was hanged in an Iraqi prison and his body dumped in front of the British Embassy in Baghdad.

But my contempt for the dictator didn't mean I'd buy into the propaganda being pushed by the anti-Baghdad coalition, most of whose partners had previously armed Saddam Hussein. Especially since it was making a mockery of our profession. When the Saudi military authorities, for instance, took the first plane-load of journalists into the area bordering Iraqi-occupied Kuwait, it was like being on a Cook's Tour with a drunken navigator. We got lost several times looking for Egyptian commandos, who didn't really want to be photographed or interviewed when we finally tracked them down. For consolation, all we had to hang on to were the neatly printed itineraries presented to us by our control-freak hosts, the Saudis.

11:45–ARRIVAL AT FIRST LOCATION.

13:00–ARRIVAL AT SECOND LOCATION.

16:00–RECESS.

Recess? It was, in fact, like a school junket, except when our overloaded bus happened by a trio of hapless Moroccan soldiers trying out their gas masks in the full blazing heat of the afternoon. As photographers piled out and charged the soldiers, one of the wobbly kneed Desert Shield defenders actually raised his rifle in self-defense.

Then, to hurry the pack along and back into the bus, a Saudi officer pressed a bayonet against the stomach of our soundman, Hanafi Hegazi. Cameraman Mohamed Muslemany, Hanafi's partner from NBC's Cairo bureau, retaliated by unleashing a few quick karate blows to teach the Saudis a lesson in restraint. Our first journey to confront the Iraqi army had produced little useable footage, but we had been on the verge of spilling Arab blood over a five-minute delay in the "program."

Far to the rear of the border zone, the Kuwaitis had a different but equally frustrating approach to the propaganda game. They concealed their "government-in-exile" in the southwestern Saudi resort of Taif and hired a high-powered Washington consultancy firm, Hill and Knowlton, to help win the hearts and minds of the foreign press corps. The result was that we had to talk to Lew or Nigel or Frank to find Kuwaitis who could tell us something about the occupation. But no one would help smuggle any of us overland to meet Ahmed or Abdullah or Sultan or any of the other brave Kuwaitis who had chosen to stay in their homeland to resist the Iraqis. Instead, we were invited to have Turkish coffee with idle dispossessed millionaires who had not much more to say about the situation than "When do you think the Americans will liberate our homeland?"

We knew that a number of brave men and women were fighting and dying for Kuwait, but the privileged refugees who waited in five-star comfort in Saudi Arabia with their poorly behaved children did much to dispel the myth of cruel injustice that the PR men sought to create around them. After Afghanistan and China and Romania, Kuwait seemed to me to be a nation shopping for an army of mercenaries, not a society willing to fight its own way towards freedom.

The Kuwaitis and the Saudis, though, were the amateurs of the media-control game. The professionals resided in Washington. With everyone from the Joint Chiefs to the lowliest janitor at the Pentagon warning that the American press had to be kept "on side" for this one, and not allowed to repeat the tough coverage of the Vietnam War, Defense Secretary Dick Cheney presided over the most restrictive set of controls ever clamped upon U.S. reporters in time of war.

Cheney had a small army of capable public affairs officers to operate this censorship regime, and as the system took shape in the autumn of 1991 there was an astonishing lack of resistance from the chiefs of the big U.S. TV networks, newspapers and wire services. Despite warnings from their correspondents in the field, too many top executives allowed themselves to be smooth-talked and co-opted into believing that the Pentagon would act honorably if and when the whistle blew for total war. The result: coverage packaged by U.S. military authorities.

Our network news operation stumbled unknowingly into this debate—and fell flat on its face—when producers in New York dreamed up the idea of having our crews tape impromptu "postcards" or "Hi Moms" with troops we encountered while out on assignment. The concept, once demonstrated, was an instant success in the eyes of our executive producers. Servicemen and women would stand before the camera, give their names and offer a greeting to a loved one in the U.S. These segments were transmitted to New York and inserted before and after commercial breaks in our news programs.

While the Hi Moms were an unquestioned morale-booster for the troops and their families, many of us at the Dhahran bureau questioned their legitimacy. Ours was the business of journalism, of asking questions, of digging for answers. We weren't supposed to be in the greeting-card trade, however nice it might be to put Sergeants Rock and Rita in touch with their loved ones.

The Pentagon, meantime, realizing the public relations value of the video greetings, instructed the Joint Information Bureau or JIB (their public affairs office in Dhahran) to facilitate the shooting of NBC's Hi Moms, even while they were shooting down our harder-edged story requests. This double standard should have prompted our network brass to take counter-measures. Instead, the Hi Moms became institutionalized in NBC's programming as a ratings-booster.

That was clearly a mistake. As the weeks went by, the Pentagon's public affairs strategists became more and more brazen in hindering or blocking controversial story proposals from all the networks and news agencies encamped at Dhahran. A good number of American print reporters worked around the system and turned out some important pieces explaining the complexity of desert warfare and the nightmarish political cross-winds of the region. But television news teams were more cumbersome and easier to manhandle; several PAOs shamelessly confirmed to us that control of the networks was the Pentagon's top public affairs priority.

At NBC Dhahran, consequently, most of our best shots were taken on the hotel's tennis court. Max Matteoli was stylish on the forecourt; Leon Ferguson showed he could do more with his hands than just edit, and Joe Alicastro was bursting with competitive zeal. I contented myself with the occasional jog around the soccer field, while Stefano Generali, our soundman, favored the pool. (Stefano found out the hard way that the men's sauna was off limits. An infatuated Saudi fighter pilot leapt on him when he dozed off in there one day.)

The autumn run-up to the Gulf War was one of the most boring experiences of my career, and the other twenty-odd NBC staffers in Dhahran felt the same way. Tony Wasserman, who like Gary Fairman and Brian Calvert was a veteran of Tiananmen Square, would disappear to his room for hours between shoots to sketch cartoons. Some of the guys did yoga; others went out to buy stereo gear they didn't need, and from time to time a few of the harder-core road hands got their paws on a bottle of moon-shine distilled by expatriate oil workers. But it was terrible stuff, nothing like White Lightning or Newfoundland Screech, and we all grumbled along week after week, completely sober, until our Saudi visas finally expired after six weeks and we got a chance to break for home. Which was more, of course, than the troops could hope for.

"We should get on up to Kuwait," one Marine told me. "We've had a gutful of this waitin' around bullshit. We should find Saddam, secure his ass, and then get on home."

They would get-on-up to Kuwait. And then on home, most of them. But a certain ass would be left decidedly unsecured.

* * *

I returned to Saudi Arabia just after New Year's 1991 for my third tour of duty on Operation Desert Shield. This time I had a new assignment from NBC News: I was to be Tom Brokaw's sub-anchor in Dhahran. If war broke out, I would be the principal on-air reporter Tom would turn to for the Saudi side of the conflict. That, I realized, would mean a lot of "face-time"-talking live into the camera for our shows and specials. I've never thought that this is my strongest skill, and it's certainly not my favorite. But I was glad to fill the slot, because after months of nursing the story through the phoney war, now I'd be in position to follow through with the real thing, whatever that might turn out to be.

Joe and I were geared for war. Conflict had seemed inevitable, so while we were back in Rome we had ordered in four sets of the most up-to-date chemical-warfare suits available on the civil-ian market. We placed our phone order to the British supplier ourselves because the news desk in New York was stalling on providing safety gear for the Dhahran bureau. War was still just a possibility, our executives were telling us: chem suits for a bureau full of people would cost a bomb. Joe and I argued that should war break out, there'd be no time to buy and ship into Dhahran enough helmets, flak jackets and chem gear. We were fortunate to have discretionary funds in Rome; other-wise Joe, Max, Stef and I would have been underequipped, like the rest of NBC's Dhahran staffers. The bureau never had more than one complete chem suit between two people, an unforgivable lapse in field preparation.

As the phoney war dragged into its fifth month since the invasion of Kuwait, I tried to get a head-start on another commodity that might become scarce if fighting started, namely sleep. In fact I built up such a lead in this department that when the curtain went up on war just after 2 a.m. January 17, I was a good half-hour into dreamland.

There was a pounding at my door, and I heard Joe's voice calling to me through the roar of jet fighters that seemed to be blasting off through my bathroom.

"It's on," Joe shouted. "*You're* on! The bird's up! C'mon, get movin', *hurry!*"

I leapt out of bed and said goodbye to my pillow for three days. At some point in the proceedings, to counter the wintry Gulf breeze, I was forced to dig into my suitcase for a brown leather jacket I had bought a year earlier in Rome. The boys had never let me wear it on camera before. They said it looked too slick.

Our camera platform was just outside my hallway on a small sub-roof to the main hotel building. When I got there, Mike Boettcher was already under the lights doing live cut-ins–and doing well, considering we only knew at that time what we could see with our own eyes. British Tornado ground-attack planes were bellowing off on into the night from the runway nearest the hotel, while a stream of flaming rooster-tails in the sky to the west was all we could make out of the squadrons of U.S. and Saudi F-15s flying off towards Kuwait and southern Iraq.

As I mounted the platform to make my own first report of the war, hard facts about the allied attack were out of reach. The satellite was up and we were on the air, but U.S. military authorities had us right where they wanted us–far to the rear and waiting for an explanation of the air assault from official sources. For what seemed like an eternity, all I had to go on in Dhahran were wire-service reports on the computer and NBC's program audio in my earpiece. I learned much more listening to Tom Brokaw in New York and Fred Francis at the Pentagon than I did from our own limited sources in Saudi Arabia.

The JIB was locked up tight on useful information. A few PAOs shuffled paper or strolled among their desks, saying they knew only what they'd heard on the radio. The British were just as bad. The RAF's idea of a press release in those first hours was five limpid sentences ending with the revelation "Operations continue," which our own eardrums confirmed as they popped and rattled in the constant thunder of Tornado exhaust.

As I listened hard to the crackling voice of my colleague Tom Aspell in Baghdad, telling Brokaw and our viewers in the U.S. of the firestorm of anti-aircraft fire over the Iraqi capital, the war was very real to me. I couldn't smell explosives or hear cries of pain, but I could describe the bomb-racks on the underbellies of the Tornados, hung heavy with the best, most destructive conventional munitions money can buy. And it was hard not to think about the possibility of Aspell and his unit in Baghdad being on the receiving end of those bombs or others like them.

And then, at last, a story dropped into our laps in Dhahran. When the first SCUD swooped down in an arc of brilliant red within view of our camera platform, none of us knew what kind of warhead it would deliver, or how many more rockets might follow. Saddam Hussein's souped-up missile system based on the Soviet SCUD-B (and dubbed "Al Hussein" by its proud patron) was nothing like a secret weapon, but it was certainly an unknown commodity. Western arms specialists doubted Saddam's ability to launch a nuclear weapon, but the SCUDs were almost certainly capable of carrying chemical warheads.

Mike Boettcher and I described the first attack together. If this demonstration was anything to go by, we said, the SCUDs amounted to little more than a sensational-looking form of random violence–terrorism, not a tactical threat. Our hearts were pounding, not only from fear of the unknown but also from the loud and unexpected blast of the Patriot missiles launched to intercept incoming SCUDs.

The Patriots, we reported, had hit but had not completely destroyed their targets, and fiery debris had fallen to earth. We had accurately reported the first instance of missile/anti-missile warfare broadcast live on television.

Trouble was, we were describing a war that none of us in Dhahran could see first hand. Virtually all official comment was coming from Washington. Sure, I had lined up alternate sources: ex-generals in Britain and the U.S. who were reachable by phone to comment on what they were seeing and hearing; a coalition Tornado pilot; a Defense Intelligence Agency analyst in DC. But pure, raw information was scarce, rationed by the Pentagon. The only time that control system broke down was when the Iraqis fired a SCUD or two through the cone of silence, as they did on the wild night of Sunday, January 20.

I had taken the platform to do a live one-minute cut-in with Garrick Utley in New York during the half-time show of the AFC playoff game, which was telecast live in Dhahran on Armed Forces TV. Joe and Leon had cut a tape "core" for the report, and I was reviewing my script while keeping my eye on the game. Suddenly the sirens blared on the airbase. Then at the hotel. The power dipped–the signal for everyone to go to the shelters. That cut the juice to our satellite transmitter, and we'd screwed up badly by not having our back-up generator up and running. Our engineers raced to get it started. We knew it'd be at least three minutes before the gear would get our live signal back into New York.

"Wham!" The first Patriot lifted off.

Our cameras were taping, but I realized at that moment that if by chance our location were hit by falling debris, the gear would be destroyed (not to mention ourselves), and the video-tape would go up in smoke. We had to get on live, instantly; it was the only sure way to get our coverage of the attack to the outside world.

"Let's go!" I yelled, as much to focus my own mind as those of my colleagues. I could see our camera's picture in the monitor now, and there was a problem.

"Focus!" I shouted.

"Wham!"

"There goes another Patriot, let's go! New York, New York, can you hear us, this is NBC Dhahran and we are under attack."

A distant thump and a blush of red in the sky revealed the first SCUD intercept. Cameraman Jim Nickless had zoomed on the tail of the outgoing Patriot and got a fine, clear shot of debris raining down. I started describing the scene–by this time I could hear the voices of our New York control room assuring me that they had regained our signal. I called in the rest of the action as we saw it. The whole episode was a little raw, and it required a lot of refeeding of taped video and replaying of it in New York, but over the course of the next half-hour or so, NBC Sports interrupted the football game five times, first with Garrick in the anchor chair in New York, then with Tom Brokaw sitting in.

By the time the Pentagon put its first official spokesman on the air, we had given about fifty million Americans an accurate account of the attack on Dhahran. I hadn't screwed up on the facts, thankfully, and the rest of the unit had performed flaw-lessly under fire. Standing up there after it was all over, I looked down into the tent housing our satellite gear and listened to the engineers whooping it up and trading high-fives. It was them I felt pride for—techs don't get combat training, nor do most of them experience the field school of hard knocks reporters and cameramen go through. Yet no one had run, despite the risk of chemical weaponry, and they had kept their minds on their machines.

Then, next day, a surprise.

"It's *crazy* around here," John Stack laughed down the phone from our news desk in New York. "Calls are comin' in from women all over the States!"

I threatened to hang up on him.

"It's *true*! Honest. I do not *lie*!"

A sheaf of faxes was thrust into my hand by Leslie Edwards, who managed our Dhahran office. She was snickering wickedly. No wonder. There were poems, love notes and at least one proposal of marriage. Then radio stations started phoning from the States.

"*Hiya*!" a top-40 voice announced from St. Louis. "We just called to say, *We Luv Ya*!" And for a phone interview—I did about three of those before I decided enough was enough. I had a peanut-butter sandwich for breakfast and went back to work on the platform.

"*Fan clubs*!" Leon leered at me, raising his piratical Australian eyebrows.

Ginny Harris, our satellite co-ordinator chimed in, "Gee, can I have your autograph?"

The teasing got worse, but it helped relieve pressure. I didn't mind—this was, after all, a war, and we were lucky to have anything at all to laugh at. And the SCUD mishaps gave my girlfriend Deborah, in London, a unique way to keep up on my escapades. She was watching the whole story unfold from her slot on the foreign desk at Britain's Channel Four News—she had been screening all the network feeds from Dhahran the previous night. Someone in the newsroom cried out, "Hey, who's that guy on the rooftop?" Deborah looked up to see me.

"Every TV station in Europe is replaying your SCUD-dance over and over again," she told me. "But I don't know if I care much for this nickname business, Mister SCUD Stud."

My mother didn't think much of the label either. "Undignified," she told me when I called her at home in Calgary. Reporters had been calling her to nail down my life story. But Mrs. Kent was referring most of the calls to my brother Peter in Boston. "I'll make it up to him somehow," I told her.

I was on the phone, in the process of reassuring my mother of our safety in Dhahran, when the sirens blared to announce another attack. I swiftly excused myself and hung up; my mother did the same and walked over to her TV set, turned the dial to NBC, and watched me pop up seconds later describing the latest SCUD attack. Day by day, the "Desert Fox" craze grew.

"We *love* you," one fax from Boston read.

"*Love* that leather jacket," was the message from San Francisco.

"Come see us when you're Stateside," said Chicago.

"Please don't get married," said Fort Worth. "Save yourself for all of us!"

A number of women wrote to inform me that I had "visited" them in some astro-traveling netherworld during those first long nights of war. "I've had a series of dreams," one letter from Milwaukee read, "wherein we held long conversations."

Love letters came from nurses and anthropologists and pilots (all female), and one of my long-lost lawyer buddies from Los Angeles wrote, "Now you've really gone and done it. You're famous and I can't even go into Stanley's anymore without all the women at the bar wanting to know when you're coming back." (The strange suggestive powers of television: the women at Stanley's Bar hadn't shown the slightest interest in me during my haunts there years earlier.) Back in Toronto my sister Susan got a phone call from old friends in England, who wanted to know whether her brother had become a sex symbol in Canada too. Befuddled, she said the first thing that came to her big-sister mind: "I don't think we have much symbolic sex in Canada— just the ordinary kind."

The messages that meant the most to me came from school-children in the U.S. and Canada who were confused and frightened by the war, and clearly needed older people they could identify with to help explain what was going on. These kids gave us all a reason to work harder. And some of them had a sense of humor, like the kids from Melanie Crane's second-grade class at Washington Elementary in Birmingham, Alabama.

"We have been studying about the news in social studies," they wrote. "We thought you might like a little respite from all those adoring female fans. So, here are some letters from the future journalists of America."

In the days and weeks that followed, I received a small mountain of faxes, telexes and, eventually, letters, which came courtesy of the U.S. military airlift. There were appeals for my services from aspiring actresses; greeting cards tucked into wildly imaginative women's underwear; formal requests that I represent companies producing bullet-proof vests and leather jackets; finger-painted Valentines; and photographs of topless women accompanied by messages suggesting clandestine post-war meetings. At least two families wrote to tell me they'd renamed their dogs after me. There were invitations to "come and make movies in Alaska"; cassettes and CDs of everything from Bach fugues to Willie Nelson; offers of free airline flights and "hide-away" hotel rooms in Washington, DC, or Austin, Texas; sweatshirts from Kent State (thank you), Minnesota and Florida state universities; serious cash offers to anchor local TV shows in the States; word that the nursing sisters of a Catholic hospital in New York had formed a fan club for me; and pleas to support dubious legal proceedings involving lovelorn matrons in the midwest. And an Italian-American porn queen sent along her X-rated audition video, hoping that I'd help to boost her career, which, she claimed, was just her way of raising money for animal welfare.

If all this was a welcome diversion and morale-booster for me and our unit, and even for the folks in the New York newsroom, who were, like us, working long hours, the real benefit of my instant notoriety was being put on the air more often. There, I hoped, I could contribute something different. Which is exactly what our unit was given a chance to do one week into the war.

NBC wanted to mount a one-hour special for the night of Sunday, January 27, day ten of the allied air assault on Iraqi forces. The time slot for the show was unenviable—opposite the Superbowl broadcast—but the executive producer of the special, Sid Feders, offered Joe and me complete freedom of expression. We could focus on the issues we thought were important, and attack them from any angle.

"You really mean that?" I asked Sid. His counterpart at "Nightly News," Steve Friedman, had been keen to get my face on air, but groaned every time he saw a reference to censorship in my scripts. But Sid was encouraging. He told me, "This is your opportunity to cover ground you think we've missed so far."

"Then get me Mr. Williams for a live interview, please."

Sid liked the idea. Pentagon spokesman Pete Williams and his superiors at the Department of Defense had been skilfully fending off reporters' complaints about censorship. But with CBS correspondent Bob Simon and his team missing and presumed captured by Iraqi troops, I felt that the Bush administration was in an indefensible position regarding its draconian reporting restrictions—which had forced Bob and others to try "back-door" routes to the front.

The show opened with a long piece that Joe and I put together, which detailed mishaps in the allied war effort. After eleven days of bombing, I said, there was no way of knowing what had been accomplished by the most lethal air armada ever assembled. Saddam Hussein's forces had created a giant oil slick in the Gulf, and had set oil fires and painted mock-damage on buildings to confound allied pilots. The number and location of SCUD launchers remained a mystery to coalition intelligence analysts, with the Iraqi rockets continuing to harass Israel and Saudi Arabia.

After Faith Daniels, co-anchoring from New York, took a look at the anxiety the war was causing on the home front, we explained how the U.S. military was enforcing the tightest wartime reporting restrictions American journalists had ever been subjected to. We explained Bob Simon's predicament and featured a soundbite provided by CBS, recorded a day before their crew had gone missing, in which Bob expressed his frustration with the reporting restrictions. Then I introduced Pete Williams, who was hooked in live from our Washington bureau.

"Why are you trying to put your hands so far into our business?" I asked him. "We're not trying to tell you how to run the war; we're just trying to cover it."

"First of all Arthur," he said, "I keep hearing a lot about military censorship. I assume there's no one standing next to you now with his hand on the switch and what you say."

When I responded that it was through denying us access to the front that the Pentagon was achieving censorship, Mr. Williams dodged the issue, claiming, "We don't have ultimate control of what goes on the air–you do."

This was another dodge, of course. It wasn't a question of ultimate control but rather of primary control. We couldn't broadcast what the generals prevented us from shooting in the first place.

It was a heated exchange. Pete fought his corner well, and I think we said about all there was to say about the threat in the desert to freedom of the press and freedom of speech. But viewers in the U.S., at least those who felt strongly enough to pick up their phones, were furious. NBC received six hundred calls against and only three in favor of our approach.

"That was the most unpatriotic thing I've ever seen," one man yelled at an NBC operator.

"Shameful," said another.

"About time," said one of our three lonely supporters.

In Dhahran we consoled ourselves with the belief that one day Americans would understand that the Pentagon had cheated them of a free and open view of the battle for Kuwait. It certainly wasn't the next day, Monday, January 28. That was the day the single most depressing response to our show came from Steve Friedman, the bombastic executive producer of "Nightly News."

"OK" he said on a conference call. "Now it's time to move forward. I think we should stop whining about this censorship thing and just get on with the show."

At NBC Dhahran we continued making on-air references to the policy, and often. We always wondered: when will our executives and the public wake up and send a message to the president and his generals–the message that so many U.S. servicemen and women asked us, pleaded with us to broadcast. That you can't sacrifice your own ideals while fighting for someone else's territory and oil.

But in the midst of all this, another dilemma in media politics loomed. "*People* magazine have got a reporter and photographer on the way to see you right now." It was Peggy Hubble, the News Division's spokesperson, on the phone from New York. She sounded thrilled. She usually received interview requests for anchors–now she had a star correspondent in the making.

"I dunno," I told her. "We're in the middle of a story. It could be disruptive to everyone else here..."

"What's disruptive?" she exclaimed. "They want to know who the real Arthur Kent is. You'd be helping NBC, helping everyone on the team." Peggy knew all the right things to say, all the buttons to press. I had met her about a year earlier, on my way through 30 Rock. An attractive, cheerful woman in her late thirties, she'd impressed me as more than just a competent public-relations guru. She also seemed to care about the division's staffers overseas, to share our concerns that the opinions of seasoned journalists in the field weren't valued highly at NBC News. "Remember Arthur," she told me, "this is a chance to get your thoughts and feelings across to a huge audience."

Soon, Peggy had our vice-president Don Browne on the line pleading with me to do the interview. "It's not all pass-and-run," he said, resorting to one of his infamous football metaphors. "Sometimes a good quarterback has to stop and talk to the guys on the sidelines."

I grimaced; the front line in Kuwait and our considerable distance from it was the only boundary I felt Don should have been concentrating on. Finally, though, I was persuaded by his argument that doing the *People* interview would reflect well on all of NBC's operations in the Gulf.

Realizing that this degree of media attention on one field reporter would likely reverberate in unpredictable ways later on,

I told *People* magazine that I expected to pay for all this somewhere down the line. "Even within our own happy little community," I said, "there will be a backlash." After all, journalism generates great rivalries, and the flip-side of success is the envy and jealousy it can provoke in those who see themselves as your competitors. Or, as one of my British newspaper colleagues, Colin Smith, says, "Let's face it—we work in the bitchiest business in the world."

Sure enough, within a year, a few people would try to make me pay for my moment in the spotlight. Some of the same people, in fact, who had done so much to vault me into it in the first place.

* * *

As the air war approached its climax, I was presented with an opportunity to put my body where my mouth was on the censorship issue. The next phase of the coalition assault on Saddam Hussein's forces—the ground war—could be covered one of two ways: from outside the coalition, by cheating the system of restrictions and no-go areas, or from the inside, by trying to force individual U.S. ground commanders to ease up and permit more open reporting. I thought I had a chance of pulling off something with the latter approach, and so on Saturday, February 23, as allied land forces began their push into Iraq and Kuwait, I joined the First Cavalry, an elite armored division that wound up invading Iraqi territory not once but twice.

With me was cameraman Tom Baer, a big, tough-talking bear of a guy from New York, and soundman Martin Schmidt-Bleek, an American student from Berlin who had tied up with NBC when the Wall came down. We'd all volunteered for duty on the 1st Cav TV pool. A good thing, because the division's public affairs officer, Jeff Phillips, had quickly agreed to put us up front where the action would be.

Unlike the brass in Washington, many field commanders and their unit PAOs were eager to have reporters and cameramen along for the ride. They'd roasted for months in the desert waiting for this moment, and now that they were about to ride into history, they wanted everyone back home to know about it.

Artillery was firing at Iraqi positions as we rumbled across the border into the Wadi Al-Batin—the desert wash offering the most direct invasion route to Kuwait. A pall of black smoke was suspended on the horizon before us. Apache attack helicopters rushed overhead, and passing us, heading to the rear, were several Bradley Fighting Vehicles, the army's light armored troop carriers, with some unlikely looking passengers on top.

"Iraqis," I heard over my headset. "Prisoners. We got a few dozen this morning."

The captives were scrawny youths in rags who were clinging to the Bradleys for dear life. Hardly Republican Guard stock, but the smoke and noise up ahead told us that some of their colleagues were putting up serious resistance. We pulled into a widely spaced formation of Bradleys waiting for the signal to advance. The helmeted officer in the vehicle nearest us turned his attention from the battle for a moment and waved hello.

"Welcome to the Wolfpack," he said genially. "Better hurry aboard. We're going in." This was Captain David Francavilla, Charlie Company, First Battalion of the Fifth Regiment. The way he and his men were casually scanning the desert, they might have been out for an afternoon of four-wheeling.

But as Tom and Martin and I scrambled into the back of our Bradley in full chem suits and helmets, we knew we were going for more than a drive in the country. The 1st Cav was General Schwarzkopf's "force reserve," made up of some of his toughest, best-trained troops, with the newest tanks and weapon systems. On the big battlefield chessboard, the two brigades of the 1st Cav were like killer knights Schwarzkopf could pull out of his sleeve, either to avert disaster if the Iraqis counterattacked or to exploit the success of allied divisions leading the ground assault.

The 1st Cav represented one of the general's best knockout punches. But it could do other tricks too. And that's what we were part of now. Schwarzkopf had ordered our half of the division, the "Blackjack" Second Brigade, to perform a feint. Bradleys and M1-A1 tanks were to drive headlong into the bomb-weary remnants of four Iraqi divisions and make the commanders on the other side believe that the entire allied ground assault was coming their way. It wasn't, of course; the main thrust was in a massive flanking maneuver far to the west. The hope was that the

Iraqis would either surrender or pull in reinforcements, which would weaken their defenses at other key attack points on the Kuwaiti front.

Deception or not, things were looking pretty hectic for Charlie Company as Tom and Martin and I scrambled out the rear hatch of our Bradley. We'd made a ten-mile advance along attack channels ploughed through minefields and over abandoned Iraqi trenches. Criss-crossing trails of rifle fire were flashing through the sand about a half-mile in front of us, and word came down the line that an Apache helicopter had just been shot down. Its two-man crew had been rescued.

Suddenly a streak of bright light shot out of the smoke up ahead. A hovering Apache side-slipped just in time and dodged the Iraqi surface-to-air missile, fired from a bunker somewhere beyond the blazing fire-trench before us. Having missed the American gunship, the missile exploded harmlessly in the air.

"Holy shit," Martin said quietly.

"Let's get a stand-up real quick," Tom said, "and get the fuck back inside!"

That's how we played it—safe, but with enough pictures to tell the story. The three of us weren't out to be heroes. Martin wanted to see Berlin again, and he wanted to do it without a Purple Heart on his chest. Tom, it's true, had joined the pool to give his combat experience a workout. He'd been an army photographer in Vietnam and had been wounded in action there. Like me, he believed the ground war was the ultimate assignment of the Kuwait story.

"Boys, you better tie yourselves down for a while. We're all goin' for a little drive." The lazy Georgia drawl belonged to Sergeant Mark Taylor, the gunner of our Bradley. He was crouched down, talking to us from the turret, where we could just make out the legs of Lieutenant William "Brother" Ratliff, Charlie Company's executive officer.

"We just heard that we're not gonna go through the middle," Mark told us. "We're pullin' back into Saudi territory and headin' west."

So the feint was over. Schwarzkopf had left it to the 1st Cav's field commanders to decide whether or not they wanted to turn the bogus assault into a straight-ahead push for Kuwait City. If, as now, they encountered too much Iraqi opposition, they could choose to go back to plan A and join the big allied advance to the west. That meant that all of us were in for a different kind of battle—namely, keeping our tailbones and our balls from breaking as we rushed across the desert, back through Saudi Arabia, up north into Iraq and east to Kuwait.

After sixty-four hours of driving, with only six hours of rest along the way, we were in much worse shape than sardines—we wound up feeling like fishmeal in an armor-plated can. The sight of more than 2,200 vehicles and roughly 8,000 men moving across 350 kilometers of desert was an amazing spectacle. When our backsides began burning with the pain of the journey—which was early on—we stood in the open hatch, braving the cold night air or the drizzle of the daytime, and the desert was in motion all around us. It was more like a seascape than open wasteland, with endless wave-lines of armored vehicles running constantly forward all around us, rising and falling over the gently rolling terrain, creating a vast metallic ocean undulating in the starlight. For the soldiers of Charlie Company, this was the pay-off for all their training and waiting. For us, it was agony, and not just physically.

First Cav's speed meant that we had outrun our ability to get our pictures and words back to the rear, where our stories could reach the satellite to New York. True, the army's public affairs courier system had delivered the story of our initial attack back in time for "Nightly News" on the third night of the ground campaign. But since then we'd had no way to get our tapes out—we were moving forward too quickly. We had anticipated this problem, but the PAO brass back in Dhahran turned down our offer to design a pick-up routine using army helicopters. The military's priority for news was control, not speedy reportage. It was only when the war stopped that we were able to get the rest of our stories out.

Still, Tom and Martin and I were proud of the last few stories we produced. The pictures of the armored columns rushing through the desert were terrific. And we got some powerful footage of Iraqi troops surrendering to Charlie Company's Bradleys on the last afternoon of the war, when our division over-ran an Iraqi army command post that had been ravaged by allied bombardment. As well, I think we captured the anti-climactic atmosphere of the ceasefire: the men of Charlie Company couldn't believe the war was ending so soon. Sure, they wanted to come out of this alive and get home as soon as possible, but they'd had their hearts set on blazing into Basra, in Iraq, or at least into Kuwait City, which was still a hundred miles southeast of their position. Most frustrating, at the one-hundredth hour, when President Bush had called off the ground offensive, Charlie Company's brigade had been poised to take out an escaping armored battalion of the Hamarabi Republican Guard. Instead, they were ordered to sit tight as the Iraqi force passed by only five miles away.

"Dammit, Captain, them was my Eye-raqis!" Mark Taylor cursed.

By far the most powerful story we did out there, however, was about the death of one of Charlie Company's young men and the wounding of two others on the first afternoon of the ceasefire. The men had stepped on unexploded cluster bomblets, remnants of the U.S. air attack on the Iraqi post. We photographed the helicopter evacuation of privates David Weiczorek and Alcides Robledo and a third soldier. Tom's shots evoked strong memories of Vietnam—uniformed men collapsing in one another's arms with choppers swirling up through dust in the background. Weiczorek died of his wounds; Robledo lost a leg. I was careful in writing the story not to cast blame. Just before we'd heard the explosions, Blackjack Brigade's commander, Colonel Randy House, had warned all his men that ceasefires are often more deadly than open warfare and that extreme caution had to be taken by everyone. It turned out that the ground we were camped on was littered with hundreds of the bomblets. Our own footprints lay in the mud just inches from three of the small grey canisters. The bad luck of stepping on one of these was just another mad chance of war. I knew that, and I said so in my script.

But even in death, there was conflict over news coverage. While the men of Charlie Company felt we belonged at Weiczorek's memorial ceremony, the 1st Cav's top commander didn't see things that way. Brigadier-General John H. Tilelli Jr. issued an order: no cameras at the service; no exceptions, no discussion. It didn't matter to him that Tom and Martin and I had journeyed over the desert with Charlie Company, or that we had shared the dangers of the mission, or that the soldiers regarded Tilelli's order as arbitrary and wholly insensitive to Blackjack Brigade's legendary codes of honor and camaraderie. By that point in time, the GIs said, excluding us would be more of an affront to the unit's dignity than would any possible intrusion posed by the camera.

In the end, we were reduced to watching from a distance one of the U.S. military's most historic and touching ceremonies. A company of soldiers stood at attention on a lonely hillside, with the Stars and Stripes, and cavalry flags dating back to the American Civil War, rustling gently in the breeze. A bugler committed the Last Post's eerie lament to the foreign desert, while the dead First Cavalryman's boots and weapon marked his place in the troop's formation.

It was a tragic moment, and a death that can be argued to have been either a brave sacrifice or a useless waste. But unquestionably, it was a moment of history, American history. A moment that Americans never saw.

TOP: On one of our family visits to the foothills of the Rocky Mountains.

BOTTOM: My pal Dale Jamieson lassoes me in front of the Kent family home in Calgary.

TOP: WITH MY MOTHER (HOLDING DOG GEORGIE). THE BEARD WAS
A LEFTOVER FROM MY FIRST SOJOURN IN AFGHANISTAN IN 1980.

BOTTOM: A. PARKER KENT, ARCH-CONSERVATIVE COLUMNIST,
BUT ALSO A MAN WARMLY RESPECTED BY HIS MORE LIBERAL-MINDED
COLLEAGUES AND RIVALS.

WITH MY BROTHER, PETER, IN DECEMBER 1978, WHILE WE BOTH WORKED FOR CBC NATIONAL TV NEWS.

Arthur Kent

Arthur Kent

TOP: WAITING. IN AFGHANISTAN THERE WERE LONG PERIODS OF
INACTIVITY PUNCTUATED BY TERRIFYING ATTACKS BY SOVIET FORCES.

BOTTOM: HOW TO GET A $50,000 TV CAMERA OVER THE HINDU KUSH:
PROTECT AGAINST SHOCK, SEAL IN PLASTIC, COVER IN A BACKPACK
AND WRAP IN A BLANKET.

Arthur Kent

BIBI ZABAYRA AND HER CHILD ROSHAN TREKKED MORE THAN SIXTY DAYS TO ESCAPE SOVIET BOMBING IN KUNDUZ. NOT YET THIRTY YEARS OLD, HER FACE REFLECTS THE HARSH REALITIES OF LIFE IN THE AFGHAN COUNTRYSIDE.

Arthur Kent

Arthur Kent

TOP: THESE TWO AFGHANS DIED IN THE QUAGMIRE OF JALALABAD
BECAUSE THEY WORE THE UNIFORM OF THE SOVIET-BACKED
GOVERNMENT ARMY.

BOTTOM: AFGHAN CHILDREN, REFUGEES FROM THE FIGHTING, ENJOY
A MAKESHIFT MIDWAY.

Arthur Kent

Arthur Kent

TOP: AN AFGHAN GUERRILLA GUIDE RESPONDS WITH HIS KALASHNIKOV
TO SUDDEN MACHINE-GUN FIRE.

BOTTOM: CAMERAMAN JIM BOWEN CAPTURES THE DRAMA OF THE
SOVIET WITHDRAWAL FROM AFGHANISTAN IN MAY 1988.

TOP: REPORTING FROM THE TOWN OF LENINAKAN IN THE AFTERMATH OF THE EARTHQUAKE IN ARMENIA, DECEMBER 1988.

BOTTOM: WITH CAMERAMAN STEVE O'NEILL AND SOUNDMAN TONY COOPER, I RECORD A PIECE-TO-CAMERA DURING THE WITHDRAWAL OF THE SOVIET ARMY, NEAR THE AFGHAN-SOVIET BORDER, FEBRUARY 1989.

TOP: THE FACE OF COURAGE. A YOUNG COUPLE AWAITS THE FINAL ASSAULT OF THE PEOPLE'S LIBERATION ARMY IN TIANANMEN SQUARE, JUNE 4, 1989.

BOTTOM: IN AUGUST 1989 I PACKED UP MY ONE-MAN BUREAU IN PESHAWAR AND TRUCKED MY EQUIPMENT CASES TO THE AIRPORT IN ISLAMABAD, PAKISTAN.

TOP: ELECTION DAY IN BUCHAREST, ROMANIA, 1990. AN ELECTED DICTATORSHIP REPLACES A TOTALITARIAN ONE.

BOTTOM: THE NBC ROME BUREAU TEAM, AUGUST 1992. FROM LEFT TO RIGHT: LEON FERGUSON, MAX MATTEOLI, STEFANO GENERALI AND JOE ALICASTRO.

Ken Regan/Camera 5

TOP: JOGGING ON THE GROUNDS OF THE HOTEL THAT SERVED AS OUR BASE DURING THE GULF WAR.

BOTTOM: OUR POOL TEAM WITH CHARLIE COMPANY, 1ST BATTALION, 5TH REGIMENT OF THE "BLACKJACK BRIGADE," 1ST CAVALRY DIVISION, PARKED ON A CAPTURED IRAQI COMMAND POST.

TOP: A U.S. BRADLEY FIGHTING VEHICLE SERVES AS A MAKESHIFT
NEWSROOM DURING THE GULF WAR. JUST ONE HITCH: NO WAY TO GET
OUR STORIES OUT OF THE BATTLE ZONE.

BOTTOM: DURING COVERAGE OF THE ATTEMPTED COUP IN MOSCOW IN
AUGUST 1991, OUR NBC TEAM VIEWS A SECRETLY RECORDED HOME
VIDEOTAPE SHOWING GORBACHEV DETAINED AGAINST HIS WILL.

TOP: WITH MY DRIVER MLADEN (RIGHT) AND GUIDE MILOSH IN TRAVNIK, BOSNIA, NOVEMBER 1992.

BOTTOM: THE END OF LIFE AS THEY KNEW IT: BOSNIAN MUSLIM FAMILIES SEEK REFUGE IN TRAVNIK FROM ADVANCING SERB FORCES.

TOP: MICHAEL GARTNER, FORMER PRESIDENT OF NBC NEWS, PROVIDES VIDEOTAPED TESTIMONY REPLETE WITH MEMORY LAPSES.

BOTTOM: PEGGY HUBBLE, FORMER NBC PUBLICIST, RESPONDS IN AN ICY MANNER DURING HER VIDEOTAPED DEPOSITION.

Michael Caulfield

CLOCKWISE FROM TOP LEFT: BRUCE LILLISTON, WHO CHALLENGED NBC MANAGEMENT'S ACTIONS; BRIAN LYSAGHT, LEAD LITIGATION ATTORNEY FOR THE PLAINTIFF IN KENT V. NBC WITH HIS ASSOCIATES ANDREW COOMBS AND FRED FRIEDMAN.

WITH THE CASE BEHIND ME, ON THE BANKS OF THE PANJSHIR RIVER, JULY 1994, SHOOTING "RETURN TO AFGHANISTAN."

CHAPTER ELEVEN

Fade to Black

Dear Mrs. Kent:
Your son has accepted risks, discomfort and fear in order to serve the
public. We are very proud of his achievements and we want to
thank you for your support and understanding in this difficult time.
Sincerely, Bob and Suzanne Wright.
          —letter from the president of NBC, January 30, 1991

It is enough to make one wonder: Is network news' most glamorous
male star-of-the-moment being groomed for bigger and better things?
    —New York Newsday *and* Vancouver Sun, *August 9, 1991*

I want to practice my craft. To try to cash in on the celebrity thing,
in my way of thinking as it's been passed down by my father and
family, would be crass. And I don't think I could pull it off, anyway.
          —Arthur Kent, USA Today, *April 3, 1991*

MY SUDDEN VISIBILITY swept me into a media galaxy many
light years away from the Third World TV stations I had stalked
as a foreign correspondent. The reporter who had fought for a
minute and forty seconds of air time now found himself sought
after by Johnny Carson, David Letterman and Phil Donahue.

I had never viewed myself as talk-show material, but when I
visited the U.S. just after the war, I was delighted to speak publicly
about international news gathering. Peggy Hubble told me her
office had been besieged with interview requests. She'd been
careful, as before, to discuss the options with me and not to agree
to anything I wasn't comfortable with.

"But maybe you shouldn't talk quite so much about the censorship issue," she whispered as I headed into one of the tapings.

"Try to be more upbeat, more positive."

"Peggy," I told her, "nothing makes me feel more upbeat than telling people what they need to know. And they need to know we were gagged out there."

Applause is a sound we never hear at the business end of a satellite link, and I was startled by the howling approval of the studio audiences. But if they were curious about me, I was even more fascinated by them. Why were they responding so warmly to a lowly field reporter? The Gulf War hadn't been my biggest story, and it certainly hadn't been the most difficult or interesting.

Johnny Carson explained it best, I think. He ducked into my dressing room to chat just before his show. "I really had to judge the mood of the audience each night during the war," Johnny told me. "You had to be careful not to squeeze too much humor out of what was going on—people were pretty sensitive."

So that was it. Collective anxiety; ultra-sensitivity. Johnny Carson has had his finger on the pulse of the American audience since I was in diapers—he was aware that the war had caused a phenomenal kind of nervous expectation among the American public. I was just a walk-on player, a guy who had shown up when the nation was already on the edge of its seat. Any pride I had in the experience centered around this fact: the reporting stayed simple and clear; no member of our unit did anything gimmicky to boost the thrill factor of our work.

I reached Alberta not long after my visit with Carson, and took my mother along to the Banff Television Festival, where I was to present an award. Before the ceremony, however, there was a chance meeting with a distinguished guest of honor: Mr. Walter Cronkite. "You did some good work out there," he told me. But it wasn't what Cronkite said that mattered most to me. It was his voice—just the way I'd heard it as a kid on our black-and-white Electrohome with its four-inch mono speaker. Strangely, wonderfully, I felt transported to a special place in my memory. My father might have been there with us, listening, ready to explain. My mother was there, nearly ten years a widow now, but looking radiant and proud as we drew up a couple of chairs, sat down and chatted a good long while with Walter and Mrs. Cronkite. I was no longer a reporter in the spotlight, just a wandering son at a very special homecoming.

That springtime of 1991 was, overall, a time that galvanized my faith in the very special public service our profession can and should deliver. And vindication for the tough stance many of us had taken against military censorship came by way of some spectacular reporting by my fellow correspondent Mike Boettcher. Mike was in northern Iraq covering the flight of Kurdish refugees from Saddam Hussein's Republican Guard. His reports cried out with powerful images of human suffering, but much more, they constituted a chilling indictment of U.S. and United Nations policy. President Bush had encouraged the Kurds and the Shi'ite populations in southern Iraq to rise up against Saddam Hussein. They had done so, only to be deserted by the West when the balance of power in the region threatened to swing too far in favor of Iran. Saddam put down the rebellion, with great brutality, as the "victorious" coalition forces stood by and watched.

Mike's reports were graphic evidence of what free and accurate reporting can achieve: the Kurdish disaster was the first conclusive evidence that the operation known as Desert Storm had been a failure in terms of achieving security in the Gulf region. But it would be months before the Pentagon—which had so effectively cast an image of success on the war—finally admitted the truth. The "storm" had been a whirlwind of intelligence foulups and mixed signals. And the aftermath was in many ways as troubled as the political climate that had caused the war in the first place.

* * *

Despite the attention drawn to my reporting by the Dhahran SCUD episodes, three factors would work against me as I sought to continue my work in foreign news through the remainder of 1991.

One was the long-term nature of my contract with NBC News. The network News Division and I were tied together for another three full years. This should have brought stability to the relationship. That was certainly my wish—I rejected the advice of some of my colleagues to cash in on my new-found notoriety by demanding a higher salary. I asked only for the opportunity to continue reporting. But the lengthy term of my contract wound up lulling my superiors into the belief that they had me sewed up tight and that there was no great hurry to determine how best to employ my skills overseas, or even to ensure that I was kept on the move and on the air.

Secondly, there was a fundamental change in the commitment towards foreign news coverage by the commercial networks, particularly NBC. At "Nightly News," Steve Friedman made no secret of his preference for domestic American topics and newsmakers over stories about "people and places nobody really cares about." As a foreign correspondent, I was a craftsman in a shrinking trade.

Third and most important, our foreign news infrastructure was about to feel the axe as never before. There'd be no more chipping away at people and equipment and office space. The new cuts would go beyond the gradual "streamlining" process that had reduced staff levels at our foreign bureaus from 180 staff and 82 freelance positions in 1988 (when I was working in Afghanistan) to 123 staffers and 52 freelancers by the start of the Gulf War three years later, an overall cut of some 35 per cent.

The summer of 1991 ushered in a season of drastic "downsizing" or "right-sizing" or "rationalization" of resources, to quote the corporate double-talk of the time. To help justify the coming blow, our normally secretive network management went public with its estimates of the cost of covering the Gulf War. In internal memos and interviews with media writers, senior NBC executives came up with the figure of $55 million, representing a combination of expenses incurred by the News Division and lost advertising revenue due to pre-emptions of sports and entertainment programs.

Despite explicit promises made during the war by the General Electric Company that they would absorb most of these extraordinary costs, within weeks of the war's end it was clear to all of us that people, not corporate reserves, would be used as the company's financial shock absorbers. And to reduce expenditures even further, the entire bureau system—the web of news-gathering sub-stations around the world—was on the chopping block, too.

The cuts began in late June, when three officers of the News Division's New York headquarters arrived unexpectedly in

Europe. Frankfurt took the biggest, most painful hit. The office was to be closed. There was no chance of a reprieve. Only two people, producer Michelle Neubert and cameraman Jeff Riggins, would remain in the city, working from home. All the rest would go, including staff cameraman Joe Oexle, the gritty NBC veteran of forty-two years' standing and a father-figure for most of us. At the time Joe was two years shy of sixty-five and retirement. The fact that NBC management could simply blow Joe and his soundman, Heinrich Walling, and the others right off the payroll sent a message to all of us: everyone was expendable.

But there was more. Tokyo was cut drastically. London, too, lost five heads, including Derrick "Skull" Herincx, the veteran soundman I'd worked with in Armenia and Kabul. Perhaps most brazen of all, the budgetary axe sliced into the South African bureau, coming down on three of the hardiest road-warriors in the foreign news corps. Cameraman Tony Wasserman, sound-man Maurice O'Dello and editor Roy Meyer were eliminated from the payroll. Fired. Cut loose only a few months after the Gulf War, in which all three had yet again demonstrated their reputation for courage and skill. Tony and Maurice had been in Saudi with us and had gone into the ground-war pool as volun-teers. Two years before, they had worked through the Tiananmen Square massacre, and had bulled their way through countless other hazardous story-campaigns for NBC News.

I felt revulsion at the way they and Joe and Heinrich and Skull and all the rest were being treated. In Rome I picked up the phone and called Don Browne in New York. How, I asked him, could we possibly compete in future if we threw our most talented people into the street?

"Arthur," he said sternly, "we've thought long and hard about all of this, and believe me, there's no other way. We've had to do this. If we don't streamline the team, if we don't make the hard choices in the locker room, then GE will do it for us. And believe me, you don't want that.

"But remember," he emphasized, "we promised you that we wouldn't touch Rome, and we haven't, have we?"

So that was it. I was to be content that our own bureau hadn't felt the knife. Don practically spelled it out for me. In the choice over which European bureau to close down, Frankfurt's number had come up and ours had not, because we were a fully integrated unit—correspondent, producer, camera, sound and tape editor—whereas Frankfurt was minus its correspondent at the time. And because we were delivering the goods.

My argument that maintaining a German bureau was imperative to coverage of the new Europe counted for nothing. The implied threat was that I should shut up and keep working or the budgetary grim reaper would come calling to Italy too. One of our most respected executive producers in New York, Gerry Solomon at "Sunday Today," was himself deeply disillusioned at the way things were going. He put it to me straight.

"Get used to it, Arthur. NBC's getting out of the news-gathering business. The buzzwords now are 'programming' and 'packaging.' The shows will decide what features they want overseas, and they'll send people out from New York or London to get the material. And when 'Nightly' needs breaking foreign news footage, they'll just dip into the 'video river' and script it from the wire services."

Depressing. The "video river" is formed by the many streams of pictures from story locations all over the world that converge in news agency offices in London each day. It's a flood of images that are rarely accompanied by a written or spoken explanation of the scenes and people shown. The vital questions of who, what, when, where and why must usually be answered by reading wire-service reports, from AP or Reuters, about the same event. Writers and announcers can then patch together second-hand—and too often, second-rate—reports. It is a bloodless process totally devoid of first-person reportage.

Watching the downscaling of NBC's foreign capabilities, all of us in Rome, particularly I and my producer and bureau chief, Joe Alicastro, wondered what to do next. Then on the 4th of July, evidently ignoring the all-American values that date symbolizes to Italians, at least, representatives of ABC News flew into Italy and abruptly announced the closure, with immediate effect, of their Rome bureau. That hit close to home, and the explanation from New York that "all the networks are doing it" was meant to assure us that the cuts were part of some brilliant strategic design.

We didn't believe that for a minute. There was no sign of new initiatives to address the other side of the ledger–revenue, which could be created by coming up with inventive new programs, and with them more money from advertisers. Our management's thinking was on one track only: cuts.

Soon the axe started sweeping across domestic bureaus in the United States as well. Top shooters, producers and correspondents were laid off across the country. Bureaus like Miami were shut down cold–surprising, since Don Browne had built up and run the place prior to becoming the News Division's vice-president. And according to several staffers serving there at the time, Don had assured the Miami team that their base was safe only weeks before the bad news was announced.

One of those bumped off the payroll in Miami was Jim Nickless. Jim and his soundman Joe Valle had been with me on the live-SCUD platform in Dhahran. They'd driven with Tom Brokaw up to Kuwait City too, just after the entry of coalition forces into the emirate. But now Jim was one of the numbers in the savings column of a spreadsheet in New York, a statistic of "right-sizing."

Morale plunged throughout the News Division. It was impossible not to feel that we were all being punished for our many successes. After all, the journalists at NBC News had seldom failed to be first, or among the first, at any big story, at home or abroad. The failure to translate that success into a winning program roster rested with management–the very same people who were now subjecting us to a GE-style purge and rendering our company uncompetitive in the process.

All this bloodletting led to a steep downturn in viewership for "Nightly News." Anyone with a television set could see our product cheapening in value and content. By the end of 1991 "Nightly News" had secured undisputed possession of third and last place in the evening news race. Meanwhile, a new breed of middle management had been installed. Don Browne boasted of stealing two highly prized deskmen away from ABC News, David Verdi and Alex Benes. But when the careers of the new arrivals were held up to close inspection, nobody could understand what Don was bragging about. What had they accomplished, on or off the air? None of our colleagues at ABC could recall anything of significance. So in the NBC newsroom at 30 Rock, Verdi and Benes became known as "The Pretenders." And everyone watched, amazed, despairing even, as the pair swiftly climbed Michael Gartner's management ladder.

* * *

All we could do as individual journalists, meantime, was to continue working our stories. In Rome there was one thing we most definitely did not want to do: chase the dish. Satellite links and the live reporting they make possible are fine, in their place. But we wanted to get off the beaten TV news track to spend some time on a story, and turn in some crafted, visual pieces. This plan got off to a rocky start when we traveled to Iran.

"Nightly News" sent us there to have a look at Kurdish refugees who had fled from Iraq. But when we fed our first edited stories from Teheran, the foreign producer at "Nightly," Marc Kusnetz, rejected them out of hand. Strange, we thought, since the network's other programs–"Weekend Nightly," "Sunday Today" and the "Today Show"–featured our spots prominently in their broadcasts. Some of our contacts on the news desk said they'd seen this kind of roadblock thrown up at "Nightly News" before. They told us that Marc had ditched the Iran piece to trip up a rising star, to protect his close friend and mentor on the show, Tom Brokaw.

Unknown to me at the time, management's pollsters and consultants had come up with some intriguing new statistics. An NBC sampling report following the Gulf War read: "Arthur Kent (33% awareness) and Katherine Couric (26% awareness) posted appeal scores (17% and 16% excellent respectively, with low negatives) that exceeded those of all but two of the NBC talent we tested–Jane Pauley and John Chancellor."

Whether this notoriety influenced Marc's attitude on the Iran assignment or played no part whatsoever, I'll never know. But in the months following the incident, Joe and I worked hard at patching up our differences with "Nightly's" foreign producer in New York. Beyond all else, we shared with Marc a love of international news reporting. And by that time, with NBC management throwing the entire discipline into question, it was clear that if we wanted to continue following the foreign story, we'd all have to work together.

No single story showed off to greater disadvantage our company's new weaknesses in world news than the attempted coup in the former Soviet Union. The abortive takeover by hard-line communists in August 1991 crushed Mikhail Gorbachev's hopes of holding his crumbling political empire together. And in our own disorganized response to the crisis, NBC News too lurched like a dinosaur on its last legs.

I was in New York on substitute-anchor duty at the time. I had sat in for Bryant Gumbel on the "Today Show" for a week and was about to move to more familiar ground on "Nightly News" as Tom's vacation relief when the coup plotters made their move. The moment I heard that Gorbachev had been bumped by a band of boozy throwbacks to Brezhnevism, I knew where my place was: overseas.

Tom rushed back from vacation, and Joe and I made our way immediately to London to cover European reaction to the story. From London we contributed to three days of coup coverage, unquestionably the most poorly co-ordinated operation I have witnessed at NBC News. One evening our program came close to falling apart, melting down, right before our viewers' eyes. The show several times cut to black; over my earpiece between reports, I could hear Tom Brokaw in the studio in New York shouting angrily about lack of technical and editorial support. Confused voices merged in a jumbled response. Luckily, as New York fumbled, the staff of our Moscow bureau saved us from dying a most public on-air death. Cameramen Steve O'Neill and Kyle Eppler, together with soundman Tom Dumsdorf, captured footage of several key moments in the Gorbachev drama before anyone else. Our producers, correspondents and tape editors in Moscow, pumped on adrenalin, got the stuff on to the satellite and into our shows. The Moscow team barged through those nine or ten sleepless days and nights with great spirit and ingenuity, once again showing the value of well-staffed, on-site foreign bureaus.

Meanwhile, indecision and outright amateurism racked management at 30 Rock. Should we send Tom Brokaw to Moscow? Should we send Kent? Should we send them both? Can we "crash" into Russia without visas? What about those other reporters who've tried that and been sent packing back to London? These and other uncertainties plagued our broadcasts for more than four full days, culminating with the farce of a satellite uplink being sent into Moscow without an engineering team there to assemble and operate it.

Things finally fell together on day seven of the coup, a Saturday. The bird was up and operating. Gorbachev had been freed, and the coup was over. The Moscow bureau was on top of the complex political-aftermath story, guided, thankfully, by the News Division's veteran diplomat, Gordon Manning—perhaps the only NBC News executive capable of divining a path through chaos. And chaos ruled: Joe and I arrived just in time to report the independence of Ukraine.

NBC's coverage was just beginning to look as though someone at the top was finally getting a handle on things when suddenly, at least three days late, the decision was made to fly in Tom Brokaw and the "Nightly" gang to anchor the show from Moscow. The story was on the downswing by day nine, the day of "Nightly's" first broadcast. We were covering the same aftermath angles, over and over again. We couldn't seem to get the big interviews with Yeltsin or Gorby or anyone of note, for that matter, to break fresh ground.

Thankfully, Joe, Kyle Eppler and I were sent to Leningrad—soon to be St. Petersburg again—where we shot several stories about the Russian people and what the impending collapse of the Soviet state meant to them. But when we were ordered to return to the confusion of the Moscow operation, I called Don Browne in New York. We had become fifth wheels on the story, I explained: coverage was winding down, and since our colleagues at the Moscow bureau were the only consistently strong performers in our coverage, the next phase should be left in their hands.

Don ordered me to stay put. We had a blazing argument—both of us let fly all the frustration and tension that had built up since the war. I told him bluntly that he was helping to preside over the downgrading of a news network. Safety and focus and determination, I said, were regularly compromised in NBC's overseas operations. But he rejected all of this, and when we finally hung up on each other, Don was bitter, and I had become an outcast, an unwanted dissident.

* * *

The following autumn was unquestionably the most rudderless season in the history of the News Division. Joe and I and the rest of the Rome team managed to get back to Afghanistan—our first update in nearly two years. We returned to find NBC still racked by inertia. There were no new initiatives coming out of New York. No new ideas, no sign of renewed energy. Just a team trailing badly at the bottom of the three-network race.

Then suddenly, in December, things changed. I was summoned to 30 Rock along with Joe. There, Don Browne, with whom I hadn't spoken for three months, outlined things slowly, one step at a time. He had a new assignment for us, he said. A promotion: we would become senior European correspondent and producer, NBC's new big guns overseas.

"We want you guys to go to London and report into 'Nightly News' just as often as you can—every night, if possible."

Joe and I could hardly believe our ears. It would be a rough assignment; we'd be looking at more road-time than ever, and there would be danger too. The civil war in Yugoslavia was shaping up to be the central story of the coming year. A lot of our friends from Britain had been braving the ugly conflict in Croatia, which had claimed the lives of more than fifteen journalists in the previous eight months. With a firm mandate such as the one Don was describing, I would feel obligated—and eager—to go there too.

We accepted Don's proposal enthusiastically, and shook on it. Steve Friedman at "Nightly News" praised the new arrangement. "The most important assignment in the News Division," he called it. Brokaw ushered us into his office to give us his blessing, and with Marc Kusnetz joining us there, we all put the scrap over the Kurds-in-Iran incident completely to rest. 1992, we agreed, would be a comeback year for foreign news at NBC.

Finally, it looked as though we were back on track, and I'd be back in the reporting groove once again. The only question mark was the untested new management layer we would have to deal with. Don Browne had installed David Verdi, one of the newcomers from ABC, as his second-in-command. Verdi seemed a bit too sure of himself, cocky even, when we met him. His shirt was pressed and starched to a cardboard-like stiffness, and his tie looked very tight around his neck. He jerked up his chin and stood up straight when he told us: "I'm here to knock down every obstacle in your path."

It was a pretty effective echo of his bosses' words, but as we listened to him lecture us on the new "system" dawning at NBC News, Joe and I didn't hear much beyond that echo. We decided he was just an insecure guy feeling his way in new territory. But he was also hungry, very hungry, to get ahead. While we said we would work with him closely, our field instincts told us that Verdi, full of ambition and short on experience, was clearly a person to be wary of. Not unlike his ultimate boss, Michael Gartner, who sounded the only sour note of our visit that day.

"You're volcanic, Arthur," he told me pointedly after he outlined his "vision" for the future of NBC News.

"I think it might be fair to say," I responded politely, "that I can get a little steamed when observations and analysis from the field are ignored."

"You're volcanic," he insisted.

"Well, Mr. Gartner," I told him, "you're the first man I've ever worked for who has said that about me. There must be a reason why."

Michael changed the subject. He didn't want to know what I thought that reason might be. He'd taken enough heat around 30 Rock about his prickly style–not least from Bob Wright, his boss. So he wrapped up the meeting, and Joe and I set off for Rome, acutely aware that we had much to prove to Gartner and his team. We were also confident that we would do just that.

At last we had a clear goal. We would move to London early in the new year, keeping the Rome operation going as one of our own story-mines. It was a good plan, a way to participate in what we hoped would be the revival of the network News Division.

The rebuilding process, we were told, would focus both on existing programs like "Nightly News" and a new prime-time newsmagazine that Michael and Don had recently announced. It would feature Jane Pauley, whose "Real Life" show had been pulled off the air because of disappointing ratings. But this time, Don assured us, the prime-time hour would be shaped into a winning package. He had hired, he said, a couple of accomplished pros, guys with great track records from ABC's "20/20" and CBS's "60 Minutes" to do just that.

* * *

In January 1992, one year after the start of the Gulf War, Joe and I set off on our first assignment as senior European correspondent and producer while the final contracts were drawn up in New York. We were to take a look at how far Kuwait's ruling family had taken their nation down the road to economic and political recovery. Not very far, we were told by a majority of the Kuwaitis we spoke to, and the story we fed into "Nightly News" was, we felt, one of our sharpest critical efforts ever. We had edited the piece in NBC's London bureau, where we'd begun preparing for our move from Rome.

Then Don Browne called from New York. Great spot, he said. And he had some exciting news for us, too.

"We're going to ask you to *adjust* yourselves a little. We need you for the new show. They want you badly over there."

By "adjust," Don meant that there would be no "Nightly News" gig, that I would move to New York and be the sole property of a prime-time program called "Dateline NBC," an unknown commodity.

Dejected by the sudden change, I resisted the suggestion. But resistance of any kind had become futile at NBC. Momentum had grown for Michael Gartner and Don Browne and their program of radical change in the News Division. After a full year of deep staffing cuts and bureau closures, few staffers dared get in their way for what was set to happen next—the wholesale redefinition of the News Division's practices and programming.

Keeping the pressure up, Bob Wright exhorted Gartner and Browne to develop new sources of income. The recession was hurting all the networks, he said. Advertising revenues were down. More than ever, it was time to act on Jack Welch's philosophy of bringing down barriers within the corporation. Ideas and energy and inspiration would flow more freely from division to division. Inevitably, growth and profits would follow.

At the correspondent and producer level of the organization, this concept was handed down by way of Don Browne's characteristic jock-strap bravado. Don exhorted all of us to "get on the team" and "get on the same page" with the GE plan.

"I'll tell you, Arthur, there isn't anything we can't achieve around here if we really try. We're going to get the best people, move the football and score big points. We're going to win!"

As always with Don, the hype was at odds with available evidence, especially where we were on the other side of the Atlantic. Our remaining bureaus had been cut so deeply in staff and resources that our entire mandate had changed. Hard-news coverage on a global basis was out. The "one-big-story" capability was all that was left—we had enough people and gear to cover a single breaking international story, but beyond that, feature items without an immediate news-peg would be our daily bread.

"I call it value-added coverage," Steve Friedman announced from his "Nightly News" office. "You know what I mean—more information, less panic, no pressure to just run out and get it on the air."

I got the message, but I had to recall George Orwell's *Nineteen Eighty-four* to decipher it. "War is peace. Ignorance is strength." Now Steve had his own newspeak catch-phrase to live by: "Old is new."

From the beginning Welch and Wright had been more comfortable with NBC's Entertainment Division in Burbank. The manufacture and selling of an entertainment product was less alien to them than news. Package the product and sell, sell, sell. Burbank's executives didn't throw up troublesome phrases like "public service" and "balance" and most especially not "separation of church and state," the concept of keeping the business and journalism components of a news company separate and distinct—a concept Henry Luce had championed while building his publishing empire at *Time* magazine. To Welch and Wright, Burbank's show-business savvy could only help Gartner and Browne to get their news product on the money.

Steve Friedman, who had won executive-in-charge status at "Dateline NBC" while keeping his top spot at "Nightly News," informed me that I had, in effect, no choice but to accept the position on the prime-time magazine show. Meanwhile Steve's subordinate and the chief creative mind behind "Dateline," Jeff Diamond, formerly of ABC News, convinced me that the program would be a serious, responsible new production along the lines of "60 Minutes"–a show I'd always admired.

Jeff had left a mixed impression on Joe and me when we'd met him briefly that previous December. He talked a bit too smoothly; he had a habit of stroking his neatly manicured beard while he spoke about "programming the broadcast" and "booking the big interview" and "casting the right characters." It wasn't easy to get a fix on who Diamond was and what he really represented, especially with New York pressuring us. Everyone from Michael Gartner down to the doorman at 30 Rock was making it clear: either Kent and Alicastro sign on with Diamond and "Dateline," or the Rome bureau is on the chopping block.

Through six weeks of difficult negotiations, my agent Stu Witt and I cut the best deal we could manage. I flatly refused to move to New York, as Jeff Diamond had initially insisted. Instead, Joe and I would remain in Rome, and it was agreed that more than half my stories for "Dateline" would be in the realm of foreign news. That was not only where I felt I belonged, I told them, but where our viewers would expect me to be, too.

To help put the deal away, NBC's management offered me a substantial pay increase. But in return they demanded, in writing, another full year of my time. I would be tied to the News Division until 1995. Aware that refusal on my part would almost certainly commit the Rome bureau and everyone in it to broadcast history, I reluctantly signed on with the new show.

Things went badly from the start. For one thing, "Dateline" turned out to have very little in common with news, especially foreign news. The first story I did for the show–an examination of the suffering inflicted on civilians by United Nations sanctions against Iraq–was held on the shelf for two months. Mysteriously, Jeff refused to run the piece, even when new developments in the Gulf would have given it added timeliness and impact.

A much worse fate awaited our Afghan story. Together with fresh material from the mujahideen/refugee side of the war, we had resurrected the story of the mine-boys, Raz and Lal, for "Dateline." It was available for air the night of April 21, 1992, when mujahideen guerrillas finally swept into Kabul, capturing the capital after fourteen years of war.

Incredibly, the Afghan spot was held off the air and my piece on Iraq was run instead. Not just a dumb decision then, but double-dumb: the Afghan news-peg was passed up; a peg for the Iraqi spot just didn't exist at that point.

Equally incredible was the heavy-handed, manipulative system of editorial control on the show. Stories were turned upside down and inside out during the writing and editing process. Jeff called this "crafting." I felt "corrupting" was a better word for what I was experiencing, at least in an editorial sense. I realized that it wasn't our reporting, our style that was wanted for the show. It was *their* style, with my face and voice grafted on to present it. The story itself, any story, was of only secondary importance—just a stage on which the show's anchors and correspondents were to appear, dancing to rhythms dictated by a committee of producers, all of whom deferred to Jeff Diamond and Steve Friedman, the maestros, for the final cut.

The critics aimed broadsides at "Dateline" from the start. Jeff Jarvis of *TV Guide* wrote of one segment: "How exploitive. How unconscionable. How sick." He was railing against the shaping of a story about AIDS sufferers in Uganda; blood tests on two couples had been hyped in the story with a voice-over line that said: "You'll find out the results—who will live and who will die—later." To Joe and me, that piece of narration was bad enough. But beyond that, the "Dateline" account of Uganda's heterosexual AIDS tragedy wasn't about Uganda at all. It was about shocking an American audience. A phrase kept coming up like a recurrent scare-theme in the soundtrack of a low-budget horror movie: "Can this happen in *America?*"

Joe and I had watched NBC News programs from childhood. We agreed we had never seen or heard anything like this before. As much as we fought for the integrity of our own work, the new editorial order at "Dateline" was biting deeper and deeper by the early summer of 1992. Finally, Jeff Diamond announced in late May that our Afghan story would be abandoned.

When Joe and I next visited New York in early June and pressed Jeff for a full explanation of his decision, he and his subordinate David Rummel broke down and offered up their excuses.

"You guys have had a difficult time," Jeff sighed, "and I can see that I'm responsible for a lot of that."

We said nothing. Jeff paused uncomfortably. The next words

out of his mouth came like a confession, or at least an admission that he'd kept bottled up inside too long.

"It's Burbank," he said. "They're much more involved in this show than I expected. Much more than Entertainment's involved in news at ABC."

"And Burbank doesn't want the piece?" I said.

"They just don't think they can promote it," Jeff told us.

I looked at Joe. No one had told us anything about shaping our work to the Entertainment Division's concepts of market-ability. But in an odd way I had to agree with Jeff on one point: the Afghan piece didn't belong on his show. It was a report through human eyes, the eyes of Raz and Lal and the Afghans. It was not, and would never be, an exploitative piece of tabloid journalism.

Jeff's next statement came with an air of finality, of resignation: "I can't see being able to program as many foreign spots as we talked about." He and his top editors had caved in—they weren't going to fight Burbank.

Throughout the "Dateline" affair I put our experiences in writing and delivered these letters to Don Browne. On April 21, 1992, I detailed the obstacles we were running into over the Afghan piece and the delays with the Iraq story. On May 27, after receiving the word that the Afghanistan story had been killed, I sent him a tape and suggested how it might be salvaged elsewhere on the NBC News schedule. And the next day, May 28, I formally notified him that I wanted to be reassigned back to hard news. "Unfortunately," I wrote, "my projects have been hampered by a confused, manipulative editorial process, one that threatens the standards and ideals that have been, until now, the bond that has held me to NBC News."

CHAPTER TWELVE

"No Such User"

Arthur Kent is feuding with his producers at the newsmagazine Dateline NBC. Kent won't talk specifics: "It would be improper for me to discuss the concerns of my own professional circumstances in relation to the management of NBC News."
                                              —USA Today, *July 27, 1992*

A HOT AUGUST wind bathed the patio of Elio's trattoria. But the sun had been down two hours or so and the Gavi was well chilled. So Joe Alicastro, his wife Miki and I were enjoying the exquisite dinner of pasta melanzane.

Most people go to the small perfect restaurants of Rome for good food. Joe and I and the rest of our team all too frequently were looking for relief from tension, too.

"Evil Empire?" Elio had overheard us as he cleared our plates. "You guys working on another Mafia story?"

Joe laughed. "We wish it were that simple."

Actually, neither of us felt any satisfaction for the "Evil Empire" nickname that we'd borrowed for GE from one of Joe's buddies, a banker who'd recently been shafted by his own corporate hierarchy. It was trite and bitter. Bitterness means excess baggage, and we had more than enough of that on the road already.

Still, there was no mistaking that the Empire of GE had reached across the globe and was present there among us that night in Rome. Miki, in particular, looked gloomy and on edge.

It had been an unhappy year for all of us. Our Rome bureau had been variously enticed and cajoled into signing up with

"Dateline NBC." But our specialty, foreign-based news, had since been relegated to the spike.

Steve Friedman put it plainly: "Burbank wants happy endings—Hollywood stuff." Viewer statistics, according to the network's experts on the west coast, proved the show couldn't hold an audience with tough international news pieces. And because the Entertainment Division in Burbank controlled the air time on which "Dateline" was broadcast, the News Division was forced to submit.

Don Browne did not reply to any of my letters. Indeed, all my efforts to resolve the situation were ignored by NBC. Until, that is, they shunted Joe and me back into NBC's general reporting pool. This was in clear breach of our contracts, which specified that reassignment from "Dateline" could be in only one direction—to the senior European posts at "Nightly News," the deal we'd accepted from management at the start of the year. Since this key clause of my contract had been broken, I had no choice but to instruct a lawyer to make my case to management in writing. The response from New York had been unlike anything any of us had ever experienced or heard of.

Within two days of receiving my lawyer's letter, David Verdi, the ambitious, inexperienced Gartner appointee who was doing summer relief on the foreign desk, declared that we were to go to the nearest airport and fly to Zagreb immediately and move on into Bosnia. Verdi hadn't a clue when or where we might get protective gear like bullet-proof vests and helmets. No translators or guides awaited our arrival. No first-aid gear, no maps, no background files on the conflict and its combatants. And we'd be given no time to assemble any of this. Verdi's command was explicit—tie up immediately with the UN investigating team in Zagreb and proceed to the Bosnian Serb prisoner-of-war camps in Bosnia.

Since my lawyer's letter had made clear that I would refuse assignments to war zones until the "Dateline" debacle was resolved, the Bosnia trip was clearly nothing but a brazen set-up, a means of punishing us for not falling into lock-step on "Dateline." But it was a most dangerous form of punishment: some twenty-seven journalists had been killed over the previous year in the former Yugoslavia.

We refused the assignment. A few days later Mr. Gartner sent a letter to Joe and me threatening each of us with suspension. But in his zeal to strike out at those who would challenge the company's editorial direction, Mr. Gartner had overlooked the provisions of NBC's own policy book, which states that all hazardous assignments are purely voluntary–the choice to go or not to go is strictly that of the individual journalist.

It was in the midst of this intrigue, one week after we received our letters from Mr. Gartner, that Joe and Miki and I had trod the ancient cobblestone passageways to Elio's place. We walked in silence past the ghostly ruins of the Forum. Like the phantoms there, we were in limbo: in spite of Mr. Gartner's threats we had continued working, and had put the finishing touches on a story that very afternoon.

The producers of "Nightly News" had encouraged us to finish the investigative piece we'd been working up on Mafia investment in Germany–the assignment we were completing when the strange order to go to Bosnia came through. Hoping my lawyer could somehow persuade Mr. Gartner of the wisdom of a constructive resolution of our dispute, we put every ounce of craft and experience into writing and editing the Mafia piece. As we worked on, we had no way of knowing what was being planned for us in NBC's executive offices in New York.

When Joe's beeper sounded around 9 p.m., we looked at one another across the table. Joe sighed and went to the phone to call the news desk in New York. He came back scarcely a minute later.

"They want us to go home, then call in again. They said they weren't going to discuss anything on a phone in a restaurant."

"Terrific," I said.

"I guess they don't want us passing out in public."

Miki's eyes welled up with tears.

As I walked home, as I passed the Temple of Apollo and crossed the Isola Tiburina, over bridges that have spanned the Tiber since the days of the Roman Republic, I knew that what NBC News was and would be was no longer determined by the company's journalists but by executives who had no knowledge of–and worse, no love for–the business of network news.

* * *

"We're suspended without pay." Joe's voice on the phone was low, shaken.

I had waited five minutes after getting in the door to call him. "What else?"

"We're locked out of the bureau," he told me. "Someone's flown in from London to take away our keys."

"Christ," I said. "They've been planning this for days. Even while we were finishing the Mafia story."

"Yeah. And get this—we're shut out of the computer. I tried to log in a minute ago. It said 'No Such User.'"

So we'd been erased from the NBC News computer system, which links all overseas and U.S. bureaus to headquarters in New York. The same computer system I had used that afternoon to rewrite the Mafia Germany script and duplicate it to the New York files of "Nightly News with Tom Brokaw."

"How's Miki?" I asked.

"She's crying." Joe had served NBC News faithfully for four-teen years. Miki had worked there herself for ten. Neither had a blemish on his or her record until now, until this.

"They can't make it stick, Joe. It's the crudest lie of the worst management team in the company's history. Let me get on to my lawyer. I promise you I'll clear this up, no matter how long it takes."

There was nothing more to say. We agreed to talk the next morning and hung up. My phone rang almost instantly. I picked it up.

"Arthur...David Miller here."

It was Mr. Gartner's foreign-news director in New York, the same man who had informed Joe of the suspensions. There was a funny sound in his voice. Gleeful, almost. David had been off the desk, away on vacation through the Bosnia affair, and I wondered how much he knew. "Arthur...you there, Arthur?"

Whatever Mr. Gartner and his associates had told him on his return, David's mocking tone indicated to me now that he had been thoroughly disinformed.

I placed the receiver down gently, and broke the line. No use talking to David. They were just using him to deliver the blow. And I was already thinking of how we could extricate ourselves from this mess.

The next morning, while I was cut off from virtually all communication in Rome, Mr. Gartner's publicity machine told most of America's top TV critics and writers that we had been suspended for refusing a legitimate and safe assignment. Not to Bosnia, they claimed, but to Zagreb, Croatia.

It was a lie, and a very damaging one. But I would have to prove that, in a lawyer's world and in my own.

CHAPTER THIRTEEN

Into Bosnia

The trouble might be that Kent was simply miscast at Dateline NBC in much the same way as he was when he was assigned to fill in on The Today Show—Kent showed no particular gift for sitting on a couch talking to movie stars, beauty tipsters and health advisers. Hired as a pretty face, Kent kept thinking he was a journalist.

—Globe and Mail, *Toronto, September 3, 1992*

ANY CORRESPONDENT will tell you that the night before entering a war zone is a time of mixed emotions. You're anxious, hungry to get moving. And yet you also feel an uneasy sense of foreboding. Especially if you're making a return trip to a place like Bosnia—a killing ground unlike any we had ever experienced before.

So as I picked up the phone that night of October 29, 1992, I already had a lot on my mind. Unable to sleep, I was lying there in bed in a dreary hotel room in the port town of Split, Croatia. In a few hours I would be driving overland to Sarajevo. It was the next leg of my news and documentary shoot on all three sides of the Bosnian conflict, a project I had proposed and sold, in part, to the BBC and CBC News soon after my split with NBC.

I would travel with a guide and translator, my camera gear, some food and a bullet-proof vest. And with the knowledge that as I approached the front, a gale of controversy would be rising up behind me.

"It's all set for tomorrow," the voice coming down the phone line told me. "I'll read you the news release."

Brian Lysaght, my chief litigation attorney, sounded as though he was speaking from the next town, not from the other side of the world. An intensely focused man with a reputation for leaving his opponents bleeding on the courtroom floor, Brian read through his announcement with the light-hearted relish of great legal expectations. Like me, he was about to set off on another adventure, another great hunting expedition.

"Broadcast journalist Arthur Kent today filed a $25-million breach of contract, fraud and defamation lawsuit in federal court in Los Angeles against NBC and a number of its key executives." This was as strong a lead as any journalist would compose, so I congratulated Brian on his use of language. The word fraud, though harsh, was entirely suitable in this case: we set out to show that management hadn't merely been negligent, but had knowingly disseminated false information about me. In California, that's what civil fraud is all about.

Of the "Dateline" dispute Brian had written: "Kent's groundbreaking stories on the Afghanistan war, Iraq and Guatemala were all ignored. He was advised that 'Burbank likes happy endings.'"

Of the Bosnia subterfuge: "In order to evade its contractual obligations, NBC attempted to destroy the reputation and career of a world-renowned war correspondent by deliberately sending him unprotected and unprepared to frontline war-zone danger and then accusing him of cowardice for declining such a suicide mission.

"We want to present Arthur Kent's story to a jury at the earliest possible time. We are confident that Mr. Kent will be vindicated by means of a substantial judgment in his favor."

The release would hit the streets in the morning, when my formal written complaint would be filed at the U.S. District Courthouse in L.A. Just about the time I'd be driving across the Croatian frontier into Bosnia.

"Be careful out there," Brian joked as he said goodnight. "We'll need your testimony."

I felt encouraged. As scandalous as the NBC situation had become, we had made good on my promises to retaliate with a forceful legal initiative. That night, in my dark unheated cell of a hotel room, I slept remarkably well despite the unusual prospect that lay before me in the morning, when I would step on to two very different battlefields at the same time.

* * *

The mountain track leading into Bosnia's central Croat and Muslim enclave wasn't built for speed. It was devised to keep military and civilian aid traffic out of range of the Bosnian Serb artillery. But every mile further inland from Croatia's Dalmatian coast brought us closer to the many scattered flashpoints in the interior. So the three of us talked to keep our nerves in check—Milosh, my translator and guide in the back, and Mladen in the driver's seat of the little Lada jeep.

The guys found the background to the NBC case to be a welcome diversion from the prospect of conflict ahead. Since war had broken out in the territories of the former Yugoslavia eighteen months earlier, they had picked up the odd few weeks of work here and there for the big foreign news teams crashing in on the story through their hometown, Zagreb. So they were familiar with journalists' horror stories about network bosses in New York. My tale, though, had some twists they had never heard before.

To be assigned to go unprepared into Bosnia was strange enough. But to be publicly branded a coward—the act seemed to confirm for them the worst excesses of big American corporations.

"We have the secret police," Mladen joked, "and you have your big men in boardrooms."

As we rolled along, I went over the tale once again.

Mr. Gartner had moved against the Rome bureau on a Wednesday night, instructing foreign news director David Miller to call Joe and me with the suspension notices. An NBC News accountant from London arrived Thursday morning to lock Joe and me out of the office. All our belongings were effectively confiscated, all our communications in and out of the bureau cut off.

Then, around noon, Deborah phoned my apartment from the Channel Four News desk in London with shocking news: ABC News producer David Kaplan had been killed by a sniper's bullet while on assignment in Sarajevo.

I gasped, sank into a chair. I had bumped into David several times in Dhahran during the Gulf War. A good guy, a very good producer. We weren't anything like close friends, but a death like that anywhere in the foreign-news corps hits close to home. As it happened, too close to home, as the next phone call revealed.

"Arthur, sit down." It was Stu Witt, my agent, calling from New York.

"I am sitting down. Have you heard about Kaplan..."

Indeed he had. And not just from a newscast–television columnists had been calling him wanting confirmation of the Kent story that had come out of NBC. The mere timing of NBC's statements had linked my name to David's, suggesting that I had shirked an assignment while David had given his life in the line of duty.

I couldn't imagine the News Division's spokesperson, Peggy Hubble, putting out a written release without checking the facts first. As it turned out, she hadn't put it in writing, but she'd found an equally devastating way to convey management's side of the story. Stu told me: "Peggy Hubble's phone lines are buzzing. First thing this morning, I start getting calls from reporters. Is it true, they ask me–did Arthur turn down Zagreb? Peggy says he did."

It was unbelievable. The Bosnia assignment had been a sham, an act of intimidation during a contract dispute. Now it was being used as a weapon against me, against my reputation. And the attack was being led by Peggy Hubble, the spokesperson who had done so much to promote my work to the press and the public during the Gulf War–a person I had trusted, had believed to be a friend. I wondered: with NBC's public-relations machine delivering these first blows of disinformation, who would believe me when I tried to set the record straight?

Stu gave me the names and numbers of some of the reporters who had been searching for me, looking for my side of the story–among them, some of the most influential television writers in America. Early on I spoke to Jack Carmody of the *Washington Post*.

"Peggy Hubble says you chickened out," he said in his characteristic growl. "Is that true?"

At least Jack had given me the opportunity to rebut the Gartner line. Most newspapers and agencies printed the story without making any effort to balance Peggy's "confirmation" of leaked rumors of my suspension—or any mention of whether they had tried to find me for comment. That first day NBC's word was the only word seen or heard—valuable evidence, eventually, that the first crucial blast of publicity had come from the Gartner management team.

Only a few reporters, like Peter Johnson of USA Today and Michelle Greppi of the New York Post, managed to get my denials into their second-day treatment of the story. Meantime, there was a dreadful silence from my reporting superiors at NBC. Tom Brokaw, NBC's chief of correspondents, became the invisible man to me. He stood on the sidelines, not speaking, making no effort even to contact me discreetly through intermediaries, from the day the Bosnia fraud was launched and forever more. Only John Chancellor, the conscience and éminence grise of the News Division, jumped to my defense.

Speaking on the CNN program "Reliable Sources" on August 15, two days after my suspension, he objected to discussion of the case before all the facts were known. He continued: "It seems to me that what we have here is a contract dispute, and I think it maligns a very brave combat reporter's reputation to imply that he didn't want to go into combat. This kid has been in combat in a lot of places and has a perfectly fine record. End of statement. Thank you."

But despite this solitary protestation on my behalf, the damage had already been done. I was playing catch-up ball, alone, against NBC's entire public-relations machine.

* * *

Mladen pulled the Lada to a stop at another checkpoint. The grey, worried eyes of the two young Croat militiamen told us we were nearing potential trouble. So did the muzzle of the machine-gun pointed directly at our windshield from the bunker on the roadside just ahead.

They waved us through, satisfied with the identity cards Milosh waved at them. The cards bore the Croat red-and-white checkerboard shield—good on this stretch of road, but Muslim militias in some of the villages ahead were reported to be quarreling with their Croat allies. Quarreling with guns.

"Don't worry," Milosh assured us. "We can get Muslim I.D. in Travnik. We'll be all right if we can get that far."

Mladen, a well-groomed young man, a ballet student before the war, went pale as the word "if" seemed to reverberate around the jeep. For distraction, I supposed, Mladen wanted to know more about my case. What had happened after the suspension?

During my final years at NBC, I had taken up scuba diving. It's a wonderful sport, but a disciplined one too. The first rule, if you're suddenly in trouble underwater, is don't panic, don't react blindly to the problem. Think about what's wrong and how to deal with it; then take the appropriate action. That's what flashed through my mind when Mr. Gartner suddenly severed our lifeline to New York. I needed to act swiftly, I knew, but with all factors taken into account.

Michael Gartner was trying to remove me as a potential voice of dissent, even though I had not once throughout the "Dateline" debacle complained to anyone outside News Division management. But now Michael and his cohorts had dragged us all into a bare-knuckle street fight. It was time to let everyone see the truth about Mr. Gartner and his associates, time for the industry to take an even closer look at what had become of NBC News under GE. And in the most open, public way possible.

My lawyer, Bruce Lilliston, had determined that the way in which Joe and I had been suspended was itself a clear breach of our contracts. No remedy to disagreement between the two parties allowed such an act. Therefore, we decided, Mr. Gartner's actions had effectively terminated my employ at NBC.

I quickly packed up my belongings in Rome and flew to London. A few months earlier I had bought a small house there as an investment. Now, with NBC having cut off my staff housing allowance in Rome, this little cottage in Richmond-upon-Thames had become my only home. Deborah was waiting for me at the front door as my taxi pulled up.

We held each other for a few minutes, but there were no tears. Like me, Debs' thoughts had already moved forward: how would I respond; what would we do next? Doris, the kindly pensioner next door, had an idea on that score. She'd been watching our little drama on the doorstep, and when I explained something of my predicament to her, she said: " Oh well, at least now you'll have more time to tend the garden."

Debs and I laughed. All inhabitants of television-land could learn a thing or two from people like Doris.

* * *

The following day, four days after my suspension, I flew into New York. The staff at the Omni Berkshire Hotel on 52nd and Madison, my traditional haunt while on NBC business in the city, greeted me like a returning hero.

"Give 'em hell," said Peter at the door. And from Gloria and Lucy, who had years of experience fielding calls for me on the switchboard, this question about the brass at 30 Rock: "Those guys on drugs or something over there?"

A pal from the News Division had made sure a cellphone was waiting for me in my room. Next morning, Monday, I put the phone and twenty copies of a statement under my arm and walked over to the Sixth Avenue entrance of NBC Television. What happened next I'll never forget. It filled me with strength and courage for the long months of struggle that lay ahead.

It was 9 a.m., and my colleagues in News who were just arriving for the day's work greeted me with handshakes, with embraces and sometimes with tears. Every one of the fifty or so staffers and executive producers who found me there bolstered me with support. Many allowed themselves to be photographed talking with me by press and TV news photographers, including a team from News Four, NBC's New York affiliate, located just a few floors above the network newsroom. Karen Scott, producer of the five o'clock show, had heard I was on the street and rushed down with a camera crew.

Doing the interview with her seemed as strange as it was bold—a dissenting correspondent speaking to one of the establishment's own programs, another step along the unfamiliar new trail of conflict with my former bosses. The interview was businesslike. But when it was over, the cameraman and his sound engineer reached out and grabbed me by the arms.

"Bury the bastards, Arthur," the shooter said. "It's *Nineteen Eighty-four* in there."

I warned the guys and Karen not to stick their necks out too far for me. But at five that afternoon the story was there on NBC's air. Michael Gartner and his people, we learned the next

day, had been livid as they watched word of the Sixth Avenue
incident go out. Bad enough that it was on Fox and Channel 11,
on radio and in the papers. But right there on their own signal–
owned and operated by General Electric!

The headlines next day kept my story moving, and deepened
Mr. Gartner's embarrassment.

"Almost like Saudi Arabia," said the *Daily News*. And inside:
"SCUD Stud Goes Ballistic."

USA Today snapped, "Kent's fight with NBC tumbles into the
street."

My own favorite appeared in the *Wall Street Journal*: "Well,
This Reporter Named Kent is Able to Leaflet Tall Buildings."
Slightly undignified, well, yes. But after the slander and libel of
the previous week, I could see the humor in what was developing.
Mr. Gartner and his bosses were wholly unused to getting it back
as good as they dished it out. Each headline, each mention on
air was a blow in my favor. This coverage opened a stream of help
from friends inside the NBC News organization, journalists and
technicians eager to help out with information and documents,
anything that would help expose Mr. Gartner's panic-striken,
crumbling management regime.

Of course not everyone in the television industry thought my
walk on Sixth Avenue was such a good idea. Professional suicide,
some called it. The network news hierarchy was far too nervous
and conservative a world to tolerate outspoken anchors and
correspondents, no matter how justified they might be in their
words and actions.

But to me there was never any question of using a soft touch
in those circumstances. I had tried the diplomatic approach
unsuccessfully for more than four months, since the spiking of
the Afghan piece on "Dateline." Michael and his associates had
been far too brazen for the velvet-glove treatment. The president
of one of America's biggest news agencies was lying, and somehow
he'd dragged the whole management structure of the network
along behind him in that lie. And we could prove it.

It was clear to me that if I dealt quietly through my representatives, through Bruce and Stu, Mr. Gartner's lawyers would
stonewall us. They'd wind up offering a small cash payment in
return for my silence, leaving me to limp away and start over

somewhere else. That would amount to an admission that there had been something to their libelous claims–I'd just be throwing myself on the mercy of other network bosses who could take or leave me as they chose.

No way. Mr. Gartner's actions had been unprecedented in scope, and so too would be the response.

* * *

The two months between leaving NBC and arriving in Bosnia had been a crash-initiation into a new lifestyle. The law, suddenly, had become as big a priority as journalism. I had to select and brief my attorneys, listen to their advice, agree on a strategy for the case and help assemble evidence. All this on top of my efforts to launch myself back into the field with a camera and a good, hard story.

Soon after the Sixth Avenue incident, two things happened that would influence the entire course of my lawsuit. Bruce Lilliston suggested I come to Los Angeles to meet a colleague and friend with a burgeoning litigation practice. And the producers of the Jay Leno show, NBC's successor to Johnny Carson, offered to fly me out to L.A. to appear with Jay and explain my falling out with NBC News.

Not surprisingly, Mr. Gartner and NBC's lawyers were furious. In an embarrassing act of self-censorship, they issued a written order to the Leno show's executive producer to block me from the program. Under no circumstances was I to be interviewed on the show.

Ironically, the Leno show mishap became an event, a piece of the puzzle that tied my case to California. As did the announcement by Michael Gartner the next day, Friday, August 21, that I had been formally terminated by the company. These two factors would greatly help my quest to get my lawsuit accepted by federal court in Los Angeles.

So that night, as I watched the Leno show in my room at the Westwood Marquis, I had at least a few things to laugh about.

"The Tonight Show," Jay's announcer boomed out over the opening music, "and thanks to the NBC Legal Department, *without* Arthur Kent!"

Coming back from a commercial, Jay turned to Branford

Marsalis, his bandleader, waved "cut" to a musical sting and said, "I think that's Arthur Kent's favorite tune!"

Bruce and I realized, however, that we'd have to do more than shame NBC into compensating me for their libel and lies. It would take a credible legal assault, launched with great flourish and sustained with a manic attention to the many rules and precedents that could support my case. As I would discover, this didn't mean simply hiring a hotshot lawyer. No, I was embarking on an adventure of discovery, and not just of the intricacies of the law but of the mysteries of the personalities and ambitions of each of my lawyers.

When Bruce led me into Brian Lysaght's sunny offices on Santa Monica's Ocean Avenue, I immediately saw the contrasts between them. Bruce looks every inch the shrewd deal-making contract lawyer, a guy with an inviting smile and confident demeanor, as you'd expect of one of Hollywood's leading experts on independent film finance. We had met and become friends ten years earlier, when I had tried unsuccessfully to finance a costly theatrical motion picture about the Afghan war.

Brian was different. This tall, lean Irish American seemed to grin down towards me slightly, emphasizing his height and a certain, well, hunger in his eyes. Buoyant, articulate, dismissive of small-talk, this, I realized, was what an attack-lawyer looked like.

We were feeling each other out with Bruce as mediator–Brian looking to see if I'd go the distance, how convincing I might look to a jury, and I trying to measure how interested he was in my story. I knew that if Brian sensed the prospect of a high-profile victory, he'd only become more keen on the case once Bruce and I started pushing evidence his way.

"It's good energy, a good match," Bruce told me as we left that day. "He likes you. And there's no one better to win your case for you."

And so we began what would become eighteen months of discussion and debate, gathering evidence and shaping it, putting it before the court, trying to keep the pressure up on NBC and its attorneys. Within our team, I discovered, it wasn't always easy to understand one another. Lawyers and journalists are both practitioners of investigative and presentational arts, but with very different goals. Many times Brian would frustrate me with his occasionally off-hand and aloof manner, born, I think, of his intensely private view of his evidence and arguments. And I would often turn him off with my speeches about journalistic values and corporate responsibility. But early on we both sensed success against a big opponent.

That, combined with the deal we made on that crucial factor in litigation—money—tied us together, made us a team. I would pay a cash fee each month for his firm's services. But this would be limited or capped at an agreed figure to ease the financial burden, in return for which Brian would receive a contingency payment from any damage award we might win.

It was the best of both worlds for both of us. By paying a healthy fee, I would earn the right to play a more active role in my own case. And I'd keep the size of my attorney's contingency relatively low, which would leave me a larger share of any damage award. Still, Brian had a strong financial incentive to win.

* * *

That took care of legal costs. But what about my work, what about reporting? Since I'd been propelled back into the ranks of the self-employed, I would have to find financial backing for each new reporting project. And I faced another challenge, a much more sensitive one: how could I reassure my family and friends that I would prevail?

Answers to these personal and professional dilemmas began to emerge when I flew north from Los Angeles to my hometown in western Canada. Calgary's airport had been dusted by a freak August snow squall that Saturday morning, but the real chill awaited me in the pages of the *Calgary Herald*.

"Arthur Kent Canned in Dispute with NBC," screamed the headline. Here, in the daily newspaper my father had once edited, the journal for which I had once trod the street as a cub reporter, was a wire story that might have been written by NBC's public affairs hacks. It was almost totally management's story—a one-sided put-down with a dumb headline.

Arriving at my mother's door, I summoned all my strength to appear relaxed and confident. My sister Adele, an accomplished litigation lawyer, was there too, and she and my mother wore counterfeit expressions of calm not unlike my own. I put down my bags and accepted a cup of coffee before "the subject" came up. It was then that my sister, whom I respect and love dearly, made the ill-advised comment: "Now just control yourself, Arthur."

That's when the storm broke. I stood up abruptly. If I'd had a sword in my belt, I'm sure I would have drawn it and thrust it skyward as I began to speak, or more likely bellow. I said something about "control" sometimes meaning controlled aggression, and I cautioned them that they were going to see a lot of that from my corner. I promised that there would be no cringing and no tears; after all, the first thing my favorite professors had taught me in university was Don't Let the Bastards Get You Down. For every setback, for every body-check my corporate adversary might deliver, my newly formed legal team and I would inflict disproportionate damage on them in return. And we were going to have a few laughs along the way—we would fight them, I promised, with gusto.

It was quite an oath, and from the astonished looks on their faces I think I confirmed my mother's and sister's worst fear: this thing was going to go on for a long, long time. Adele, I knew, had looked across her desk at a lot of crazed litigants in her time, and so I assured her that I would be careful and, most particularly, that I would always follow my lawyers' advice. I even agreed to throttle back on the histrionics. But I warned her that because this was a case before the American justice system, there would be a much more open debate of the facts before and during trial than would be allowed under Canadian or British law. It was already very public and would continue to be so. I told them that I was about to take another step in that direction, and I marched over to the phone and got the *Herald*'s city desk on the line.

Within an hour, the paper's TV editor had returned my call and promised to sit down with me for a lengthy interview—a chance to set the record straight. Within three days, both the *Herald* and the rival *Calgary Sun* blared out the headlines: "This Means War," "Firing Back" and "I'm Going To Make These Guys Pay." Don't get mad, I had told myself: get even. With interest. And so the score in my hometown now read: NBC one headline, Kent three. Admittedly, it was a crude contest, but there was very little room for etiquette or *politesse* in a media street-fight like this one. And like my old hero Eddie Shack, I'd be damned if I was going to take an elbow to the jaw without crushing a little bone against the boards myself.

After my living-room call to arms that weekend, I apologized to my mother and sister for making a scene. As we got down to some serious Kent family updating, I began to feel calm for the first time in weeks. My strength, my true strength, was returning to me now. I was in my family home, sitting in my father's favorite chair. Arthur Parker Kent had written with outrage; he had editorialized from various postures of indignation or contempt, or, if it suited him, from less strident stances of constructive criticism. I realized that arguing my case would be like developing a lengthy piece of journalism. Some sentences and paragraphs had to question, some to discover, and some had to cut like a sharp blade.

Meanwhile, I had a family that cared, and more friends in Canada and the States and overseas than I had been able to contact in the dizzy mad week since my suspension. Proof of that came with the phone call the next day from London. The caller was a friend, and more than that—a friend anxious to help put my career back on track.

Nicholas Guthrie is one of the finest assignment editors the British Broadcasting Corporation has ever produced. Focused, honest and uncompromisingly tough, Nick keeps an open mind about the contributions freelancers and outsiders like myself can make to the BBC's impressive international TV news service. I had done a number of longer pieces for Nick in the eighties on Afghanistan, for programs like "Newsnight" and "Breakfast News." He had tracked me down by phoning my brother at his anchor desk at Global TV News in Toronto.

"Peter said you'd be sitting with Mum," he laughed down the phone line from London. Then he suggested that I come and see him once this thing with NBC was finished. There was a lot I could do at the BBC.

Nick and I agreed that Bosnia was the only real story choice. BBC News was beating the world to the tragedy, broadcasting every angle it could get a lens on. To me, the bloody three-sided war was a challenge, a test of all I had ever learned of conflict reporting. And as well as shooting news reports, Bosnia could provide a new focus for something else—independent documentary filmmaking.

Following my first conversations with Nick that September, a plan gradually took shape as I shuttled between London and Los Angeles working on the lawsuit. Taking advantage of advances in camera, lens and film technology, I would shoot the war in Bosnia on high-quality Super 16mm film. My gear package would be portable, enabling me to travel light and move quickly. And the footage could be used in two ways. It could be scanned electronically to videotape for television news, and edited as a motion picture, to reach a different audience.

I wanted to assemble a short documentary film that could be enlarged to 35mm projection prints—the standard used by movie theaters and cinemas around the world. Audiences would see the staggering scale of war in the former Yugoslavia on the big screen. Since television news cameramen, notably the BBC's, were by that time turning out terrifically graphic videotape footage of the destruction of places like Sarajevo, my film, if nothing else, would be a different contribution to recording the carnage of Bosnia, one screened in movie houses rather than on television.

Nick bought into the idea, as did another old friend, Tim Kotcheff, vice-president of CBC News in Canada. They'd each get a series of news pieces from the remote Bosnian countryside, for which the BBC and CBC put up a share of cash and resources. But the most vital contribution to the project didn't come from the big networks.

Deborah had been dealing with the crisis in Yugoslavia since the outbreak of hostilities between Serbian and Croatian forces had beamed on to her screens at Channel Four's foreign-news desk. Co-ordinating news teams and live interviews with leaders of the warring communities throughout the region, she had formed a detailed picture in her mind of the Bosnian story, its geography and logistics. While I flew hard to launch both the lawsuit and my first independent production, Debs did some vital preliminary legwork that would pay unexpected dividends for me further on up the road.

* * *

I was on my way to the Balkans–almost. Just one thing was missing. No one wanted to rent, much less loan, a camera with the price tag of a Ferrari to a correspondent hell-bent for Sarajevo–even if I could find insurance, which I could not. (A firm backed by Lloyds of London wanted 50 per cent of the value of the camera up front for only six week's damage-and-loss coverage in Bosnia. I had to laugh–Mike Gartner and his sideman David Verdi had been willing to throw the whole Rome team unprepared into the Bosnian furnace. But try to insure an expensive piece of gear? Forget it.)

In the end, I bought a beautiful French-made Aaton XTR, slightly used, with enough accessories to push the price up to $50,000. I fell in love with the machine. It was finely balanced, and when I shot a test roll of film it felt just like a purring black cat on my shoulder.

"A lot of camera," Bruce said at the time.

"And if I get it back in one piece," I told him, "I can always hock it for a few months' legal bills."

And the legal meter was running. Brian had handed off the task of framing and writing the formal complaint to an associate, Fred Friedman. Nice enough on the surface, Fred is the kind of guy who wouldn't look out of place among a bunch of hard-bitten G-men, or a clutch of government lawyers. That's because he used to be one: Fred was an assistant to Rudy Giuliani when he was the associate attorney general at the Department of Justice, and later an assistant United States attorney in Los Angeles.

"You've got a good case," Fred told me happily. "We used to go after Colombian drug barons with less evidence than this."

Fred, I learned, was a masterful writer of legalese. Precise and persuasive, he seemed genuinely pissed off at the way NBC had treated me. More than anything, he was amazed at the way NBC's publicists, chiefly Peggy Hubble, had gone from praising to condemning me in the space of only a few months.

"But we can use that to our advantage," Fred told me in a very U.S. attorney-like voice. To him, Peggy Hubble's disinformation–the quantity and timing of it combined with the widespread use of her statements in the press–constituted one of the key smoking guns of the case.

As much as I felt sorry for the Peggy I had once known and liked, it was satisfying to hear that Brian and Fred were on her trail. More and more, Peggy's superiors and associates in NBC management were acting like culprits who needed to be reined in. The Rome bureau, we learned a few weeks after my departure, would be shut down on Michael Gartner's orders. Max, Stefano and Leon would be fired and offered limited-term freelance work by the company. Joe Alicastro's last duty as bureau chief would be to close up the office, the base of many of our past victories, and head home to New York. Given a choice between staying at "Dateline" with Jeff Diamond or leaving the network, Joe decided to stay. None of us could have guessed just how much worse things would become in the very near future.

* * *

It was a dull Friday morning in central Bosnia when we got word of a story just up the road. Muslim families were said to be fleeing advancing Bosnian Serb forces who had captured Jajce, about forty miles northwest of the splendid historic town of Travnik, the previous day. But getting out to meet the refugees with my camera meant driving straight into a free-fire zone at Turbe, where gunmen from all three warring communities, Serb, Muslim and Croat, held positions in the hills. Milosh and Mladen, my guides, who had brought me all the way from Zagreb through Split, hadn't signed up for this kind of jeopardy.

A local teacher named Stjepan Lozic, a Croat, stepped forward. He didn't know how to drive, but he could show me the way to the front. He knew the hills well. And there was word, he said, of a temporary ceasefire to let the refugees pass.

"Terrific," I groaned, steering the Lada up the shell-cratered road. "Another ceasefire."

I had learned a few weeks earlier while traveling on the other side of the conflict with Serb gunmen how worrisome an agreed cessation of violence in the Balkans can be. We had just taken the high mountain trail around Muslim-held Sarajevo. The besieged city looked painfully vulnerable in the natural bowl formed by the Serb-controlled heights.

Svetlana and Nele had some friends they wanted me to meet.

Svetlana, a sultry brunette with a .32 revolver tucked in her jeans, and Nele, her boyfriend, who drove the bullet-holed Volkswagen Golf with a Heckler and Koch machine-gun on his lap, were intimates of Bosnian Serb President Radovan Karadjic. They'd been chosen by the president's office to expose this visiting filmmaker to their side of the war.

"We Serbs were so stupid," Svetlana told me. "All the while the Muslims were arming, we hoped for peace. We took to arms much too late."

Inconsistent with the evidence, I thought: as well as helping themselves to most of the former Yugoslav army's arsenal, the Bosnian Serbs had the support of Serbia proper, from whose capital, Belgrade, I had been flown into Bosnia. The Bosnian Serbs had trained thousands of heavy weapons on Sarajevo and had hammered the city mercilessly since the spring of 1992. Their forces had steamrollered much of the countryside, subjecting more than two million people of Muslim and Croat heritage to "ethnic cleansing." I told Svetlana her people hadn't much of the look of the underdog about them.

"Propaganda," she said. "Everyone is against us. You will see."

Svetlana's "friends" were Serb guerrilla fighters, so-called "Chetniks," a reference to the guardian-warriors of ancient Serb kings. I felt that old rubbery sensation in my knees, the one I get when things are about to get serious: the Chetniks looked like a cross between a motorcycle gang and seasoned combat veterans. Most of them, like their armor-plated jeeps and trucks, were liberally decorated with bullet scars. I was introduced to the group's leader, Vaske Vidivic, a wiry, limping man with sad black eyes and a straggly Chetnik beard.

"You can come with us if you like," he told me in a quiet voice. "But if they catch you with us, they will kill you."

"They" were the local Muslim forces, who were holed up in a little village nearby. There was, at that moment, a ceasefire in effect. But as soon as we approached the front-line positions in Vaske's pickup-turned-war-wagon, I found myself filming a uniformed Serb teenager spraying the place with a belt-fed machine-gun.

"Ceasefire?" I said.

"Listen," Vaske said through Svetlana. There was no return

fire. "We're just keeping them awake," Vaske smiled.

"Ceasefire," I gathered, meant an absence of all-out assault by any one party against another. Exchanging the odd shell or machine-gun burst was allowed; just hold back on the blitzkrieg.

We were driving back from the front through a so-called secured area when the semantics lesson took a more chilling turn. I'd climbed back into the Golf with Nele and Svetlana. We were in a little convoy: Vaske was leading in the war-wagon, and between us and Vaske was a compact with a two-tone green camouflage paint-job, driven by a lanky young sharpshooter named Damir. Vaske's sixteen-year-old daughter Sandra sat beside Damir in the passenger seat.

As we crawled along a dirt trail between two farmhouses, the world came to a standstill. Damir's windshield went suddenly white, and big chunks of glass broke away. Sparks splashed off the rear bodywork and then we heard it—a loud long burst of rifle fire. Damir twisted, smashed at the remains of his windshield with his rifle.

"Sniper," Svetlana breathed heavily.

I lifted my camera, rolled film and sunk deep in my seat, pointing the lens forward. I realized our cars weren't moving. We'd come to a dead stop in the sniper's trap.

"Move!" I shouted. But Nele sat motionless at the wheel. He had a pained expression, as if bracing for something. Like me, he fully expected to be shot in an instant or two.

Finally, the car jerked forward and we were past the farmhouses. Ahead of us, Damir's car lurched to a stop, and he leapt out screaming in pain. I jumped free of the cars too, still filming but glancing all around for the gunmen I felt sure were following us.

But we were alone. When we arrived at a nearby Serb field hospital, we discovered that Damir had been lucky. He'd taken only two Kalashnikov bullets in the shoulder. Only two slugs out of the dozen or so that had ripped into his car.

Vaske just shrugged. "This is normal," he said. In Bosnia, even the combatant with the upper hand is a hunted man. Ceasefire or no ceasefire.

* * *

A few weeks after my adventure with the Serbs I found myself filming life and death on the Muslim/Croat side of the war. The smashed little crossroads village of Turbe was silent and looking very much like a battlefield where hostilities had come to an abrupt, unexplained and very temporary halt. I drove slowly through deserted streets and up a narrow valley road, my school-teacher guide searching the autumn-colored hillsides for signs of trouble. Soon, the human cost of the war was trudging towards us.

Families on foot, families crammed into big old farm wagons drawn by tractors, families of three, four and even five genera-tions, from infants to great-great-grandparents, were moving away from the battle that had claimed their villages around Jajce. Through the Aaton's viewfinder it looked like a sequence from a Second World War documentary, but in color. European families fleeing war with only a few blankets and belongings, and with ragged-looking soldiers, their own defeated army, slogging alongside.

It was the counterpoint to the aftermath of a battle I had filmed weeks earlier with the Serbs. The long, bloody clash at Bosanski Brod on the Sava River separating Bosnia from Croatia had been another big victory for regular Bosnian Serb forces over their combined Muslim and Croat adversaries. I had fol-lowed the young Serb soldiers as they made their way into the captured city. Now, a hundred miles to the west, I was witness-ing the consequences of the battle that immediately followed Bosanski Brod.

Filming the mainly Muslim civilians and fighters, and with images from Serb-held territory already in the can, I was close to realizing the objective of my documentary—a brief profile of the warring parties and the nature of their conflict.

I'd been struck by a visual paradox: the people of the three communities are very much alike—in appearance, in the way they build their homes and arrange their villages. But behind subtle differences, like the frequently lighter skin tone and green eyes of Muslims, or the Cyrillic alphabet of the Serbs, there lurk divisions, deeply rooted in the past, of religion, language and custom. Divisions that had been played on by ruthless political and military leaders to create the hatred necessary to spark geno-cide. Blind, mad hatred.

That afternoon, driving back into Travnik, it felt good to return safely with fresh evidence of ethnic cleansing. I had accomplished something; I was active, fully operational once more as an independent journalist and filmmaker. Sure, it was a modest little project—one short documentary and a few TV news stories. But I was on the ground, contributing, if only as an individual, to one of the most challenging and important stories I had ever faced.

The weeks I spent in Bosnia greatly influenced my attitude towards the NBC case, which was proceeding in Los Angeles with early pre-trial motions. The war hadn't taken my mind off the scandal—my outrage at management's actions was still raw, close to the surface. But getting in touch with my reporting roots had thrown a sharper light on the journalistic aspects of the case. On the process of assignment. Safety in the field. Effective and responsible management of people and equipment. And most of all, on our duty to maintain professional codes of conduct. These issues were worth fighting for. More than ever, I felt eager to expose my adversaries in NBC management.

All around me in Bosnia were examples of the excellence we can achieve as reporters and photographers, as investigators, as recorders of history. And I don't mean examples set by foreign professionals. I mean people like the young women and men barely out of their teens who kept Sarajevo's television station on the air through the most vicious artillery bombardment seen in a European city since the Second World War. Like Harry and Changa (Muharem Osmanagic and Semsudin Cengic), the Sarajevo camera team who have shot much of the terrifying close-quarter fighting in their home town. Every major network has used their footage, almost always without crediting them.

And right in central Travnik I met one of the best-known and loved home-grown cameramen of the conflicts in the former Yugoslavia. Tihomir Tunakovic, a young filmmaker from Zagreb, was photographing the refugees' arrival in Travnik for BBC News. A tall, striking figure with what looked like brand-new equipment—expensive gear he was clearly proud of—he'd earned the rig, and the nickname "Tuna," while shooting some of the most vivid combat visuals to come out of the 1991 war in Croatia. Now his reputation was growing in Bosnia. He grinned as we crossed paths on a crowded bridge. We shook hands.

"I heard there was someone here with a film camera," he said, examining my Aaton. "It's beautiful." He told me that he wanted to direct feature films one day.

We chatted for a while, then set off in separate directions— he to record videotape that would be fed to London next day by satellite for the daily news bulletins, me to gather more film for my longer-view documentary, which I'd hand-carry home to England and edit at the BBC.

It was the next day, as I reached a village sixty miles from Travnik, that I heard the news about Tuna on the BBC World Service. He'd been killed that morning when the clearly marked BBC armored vehicle he was driving was fired on northwest of Turbe. The same road I'd been filming on the morning before we'd met. The ceasefire had broken down. Or rather, it had held true to its promise of much more bloodshed to follow.

Tihomir was among at least thirty-two journalists killed in the former Yugoslavia between June 1991 and January 1993. There have been many more since.

CHAPTER FOURTEEN

"Do you swear to tell the truth...?"

It is one of television's most blatant trends, and it is everywhere. An NBC source calls it the "cross-pollination" of news and entertainment departments. It is deflowering some once-proud bastions of TV news.
—Los Angeles Times, *August 22, 1992*

In the United States, "suck-up journalism" reigns. The firing of Arthur Kent by NBC television is only the latest evidence.
—Toronto Star, *September 5, 1992*

MY FIRST MEETING with the man who would become my principal legal antagonist in the lawsuit against NBC took on a predictably hostile air.

"I'm just trying to ask," attorney Mark Helm told me, "if you ever formed any views or had any conclusions as to whether your looks had anything to do with how widely popular you were."*

"It's not a consideration," I answered. "It's not what we do."

The attorney from Munger Tolles and Olson, NBC's power-house litigation counsel, grimaced with frustration. "My question isn't if it's what you do. My question is whether you ever had any perceptions as to whether that was affecting your reputation."

"That's been asked and answered," my lawyer Fred Friedman cut in. Fred was riding legal shotgun for me in this, my first pre-trial examination, under oath and on the record, by our opponents in the case. Like me, Fred was a bit bemused by Mr. Helm's curious manner. The man with flaming red hair in the stiffly starched shirt had a habit of shifting suddenly in his chair, his face twisting up in expressions of impatience or excitement or

---

* The testimony of witnesses quoted in chapters 14-17 is taken verbatim from official transcripts of depositions. See Appendix.

anger—all dependent on the way his interrogation was going. And with me it wasn't going smoothly.

"Just so I get it right," he repeated, "you never considered the possibility of whether your looks had anything to do with your popularity."

"What is the point of your question?" I said.

"I ask the questions and you answer them," Mr. Helm barked back at me, "so why don't we read the question back."

"If I don't understand your questions," I reasoned, "please forgive me if I ask you what it is you'd like me to say."

Helm scowled at me, and he insisted the court reporter read back the last question. Mr. Helm, acting for NBC management, clearly wanted to prove something.

"As I said," I told him, "it's not a consideration."

And so it continued into a second day. Mr. Helm wanted to know if I was difficult. If I was a prima donna. At one stage he lost his temper and angrily implied I wasn't telling him the whole truth.

"What I'm trying to do with these questions is to determine whether you have committed perjury, Mr. Kent."

"I understand perjury to mean lying," I answered, "and so my response to your outburst is that, no, I am not lying. If it is liars you are after, Mr. Helm, your time would be better spent examining your own clients in the management of NBC."

At this, predictably, Mr. Helm's pale face contorted with rage. He leapt to his feet and instructed the reporter to strike as unresponsive my remark from the record. This instruction, conveniently for Helm, also removed from the record his incendiary remark about perjury. Then he whipped open the meeting-room door and invited the attorney representing me at that session, Fred's associate Andy Coombs, to join him outside.

Andy just laughed and shook his head. A reserved, scholarly looking Canadian, Andrew Coombs was a new associate at the offices of my lead litigation attorney, Brian Lysaght. The antithesis of Mr. Helm's hot-headedness, Andy had been selected by Brian and Fred to help them prepare my case.

"He's just trying to fluster you," Andy said, following Helm outside for an off-the-record debate about my testimony. "I think it backfired, don't you?"

Backfire. It was becoming something of a symbol for NBC's

case, even at that early stage. It was July 1993, almost a year after my departure from NBC News. And what a year. Long hours spent juggling litigation with journalism were starting to pay off.

In March, Brian and Fred had won a huge victory over NBC's in-house legal department by securing Los Angeles as the venue for the proceedings. The NBC lawyers claimed that since my employment contract had been signed in New York and was covered by New York law, the case should be thrown out of court or moved back east. Besides, they said, all the News Division executives named as defendants with NBC–Gartner, Browne, Steve Friedman, Jeff Diamond, David Verdi and Peggy Hubble–were New York-based and had no connection with Los Angeles.

Brian countered with all our west-coast connections: the Jay Leno show incident; my termination while I was in Los Angeles; my ongoing residence in Santa Monica to edit and release the Bosnia short–and, most important, the key role played in the "Dateline" dispute by Burbank-based executives of NBC's Entertainment Division.

At first I had thought the judge hearing the case had looked upon the arguments of both sides with equal scorn. Judge Mariana R. Pfaelzer is a commanding presence on the bench, stern but somehow elegant at the same time. From my seat at the back of the courtroom, all I could see up there was glistening light-colored hair, long nails like red talons, and steely bright eyes that dared any lawyer to mumble or lose his train of thought or waste her time in any other way.

"I'll take the matter under submission," she said, waving us away.

"What does that mean?" I asked Fred.

"It means the suspense goes on–she'll get back to us."

"It's a good sign," Brian told us. "Take a look over there."

NBC's attorneys, Marjorie Neufeld and her boss Anne Egerton, the legal vice-president who had written the Leno gag letter, were flustered and worried. And with just cause. A few days later Judge Pfaelzer issued her decision in writing. The case would proceed in Los Angeles. With the exception of Peggy Hubble, however, the News Division executives would not be "name" defendants.

We were thrilled. It was better than we'd expected. In fact, before the venue hearing we had offered the other side what would have been a better deal from their perspective. We would drop the individuals named as defendants, Brian suggested over the phone, if NBC agreed to proceed in Los Angeles. But they had refused. And with an arrogant bluster that typified their whole approach to the lawsuit, they said the case would never reach trial, in L.A. or New York.

Now we'd won venue, plus a symbolic gain for our libel claim. We had argued that Peggy Hubble's statements about me to reporters in Los Angeles had tied her to that court district. The court found that claim worthy enough to retain Peggy as a named defendant.

"Gee whiz, maybe NBC should have taken our offer," Fred laughed.

"Maybe NBC should have come clean and paid up last August," Brian replied. But the network and its lawyers had made no serious attempt to settle the case. Early on, immediately after my suspension, Michael Gartner's number two, Don Browne, had offered Bruce Lilliston a partial payout of the remainder of my first year at "Dateline." But there had been no suggestion of a retraction of the Bosnia fraud and libel, so it was no deal. And the network had stonewalled us ever since, openly scorning our position.

If the network's GE hierarchy and its lawyers hoped to scare us with all that, two factors worked against them. First was the strength of our case. Simply put, we knew we had them. Second was the weakness of their own organization, particularly in the wake of the Gartner team's last great bungle at NBC News: the rigged GM truck fiasco.

While I had been filming in Bosnia, the same group of producers and executives that I had fought with over "Dateline NBC" had prepared and broadcast a segment on allegedly faulty GM trucks. Safety experts, the story said, had proved that pick-ups with side-saddle gas tanks were prone to exploding in crashes. The "Dateline" report included its own test, which ended in a fiery crash.

In an unprecedented televised news conference, GM revealed that the "Dateline" team had planted toy rocket

motors, or igniters, on the truck during the taping. GM claimed
that NBC had secretly rigged the crash test against them: the
"Dateline" report, as broadcast, failed to mention the presence of
the rocket motors on the truck. The audience had been misled.

After the news conference, Mr. Gartner dismissed GM's
charges, announcing to the industry and the public that NBC
stood by its story. The next day he was forced to reverse himself.
Soon the rigged-truck story was widely acknowledged to be the
most shameful fiasco anyone in the business could remember. In
the interests of damage control, NBC president Bob Wright
announced a detailed investigation of "Dateline" by a team of
prominent attorneys from outside the company. On March 2,
1993, Michael Gartner was forced to resign. So too were Jeff
Diamond and David Rummel, the two producers with whom I
had struggled to keep my own "Dateline" pieces free of editorial
doctoring.

Our legal team's evidence about Diamond and Rummel
would dovetail convincingly with the GM truck debacle.
"Dateline's" editors had severely mangled my third and last story
for the show, which focused on a Greenpeace raid in the
Mediterranean. It was a fast-moving, visual segment: our Rome
team had accompanied a colorful group of environmental
activists as they zoomed around the harbor in Barcelona, Spain, in
inflatable boats decked out with protest banners. Their objective
was to shut down a dredging operation that Greenpeace scientists
claimed was polluting the sea.

To balance the story, we interviewed the director of the port
of Barcelona, Luis Montero. He told us flatly that Greenpeace's
data on pollutants in the harbor sludge was incorrect. And
he accused the raiders of "magnifying problems where really a
problem doesn't exist."

The denials made for a better, more complete story—not
least because Greenpeace responded with even more convincing
evidence. But Jeff Diamond and his editors cut the port director's sequences from the piece. "He slowed down the process,"
Jeff explained; "he interrupted the raid sequence." And so the
entire piece was a *tour-de-force* by Greenpeace. Action-packed,
yes. But balanced? How could it be, since there was not a single
mention of any doubt expressed about the environmentalists'

claims until after the segment concluded. An abbreviated, one-sentence mention of the port director's denial was thrown in as an afterthought by "Dateline's" anchors in the studio.

This wasn't as glaring and offensive a mistake as the rocket-igniter incident, but it was symptomatic of editorial ineptitude and misconduct–a theme the network news industry and its critics howled about in their condemnation of "Dateline's" crash-test deception. The *Los Angeles Times* commented: "Far from being an isolated example of shoddiness at NBC News, the GM incident is part of a tabloidesque pattern that's been developing for at least a couple of years under the division's president, Michael G. Gartner."

Within NBC News, meanwhile, morale plumbed even murkier depths. An anonymous internal memo from unhappy staffers circulated a few days after Mr. Gartner's resignation was announced. Headed "It's Time for More Changes," it said that "Dateline's" GM truck fraud had not been just a mistake.

"It was the ethical and editorial disaster long expected from an administration that has cheapened our journalism and been driven by arrogance and ignorance."

To this day, I have no idea who penned the three-page memo. But I thank them for remembering, midway down their list of management excesses, something of my own struggle with the GE-appointed Gartner team.

"1992. Arthur Kent is fired. He refused an assignment to Sarajevo because he said no provisions had been made to safeguard him and his crew. Management intimates he's a coward, so Kent goes to Sarajevo as a freelancer and films and reports a story about Serbian militia in combat. Some 'coward.'"

Yet even in this tribute, ironically, I saw the need to set the record straight. First, that the Bosnia assignment was just a distraction, a device used by management to intimidate and punish me for my role in the original, underlying disputes–editorial mismanagement at "Dateline," and the breaching of my contract. Second, that my own Bosnia film was not just an attempt to prove my willingness to go back into conflict coverage. It simply represented my wish to keep working. I would refuse to let Mr. Gartner's actions eliminate me as an active professional journalist.

By the time we'd won our venue hearing, I had finished editing a seventeen-minute film from my Bosnia rushes. The picture was enlarged to the 35mm format, and I took a major gamble by investing still more money on the film. I re-recorded and mixed my sound tracks at George Lucas's Skywalker Sound, where big-budget motion pictures are completed. The result: documentary sound, faithful to my field recordings, but with all the power Skywalker could muster.

My gamble on quality paid off. A *View Of Bosnia* premiered in Dolby Stereo with THX Surround Sound at the Houston "Worldfest" International Film Festival in April 1993. The film won the Gold Prize for documentaries, and Kodak presented me with an award for outstanding cinematography. Soon I received enough invitations to show the film at festivals, colleges and conventions to keep me running all year. And Britain's Imperial War Museum requested a print to house in their collection.

My morale soared. I felt re-energized. And the feeling rubbed off on my family and friends–I sensed less concern about my predicament, and much more optimism. If I had managed to bounce back so quickly from the events of the previous August, maybe–just maybe–the challenger could, in fact, slay the giant. NBC and GE weren't invincible after all.

Then, two months later, I got another big boost. I answered the phone at home in London and found myself talking to Louise Lore, executive producer of the Canadian Broadcasting Corporation's highly regarded "Man Alive" series. Would I be interested in being the new host for the show, starting immediately? Within three weeks I had an apartment overlooking Toronto Harbor and an office in the CBC's new Broadcast Center. Debs agreed to come to Canada for a season; somehow we would juggle the lawsuit in L.A. and the show in Toronto and our home, now and then, in London.

The headlines were now saying that life was looking sweeter for me. But from NBC's executives and lawyers there was no joy yet. Despite our gains, they virtually dared us to keep suing them, evidently hoping I would run out of money or staying power or luck.

* * *

Funny how the mention of the word "deposition" induces either boredom or acute fear. To the innocent or uninvolved it sounds drab and officious. But to others, namely the guilty, "deposition" is the kind of legal term that reverberates in a menacing way, a signal of impending discomfort, exposure and, perhaps, disgrace.

Also called examinations for discovery, depositions are to a lawyer what practice runs are to a downhill ski racer. You break out your gear (witnesses and evidence) and test it and push it and tune it so that your gold-medal run (the trial) presents as few surprises as possible.

In a deposition, people who witnessed the events of a dispute sit down at one of those long, polished lawyerly tables and answer questions under oath. These questions are put by lawyers acting for both the plaintiff and the defendant. A court reporter taps out a written record of every word spoken. In this way, the testimony is both "discovered" and quick-frozen. When the witness is called at trial, the lawyers know generally what to expect from that person's presentation of the facts. It's a great way to find things out and to put the feet of the witness in concrete: having already sworn that every word he or she has spoken in the pre-trial deposition is the truth, the witness will be less likely to give in to the temptation to change his or her story.

I came to like depositions. Really like them. You see, as plaintiff, I had the right to sit in on all of them, to sit by my lawyer's side as he examined, one by one, the individuals who had acted against me and my colleagues in the field at NBC News. I watched their faces as Brian and the guys gently but firmly levered the truth, or better, a demonstrable lie, out of them. Brian, Fred and Andy would each remind me from time to time that the name of the game was to get *my* story out of *their* mouths.

Which is exactly what we began to do in mid-August 1993. One year after NBC management's sudden order for me to travel to Bosnia in the midst of the "Dateline" dispute, there I sat, with Brian Lysaght at my side, in a conference room of NBC's legal department at 30 Rockefeller Square in New York City. Across the table was NBC's litigation attorney Mark Helm, representing David Verdi—the senior foreign-news functionary who had issued the assignment.

To me, Verdi was a hostile member of the Gartner camp. But on this hot August day in Manhattan he became one of the best mouthpieces for my case. As the court reporter tapped out each sworn sentence of testimony, Brian set out to discover exactly what knowledge, what expertise qualified Mr. Verdi to order people into war zones arbitrarily.

"For example," Brian said, "if I asked you to tell me what countries border the former Yugoslavia, could you tell me that?

Verdi answered: "Italy is across the ocean. No, I can't tell you what is on the east and west. Turkey–I don't know."

Amazing, I thought. David was responsible for crews in the war zone. Yet even after another long year of war and daily news bulletins from the former Yugoslavia, this top NBC News assignment executive didn't know where the place is. From northwest to south and east are Italy, Austria, Hungary, Romania, Bulgaria, Greece and Albania. Turkey lies at the far east of the Mediterranean, beyond both Greece and Bulgaria. Solid geographic knowledge is vital in managing coverage and in directing emergency aid or evacuation of news personnel.

"Can you tell me," Brian continued, "what areas of Bosnia were controlled by what different factions?"

"No," David answered. "There were Muslims, Serbs. It went back and forth. So no, at the time I couldn't tell you who controlled what areas. It was a mix of different factions, all starting to fight with the regular Yugoslavian army and a very unusual situation."

"Now, the Serb detention camps were in an area, a disputed area called Bosnia, correct?"

"Yes."

"Did you understand in August of 1992 there were various forces fighting in Bosnia?"

"I understood that in August of 1992, the former Yugoslavia was disintegrating, and there were many factions mounting insurrections throughout the entire area. I did not have a handle on who was mad at whom at the time nor did I know who was partners with whom at the time."

Brian had cautioned me not to react in any way to the testimony, not to telegraph either satisfaction or disappointment to the other side. So I wore a poker face and listened.

"When you say the entire area, you mean the entire area of the former Yugoslavia; is that correct?" Brian asked.

"Yes."

"Did you know, for example, what the Serb capital of Bosnia was in August of 1992?"

At this Mark Helm cut in, "Are we going to have a geography lesson here or are we going to get to the point?"

Verdi asked, "Are you trying to determine whether I asked Arthur to go to Bosnia or Croatia?"

"I'm asking simple, objective questions," Brian said.

"I don't recall," Verdi answered.

"Do you know what the Muslim capital of Bosnia was in August of 1992?"

"I don't recall."

Unreal. Any decent foreign editor would know that Sarajevo was the Bosnian Muslim capital, and most could name Pale or Banja Luka for the Serbs.

Brian continued, "Did NBC have any equipment on the ground in Zagreb in August of 1992 for the protection of journalists?"

"No."

"Did NBC own an armored car in August of 1992 which was—"

"No."

Inwardly, I heaved a sigh of relief. Verdi had saved us a lot of investigative time and effort—he'd confirmed the total absence of safety gear waiting for us at the first stop of the mission, Zagreb. And later he revealed that the correspondent sent in my place after I turned down the assignment had proceeded from Zagreb to Sarajevo, in the war zone. Overall, Verdi's testimony appeared even more damning to NBC's case when contrasted with the official policy of the United Nations in Bosnia. Only weeks before Verdi issued his assignment to our unit, the UN commander in Sarajevo, Major-General Lewis MacKenzie, had announced that any journalists arriving so unprepared in areas under his command would be summarily returned on the planes that had brought them in.

However, Verdi had stuck to management's line on our assignment—that we'd been ordered to go only as far as Zagreb.

The truth would take more digging, and many more depositions, to unearth. Happily, we hit pay dirt on our very next stop up the Gartner team's chain of command.

Don Browne, vice-president of NBC News, swaggered into the deposition chamber, looking every inch the football-hero-turned-executive he styled himself.

"Hi, Arthur, how ya doin'?" Don shook my hand as if we were about to toss a coin at the fifty-yard line to see who'd kick and who'd receive. I smiled, remembering the good times. Despite his boosterish Ivy League manner, I had enjoyed working for Don in the years before Mr. Gartner's big foreign news cutbacks. Then he had come to personify GE heavy-handedness, the willingness to do and say anything to achieve an objective.

The experience hadn't been kind to Don. It seemed to me that he had aged in the year since our last unhappy meeting over the "Dateline" affair. He looked grey and nervous as Brian questioned him about the events leading to my termination. Don acknowledged that he and Michael Gartner had received a lengthy letter from my lawyer, Bruce Lilliston, on Monday, August 3, 1992, the day before Verdi ordered us into Bosnia.

"We discussed it, and I discussed the letter and the fact that I was not in the position to act on this, and Michael said, 'I will take care of this.'"

This was helpful. Bruce's letter had cautioned that until management's breach of my contract over "Dateline" was put right, I would continue reporting but would "decline assignments which, in [my] good faith estimation, involve unjustified personal risk and reckless endangerment of [my] physical well being..." Browne and Gartner knew full well that I'd refuse the kind of assignment Verdi dropped on us.

Don testified that Gartner had taken personal charge of the matter because the Browne family were leaving for a vacation at the Olympic Games in Barcelona the day Bruce's letter arrived.

Brian asked Don Browne, "Did you have any personal views on the subject of whether Mr. Kent's refusal to accept the assignment to Yugoslavia justified his suspension or termination?"

"I wish under those circumstances I had been consulted while I was in Spain. My view was that we should have had more discussion and more dialogue in making a decision like that."

It was the first chink in management's armor. Michael Gartner had been forced to resign five months prior to this deposition for his role in the GM truck-rigging scandal. Don had hung on as vice-president under Andy Lack, Gartner's replacement, and now, it was clear, he wanted to set himself apart from his former boss's actions and statements.

Brian played his witness out like a fish on the line. Would Don Browne distance himself, too, from charges made by Gartner when he fired me?

"Is there anything that you know of that occurred prior to the Yugoslavian incident," Brian asked, "that you understand to be a breach of any agreement that Arthur Kent had with NBC?"

Helm, for NBC, entered an objection on the record. But Browne wanted to answer.

"From my point of view as an executive of NBC, the answer would be, with the knowledge that I have, no."

A major inconsistency with Gartner. Mr. Gartner had publicly charged me with "repeated breaches of my employment agreement." Now, with Mr. Gartner's second-in-command ruling out any previous breaches, Gartner's allegations could refer only to the Bosnia assignment.

Brian turned next to the subject of a letter Joe Alicastro had written to Michael Gartner immediately after the Rome team had declined the Bosnia assignment—a letter Joe showed me just before faxing it to New York.

"Are you aware of any writing by Mr. Alicastro to Mr. Gartner explaining his position?"

"I don't recall it," Browne answered.

"Are you aware of any letter written by Mr. Alicastro to NBC to whomever?"

Don shifted in his seat. "I'm familiar with the fact that as my memory is being refreshed as you mention that, that I believe that Joe wrote to Michael appealing the decision."

"Do you know when that letter was?"

"No."

"Would it have been approximately August 8, 1992?"

"I don't know."

"Have you ever seen a copy of that letter?"

"I don't recall."

"How do you know it exists?"

"I believe it was conveyed to me in conversation."

"Who conveyed it to you?"

"I think it was Joe, and I think Michael at one point and Joe at another."

Ka-ching. Brian and I heard a sweet bell ring on that answer. Copies of the letter should have been in the files of both Michael Gartner, at one point a named defendant in the lawsuit, and Joe, an important witness still in NBC's employ. Yet NBC's lawyers hadn't produced the letter within one of the many discovery deadlines set by the court, deadlines lawyers for both sides had agreed to meet.

"We would like to get a copy of that document," Brian told Mr. Helm.

"I'll be happy to try to produce it," Helm said, embarrassment written all over his face. "Would you remind me after the depo? Because if I say I will produce it and then I forget, you'll think I'm violating our agreement."

Brian smiled. "I will remind you *lots* after the depo."

And so he did. A few weeks later Mr. Helm finally sent us a copy of the Alicastro letter. Dated August 7, 1992, just days after the Bosnia assignment had been thrust upon us, Joe's letter to Michael Gartner said, "the assignment (as I understood it) was clearly to go to Zagreb to meet the U.N. factfinders and proceed with them to the camps. When I asked David for any information which NBC News might have as to the location of the camps or the level of danger in and around the camps, I was told by David that he did not have that information."

It was a breakthrough. Evidence from the days before our suspension that corroborated my side of the story. There never had been an assignment to "peaceful Zagreb," as management had claimed. Reading and rereading the letter, I felt both the thrill of unearthing something precious and disgust with NBC management. Not just for the deception perpetrated by Mr. Gartner and his associates but for the way it had been covered up for one full year. At the very least, NBC's lawyers had to know their client's position was flawed, that my claims were at least partially justified. Yet they were holding firm, resisting a settlement, apparently hoping to exhaust my resources, or hoping I'd just go away.

NBC's executives and lawyers seemed to be living in a dream world. And until we could wake them up, my own legal nightmare would continue.

* * *

If we'd broken through on the Bosnian front, we had also moved closer to two other objectives: revealing the truth about my professional reputation within NBC and exploring the mutation of management values over "Dateline NBC."

"You rarely saw somebody that had a passion for what we do for a living [like] Arthur."

The witness was John Stack, the deskman who had been my principal foreign-assignment contact during all my years at NBC. With the departure of his boss, David Miller, the man who had broken news of our suspension, John was now the chief foreign-assignment editor at NBC News.

"At any time, in any assignment that you gave Arthur Kent," Brian asked John, "did he ever indicate an unwillingness to go into a dangerous area because of his fear of his personal safety?"

"No."

"Prior to August 1992, were you aware of any occasion when Arthur Kent ever refused an assignment from you for any reason?"

"No."

One by one, the published accusations of anonymous NBC sources at the time of my termination were shot down.

"Are you aware of any instance where Mr. Kent disappeared with a camera team on a story of his own choosing without the authorization of the news desk?"

"No."

"Are you aware of any instance where Mr. Kent refused to speak with you or David Miller about an assignment in progress or planning?"

"I have never – I'm not aware of any time Arthur refused to speak with me about any aspect of an assignment."

John testified that any arguments that I had had with New York producers over stories had been in the nature of "healthy debate." And as to my productivity on the air, which NBC's lawyers showed every sign of planning to criticize at trial, John pointed the finger at management.

John said, "There was an awful lot of negotiations involving Arthur and management as to where he will go. There was a delay process in getting him on the air as well. That was my interpretation."

"In your mind, that was one of the reasons why he wasn't on the air more during that period?"

"I think so, yes. He was sidetracked."

Joining "Dateline," I had passed out of John's assignment orbit. Then, he had been manning the news desk at the Barcelona games throughout the summer of 1992 and so hadn't witnessed the reassignment of Alicastro and me from "Dateline" or the events leading to our suspension. But here we had gained some useful testimony from David Verdi, who delivered the blow for management.

"So we rejected the idea," David testified, "of any sort of elevated status, and we promoted the idea, more insisted on the idea that the terms of this agreement were—in the absence of a 'Dateline' assignment, that they would be assignable to the New York desk and be part of the general assignment population."

This clashes with a clause in my "Dateline" contract, which states clearly that in the event that management shifted me from the new prime-time show, I would become the News Division's "Senior European Correspondent." This clause stemmed from my acceptance of management's offer of the senior London posting prior to their decision to shift me to "Dateline." Now we had Verdi confirming on the record that Joe and I had ultimately been reassigned *back* from our "Dateline" positions, which our contracts stated were limited to that program alone, and into new, previously undefined roles that required us to work on two fronts at once—news *and* "Dateline"—without the special status that our contracts guaranteed.

This testimony would help to illustrate how management reacted angrily to my protests over the mishandling of our "Dateline" stories, culminating in the Bosnia assignment. But what about the "Dateline" stories themselves? We had to flesh out that part of our case—show how hard foreign news was viewed by NBC executives responsible for the program, and demonstrate that the kind of fiddling that later resulted in the GM truck-rigging lunacy had become endemic on the show as early as our own time there.

We began by taking the deposition of Lisa Freed, a fine young segment producer at "Dateline" and the prime mover behind a piece I reported for the show on survivors of political torture. Lisa had suggested focusing on two Guatemalan survivors who were being treated at a leading clinic in Chicago. Following a shoot there, we'd traveled to Guatemala and rounded out a pretty solid piece about continuing human-rights abuses in the Central American state.

Lisa testified that she had had a "smooth" working relationship with me as we assembled the segment. Brian asked her how the piece had been received at NBC.

"I believe that the day following the airing of our piece, which was called Torture as a working title, and it had been a night where they had programmed a lot of death stories, that I recall Arthur telling me that Burbank had been unhappy. I believe he said that Jeff had told him or somebody had told him that Burbank had been unhappy with our story."

This corroborated our charge that Jeff Diamond, the executive producer of "Dateline NBC," had criticized the Guatemala story the morning after it was aired, as had Don Browne and Steve Friedman. Lisa's testimony also shed some light on tensions among "Dateline" staffers following Diamond's dismissal after the GM affair. Brian asked Lisa if she had heard co-anchor Jane Pauley speak out at a staff meeting.

"She wanted to keep standards high...I think there was certainly the feeling that, as I recall, that in the past we had gone for certain kinds of pieces."

Brian asked what Lisa believed Jane had meant by this.

"I don't remember whether she was alluding to the fact that all the magazine shows now seem to be chasing after the same sort of tabloidy-type stories...I do remember her sort of saying that we should be above it all, above the fray."

Though the inquiry into the GM incident was criticized by many NBC staffers as a whitewash of upper-management complicity in the affair, the report (released by NBC March 22, 1993) provided some insight into the way that competing news and entertainment forces exerted pressure on the show and its producers:

"Dateline" is part of the news division at NBC, but it must also work with the entertainment division headquartered in Burbank, California. The entertainment division's promotion staff decides how to promote each "Dateline" segment, proposes promotional materials, and decides how much promotion each segment gets during prime time. In addition to supervising the production of all segments, Diamond discusses these promotion decisions with executives in the entertainment division, who in turn decide how to promote "Dateline" segments on the air.

In Kent v. NBC, our challenge was to show how promotion policy influenced, and later dictated, editorial policy on "Dateline." Steve Friedman, another of the original named defendants in my lawsuit and Jeff Diamond's supervising producer, gave in grudgingly to Brian's persistent questioning on that score. He acknowledged telling me in July 1992 that promotion of the Guatemala piece presented problems.

"What did you discuss in that regard?" Brian asked him.

"That in a ten-second promo where we could only promote one of the stories on the show, that we could not promote that story because of the graphic nature, and whether or not people would tune in on a promotion to see a show about people who had been tortured and beaten and killed."

"So you had a discussion in which you discussed promotion of the Guatemala story; you said you couldn't promote it because of the graphic nature of the subject matter, namely people being beaten and killed?"

"That's what I said."

Friedman went on to describe the decision-making process in detail. "Well, Jeff told us that the people in Burbank were a little skittish about promoting that."

"What did he say in that regard?"

"He asked me what I thought."

"What did he tell you about what the people in Burbank had said?"

"That's what he said, that they are a little skittish about promoting that particular story."

"Did he tell you why they were skittish?"

"Because of the graphic nature and whether or not that would be an audience grabber or audience turnoff. "

"Did he indicate what his opinion was?"

"He asked me what I thought."

"What did you tell him?"

"Promote something else."

Sitting there, listening to this, I felt like asking Steve why he hadn't thought of arguing the journalist's side of that issue–that some stories need additional advertising *because* they're not obvious, made-for-Burbank "grabbers." But I held my tongue; my lawyer was asking the questions.

Brian continued: "Was anything else discussed in this meeting concerned with Mr. Kent or the show?"

"I think Jeff said that sometime around Labor Day, we should have some kind of resolution of whether Arthur was in or out, and I think Don and I said we will."

Labor Day. Mr. Gartner had terminated me on false charges a week before Labor Day 1992. I tried to look into Steve's eyes, but he turned away. There was so much left to discover. And so much more motivation within me, now, to keep digging.

CHAPTER FIFTEEN

Rattling the Executive Chain

My reaction was "wow," my reaction was "gutsy." I think they pushed him to the very edge. And I think you can only slap somebody in the face so many times and if that person finally stands up and pushes back, you can't say that person is crazy for pushing back.

–Stu Witt, Kent's agent, testifying about the Sixth Avenue incident

AFTER THE INITIAL round of depositions in mid-September 1993, there came an opportunity to settle Kent v. NBC. Judge Mariana Pfaelzer invited attorneys for both sides into her chambers. Mark Helm and Marjorie Neufeld, of NBC's in-house legal department, were joined by a new face–a lawyer from the General Electric Company, specifically the insurance subsidiary that covered NBC for libel claims.

"Looks like we've got the attention of the guys upstairs," Brian said with a grin.

And had we ever. Brian returned from the closed-door conference with word that Mr. Helm had held me up to ridicule before the judge, and had offered a paltry sum of $200,000 to settle the case. It was a GE-style screw-you, take-it-or-leave-it performance, illustrating Jack Welch's reputed belief that lawsuits should never be settled out of court until every attempt has been made to crush the other side. I had to admit the tactic had a demoralizing sting: NBC's lawyers were suggesting that I might be willing to bury the hatchet for less than a full year's salary, even after the company's publicity campaign had effectively ended my career in network television.

"I hope you told them to go straight to hell," I said.

Brian smiled his litigator's smile, which might resemble the grin of an urbane, Armani-clad vampire. "I didn't use quite that language in front of the judge, Arthur. I just told them that they had made a very big mistake."

We went for drinks to plan our next offensive. I tried hard not to feel down. That had been the objective of NBC's strategy—get our hopes up by suggesting the settlement conference, then drop the floor out from beneath us by scorning the testimony we'd taken to that point. With GE's lawyers involved, we were up against some seasoned behind-the-scenes operators. But thankfully their record in other cases proved that they could be beaten.

In April 1992 GE had been forced to pay $325,000 to settle a lawsuit accusing its Navy and Small Steam Turbine Department in Fitchburg, Massachusetts, of dumping photochemical waste. And at the high end of the scale, GE had pleaded guilty in July 1992 to four federal criminal-fraud charges in a scandal over jet engine sales to Israel, and paid $9.5 million in fines and a staggering $59 million to settle a related civil suit.

So Goliath wasn't impossible to trip up. And even if we couldn't score jet engine numbers, I'd be damned if I was going to settle for anything like the Small Steam Turbine figure. I decided it was best to translate the indignity of my opponents' phoney settlement offer into some good, constructive anger. Just enough anger to keep fighting.

I was becoming frustrated with the slow pace of the justice system—it had been more than a year now since my firing. But that was tempered by the encouragement I felt over the complex and convincing pattern of evidence we were building. My lawyers sensed this too. I could see that.

Brian, Fred and Andy weren't just going through the motions with my file. They talked animatedly about the finer points of the saga. The thrill of the chase had infected us all. Sure, NBC was stonewalling, resisting all suggestions to settle realistically. But they were, in effect, handing us an even larger victory down the road—as long as we could pick up the momentum of our discovery. We had to keep the testimony and the documents coming our way, piece together even more convincing arguments, substantiate the charges we had made.

Meantime, the physical and mental stresses of driving the case onward pushed me beyond any previous extreme I had known. Sure, walking for fifteen days over the Hindu Kush had caused a kind of fatigue that stays with you forever, exertion so great it scars the memory. But the eight months from the start of our discovery in July 1993 until victory in March 1994 was itself a kind of forced march. I rose at five in the morning to pore over testimony for a few hours and assemble evidence, then spent a half-hour doing laps in the rooftop pool to burn the aggression out of my limbs and mind. Then I headed over to the CBC's Broadcast Center to work with the producers of "Man Alive" for the day. In the evening I caught up by phone with Brian and the guys three time zones to the west, where they were just entering the prime working hours of another L.A. afternoon.

Through it all, I knew I had to show a happy if determined face to my family and friends and workmates—and mean it. I realized early on that I had to do more than just look confident. I really had to believe, to have true faith, not just in my chances of winning out over NBC but in continuing to learn and develop as a professional, and as a person. There had to be more to me than just a battle, a cause.

I came to understand that if I stayed whole, remained myself, that any battle could be won. And as the case progressed, the relationships I shared with the people closest to me produced the most unexpected gift of the whole undertaking. I became aware as never before in my life of the precious, vital nature of strong friendships, of the ties with other human beings that endure and deepen, if we're fortunate, as the years rush by. Whenever I checked in by phone with my mother in Calgary, I could sense that she was listening between the words and phrases: was the burden of litigation making me bitter, wearing me down, changing me? Over time, her growing enthusiasm for the twists and turns in the case, for keeping up with developments, told me that she felt I was doing all right in terms of maintaining body and soul.

Deborah was another valuable sounding-board, and she was always ready with an instant check on reality. Debs is a quiet, intelligent and sensitive young woman, and I knew I couldn't hope to hold her if I blacked out on anger, if I let the case scramble me up inside. Debs helped me laugh at myself, finding humor even in the lawyerly chase for evidence. And if I became discouraged, she gently reminded me: you'll make them give back everything they've taken away; you'll win and we'll move on.

Friends in our industry helped me to keep professional discipline in mind. Max Keeping, the Ottawa broadcaster who was my first television news editor in the seventies, can still talk paragraphs to me in only a few words about life and work. "It's the reporting that matters now," he told me. "Win your case if you can, but what will mean the most to everyone who counts is how well you've come through this. Your performance–your ability not to let them damage who you are and what you can do." George Frakjor, my TV news professor at university, assured me that he and his students were watching my showdown with NBC management closely and were cheering me on.

In a larger way, my brother Peter was there for me too. Not that the Kent brothers engage in soul-searching spiritual-support sessions. We talk more like friends and colleagues: the warmth and understanding is unspoken, but tangible and strong. Peter always answered the phone, listened to what was going on. And it was his face in the audience that I was most conscious of when I first screened my Bosnia film in Toronto. He cared enough to show up–all a little brother really needs at a time like that.

And when I felt really pushed, really tested, even strangers could provide encouragement, and I welcomed every word and gesture and took heart from them. Like the Air Canada, American and Delta ticket agents who would volunteer upgrades to first class on my shuttle-discovery missions across North America. Their bosses could be bastards, too, they told me: teach management a lesson for us while you're in court with NBC. The employees of car rental companies and hotels and restaurants that I frequented told me that they had read the papers and knew what I was up against, and wished me good luck.

Or the impeccably dressed executive who dropped his cellphone in disbelief when he saw my face and pushed through the crowd on Santa Monica's Third Street Promenade to tell me: "Go get 'em, Arthur. Believe me, I *know* what working for an invader is all about." He was a senior executive for Columbia Pictures, which had been scooped up by the Sony Corporation, as NBC had been swallowed by GE.

I was lucky–I was able to translate these random expressions of support into huge morale boosts at critical times. The support I had attracted and the gains I had made provided me with a positive focus to counter NBC's tactics. So I felt genuine encouragement when Andy Coombs reminded me of the promising sessions just ahead.

"Face it," my lawyer said, "the big fish are still to come. Gartner, Hubble, Diamond and the rest. If their depos pay off, I think Mr. Helm's clients will wake up and smell the coffee."

* * *

The next dose of caffeine for NBC: hearing the truth about "Dateline" as the court reporter typed it, line by line, into the record.

Early on we issued a formal notice to NBC to produce Jeff Gaspin, vice-president of prime-time programming at NBC News, for a deposition. It was at his examination in October that I met Jeff for the first time–his orbit in network management had been much closer to the focus of executive power than my own. I was surprised by how young he looked and sounded. He couldn't be out of his late twenties, I thought, yet he testified easily and fluently about the webs of influence and intrigue at NBC–much of which flourished across the divisional divide between Entertainment in Burbank and News in New York. The result: a blurring of traditional programming distinctions. Jeff testified: "Entertainment very often compared news shows to entertainment shows in which casting was so important."

Jeff had been appointed by Michael Gartner as the executive link between the News and Entertainment divisions. In that role he had overseen the creation of "I Witness Video," a drama-on-home-video show that had scored with audiences on NBC but had turned off many professionals in the News Division. "I Witness Video" was pure entertainment, not news. Yet Michael Gartner praised its success, and his wunderkind Jeff Gaspin was given a big role in the launch of the division's big new project, "Dateline NBC."

Andy Coombs asked Jeff if Burbank executives passed judgment on "Dateline" programs.

"Yes, they'd give me their opinion of the show, the pieces they liked, the pieces they didn't like. They were very vocal, but I would give it back. I would be very vocal about their shows." He said that Entertainment executives complained of a ratings loss in the second half-hour of the show.

"Did they make any particular suggestions about what might be done to "Dateline" in order to address this loss of share?" Andy asked.

"Yes."

"What were those suggestions, as best you recall?"

"They were usually quite tabloid in nature. Do I have to define 'tabloid'?""

"Is that softer?"

"No, it's more tabloid."

"Then you should define it."

"It grabs you more. It's sexier, sleazier, sometimes hotter, inappropriate."

"I'm sorry, did you say inappropriate?"

"Yes."

Jeff testified that Burbank had suggested "Dateline" produce a full hour on Amy Fisher, the "Long Island Lolita" whose pistol attack on her lover's wife had caused a storm of sensational coverage, especially from the tabloid press and TV magazine shows. "Dateline" covered the story as suggested.

"I think the argument from the Entertainment folks [was] that those shows were doing more than we were and if they could do it, why couldn't we."

Hearing this succinct if depressing summation of NBC's programming policy–of the network's basic instinct in broadcasting–I wanted to groan. But Andy's examination was moving closer to home now. He asked Jeff if the subject of domestic versus foreign content came up during discussions with Entertainment over "Dateline's" ratings problems.

"Yes."

"Can you tell us, as best you recall, what was said on that subject?"

"Why are you doing foreign stories?"

"Do you recall any conversations with them about any of the segments which Arthur Kent was at least partially responsible for preparing that aired on 'Dateline'?"

"I do recall the torture segment. They didn't seem too pleased with it."

"Do you recall who didn't seem too pleased with it?"

"Vince and Preston."

Andy and I exchanged a glance. Wouldn't it be fun to depose Vince Manze and Preston Beckman, two of Bob Wright's top Entertainment executives.

"Can you tell me, as best you recall, what it was they said concerning that segment?"

"You know, I really don't remember what they said. I just remember having a conversation about it."

"The gist of their comments, though, was negative, as I understand it?"

"Yes, after it aired."

The Gaspin session was very helpful. However sparingly, he had shed light on Entertainment's gradual encroachment on News' control of "Dateline" during the show's early months. Our appetites had been whetted as we sat down with our next witness, the bearded and bespectacled Jeff Diamond, the man who had pulled every string possible to get me on to his show and then abandoned me when Burbank intervened.

Meeting at his lawyer's office for his deposition, Jeff and I shook hands and exchanged pleasantries. Now, ironically, I needed this guy on my side, and my lawyers and I had been pondering some very key questions. Since Jeff's disgrace over the GM truck-rigging incident and his forced resignation from NBC, would he tell the whole truth about our own showdown the previous year? How much was he constrained by his separation agreement with the network? The company and its GE parent were well known for the secrecy agreements they thrust at departing employees.

Andy felt Jeff out on the issue of how I had been persuaded to join "Dateline." "I wanted to do foreign stories," he testified. "I know I told Arthur he couldn't do only foreign stories. We talked about ratios. I told him I would try to achieve 50/50, 60/40, foreign/domestic, and I think Arthur knew that going into the discussions on whether 'Dateline' would fit for him. I knew that you have a correspondent based overseas, and you would be using the correspondent to do foreign stories."

Jeff went on to corroborate two of our contractual claims. First, he said that his program required exclusivity: "Any correspondent I worked with on 'Dateline' had to be dedicated to 'Dateline.' That was a ground rule." Second, he confirmed that he had, like Verdi, informed me in July 1992 that I was to be reassigned from his program to the general assignment desk.

About Jeff's dealings with the Entertainment Division, Andy asked: "Did the question come up of promoting foreign stories versus other stories?"

"Yes, at times."

"Can you tell me what was said by the personnel at Entertainment on that subject?"

"Pretty much the same thing that was discussed at ABC based upon promotion of stories."

"What was it?"

"That specific kinds of stories are much easier to promote and bring in an audience to a much greater extent, and they are mostly domestic stories."

"So foreign stories were not among the easier pieces for Entertainment to promote?"

"No, they weren't among the easier. We promoted some of our foreign stories. It wasn't a black-and-white issue. It had to do with contents of stories."

"Any other content issues which arose concerning the ease of promotion of different segments on 'Dateline'?"

"After working a year doing 'Dateline,' I know that they liked promoting crime stories and stories with a sexual overtone to it, but that's promotion. They do the same thing at ABC."

Andy probed further. What had Jeff explained about "cultural differences" among the networks?

"I said that at NBC there was much more involvement with Entertainment than there was at ABC, and that it was tough for me to adjust to at first but I had been adjusting to it."

"What did you mean by much more involvement by Entertainment?"

"At ABC there is very little interaction between News and Sports or News and Entertainment. All of the decision-making and all of the changes are made within the News Division, and there are plenty of them. At NBC I had to spend more time running through promotion with the Entertainment Division and running through the broadcast with the Entertainment Division."

This was a guarded, restrained version of the kind of complaints Jeff had made to me when he spiked the Afghan piece. Still, we were getting part of our story out of one of their mouths. Things deteriorated, however, as Andy moved closer to the core of our case.

"Did you tell Mr. Kent that Entertainment wanted fewer foreign stories?"

"I told Arthur that Entertainment felt that foreign stories would not provide as big a rating as domestic stories, but I did not tell Arthur that they asked me or told me not to run them."

One out of two, I thought. Exactly halfway to the truth. I had to feel sorry for Jeff's predicament. His name and the GM truck deception would be linked forever. And now we were going to have to prove that once again, he had left out vital information, facts that should have been part of his story.

* * *

Ironically, a good deal of that proof came as the result of testimony brought out by NBC's attorney, Mark Helm. Mark notified the court that he wanted to depose my agent, Stu Witt, and his senior partner, Richard Leibner, of NS Bienstock, Inc.

"I think it's safe to say," Andy remarked midway through these sessions, "that Mark's bitten off a bit more than he can chew with these two."

Stu Witt is a trim sixty-year-old ex-Marine who survives the daily cut and thrust of the network news business the same way he runs his marathons: he overcomes the pain and just keeps going. As business agent to more than sixty correspondents and producers, he does more than just find jobs and negotiate contracts for his clients at the network news divisions. He shares our highs and lows and helps fight our battles with some of the most powerful employers in America.

Once, I overheard him on a speaker-phone delivering a verbal knock-out against a difficult network contract lawyer, who had been stubbornly blocking one of Stu's negotiating points.

"Were you ever in the armed forces?" Stu demanded.

"No..."

"Well in the Marines we had a code to live by. Never leave your dead behind. Always take 'em from the field." And then he hung up, leaving the network lawyer to wonder: what, exactly, could this sinister message mean?

It was nothing more than psychological warfare, of course—a single shot of malice blasted into the consciousness of the adversary at just the right time. The tactic turned the battle in Stu's favor. The contract in question arrived in its final form on his desk the next morning, and a few pages in, there was the clause that Stu had been holding out for. His network opponent had given in, and the provision was now part of the deal. I know. It was my contract.

Stu's boss, Richard Leibner, is funny, eccentric, and about as sharp a dealmaker as you'll find on Broadway. His office on the twenty-fourth floor is decorated with Hopalong Cassidy paraphernalia, right down to the chaps and cap pistols. But it's the collection in his filing cabinet that has made him one of the biggest guns in the TV industry—the anchor contracts of Dan Rather, Diane Sawyer, Mike Wallace and Andy Rooney, among others.

Mr. Helm looked serious as he arrived at the Bienstock office, dragging his notes and binders along behind him on a little travel trolley. After Michelle, the receptionist, showed him into the conference room, she announced in her best Bronx drawl, "He looks like fun."

Mr. Helm began by asking Stu to read into the record some notes he had taken at the time Don Browne, Steve Friedman and Jeff Diamond had been pressuring me to join "Dateline NBC": "If the magazine show is going to do Amy Fisher, we need an out as quickly as possible."

Stu testified that he and I had been worried that the new prime-time show might be soft, tabloid. "We were both very concerned, but they kept assuring Arthur and to a lesser degree me...that they wanted him for what he did best, which is the hard-hitting foreign story; that this was going to be a real journalistically sound magazine show; that they wanted him to report from places where, you know, he had done important stories; i.e., Afghanistan, Iraq and stuff like that."

Testimony from Stu and Richard painted a picture of confusion in NBC management. First came the December 1991 proposal that Joe and I be senior European producer and correspondent respectively reporting to "Nightly News" from London. Richard recalled a meeting with Don Browne. "Don essentially said, we will get it done as quickly as we can...it was virtually a done deal except for nuancing." But the "Nightly News" deal was pushed aside only one month later when Browne and Friedman insisted that Joe and I go to Jeff Diamond's new magazine show.

"It was almost like *Nineteen Eighty-four* where you don't know who your enemy is anymore. It was like we had gone from one being the most important to the other being the most important, and I couldn't understand how they had said all these things about 'Nightly' being the franchise and et cetera et cetera, now all of a sudden it was forget that, it was the magazine show is the franchise and we are giving it all of our support and we are getting top producers, et cetera, et cetera. We flip-flopped from one to the other and it was very hard to understand how the tone could change that quickly in such a short period of time."

Stu testified that NBC management played hardball, insisting that I give in to their demand of extending the prime-time show contract to four years from three years.

"I think there was certainly a threat that, you know, all of the discussions and all the promises that had been made would be out the window if we didn't give in on this point."

Then, after the contracts were signed and "Dateline" was on the air, trouble arose. Mr. Helm asked Richard Leibner: "What was your sense of what the problem was?"

"That Arthur had been put into 'Dateline,' after much persuasion by the company; that the News Division had lost some control, if not a significant amount of control, of the broadcast; that the reasons for putting Arthur on the broadcast were not being utilized other than the fact that they were getting his face and name value with the open of the show and in their publicity and press releases."

In great detail Stu testified about a luncheon meeting at New York's La Cité restaurant, immediately after the spiking of the

Afghanistan piece. Don Browne sat down with Joe and me, along with Stu and Richard, to try to reach a resolution. I had earlier suggested that if "Dateline" didn't want our stories, then we should all go back to the original "Nightly News" deal, as provided for in my "Dateline" contract. Clause 5 reads: "In the event that Artist is no longer assigned to the Program, he shall be designated as Producer's Senior European Correspondent."

"The thrust of the idea," Richard testified, "was to get Arthur back to reporting serious journalism, because they would not allow him to do serious journalism on the magazine show because they just didn't want it. They couldn't promote it."

Stu recalled that I had put another option to Don should management not go for the "Nightly" plan. "I think there was a suggestion by Arthur that the parties go their separate ways, as gentlemen."

"To the best of my recollection, Arthur said that since it is not working and that being the case, why don't we go our separate ways and terminate this contract... I remember Don Browne at that point got up very angry at lunch and threw his napkin on the table and we had to somehow quiet him down again."

Stu said that he phoned Don twice after the meeting in an effort to reach an agreement, but Don didn't return his calls.

Richard, however, testified that he had got through to Steve Friedman and made notes of every point Steve had made. This was news to me. At no time prior to his deposition had Richard told me about this. Helm had Richard read through his notes line by line.

"Then it says he will help our numbers," Helm read. "What does that refer to?"

"The ratings, the whole reason that they wouldn't take Arthur off the masthead of the show," Richard answered.

"So your recollection is that Mr. Friedman said they wanted to keep Mr. Kent's name on 'Dateline' because it would help their ratings on that show?"

"Absolutely."

"The next line says 'The show "Dateline" is, as Diamond says, different from what we sold him on.' Did Mr. Friedman say that?"

"That whole memo is a shorthand of the pertinent points of

the conversation."

"The points that Mr. Friedman made?"

"Absolutely."

"Did Mr. Friedman tell you in what ways he thought the 'Dateline' show was now different?"

"The issue was that the kind of work Arthur did overseas was not promotable and was not the kind of thing that would hold an audience."

"Did he say anything else?"

"That was the essence of the discussion."

"And what does this statement about leading with Yeltsin refer to, do you recall?"

"It meant that they were going to–that their feeling was they couldn't sell tickets with hard news but that they could do it with back of the book, sidebar or tabloid journalism."

Bingo. Program only the stories you can sell. Promotion policy becomes editorial policy. Entertainment in Burbank steers News in New York.

* * *

As a tighter web of testimony and evidence was spun around NBC management that autumn of 1993, our team took note of how criticism of tabloid television was growing in the mainstream press. Not that these outbursts were having a perceptible influence on programming; far from it. Scandal, crime and sensationalism were mushrooming on American TV screens in the form of more and more "reality-based" magazine shows. But the critics' stinging rebukes of tabloid excesses had created a new atmosphere, putting the executives and producers of these programs on the defensive, at least in terms of public relations.

In the *San Francisco Chronicle* of December 1, 1993, John Carman hit the show doctors squarely on the head with only four words: "It happened in November..." He followed with a list of that month's TV milestones: "'A Current Affair' screened a rock video called 'Snake Skin Voodoo Man,' starring Joey Buttafuoco, his wife Mary Jo, and an Amy Fisher lookalike... 'American Journal' profiled a Florida man who held his wife hostage after he saw her picture on the jacket cover of a porn video... and 'Inside Edition' aired a three-part interview with 'Son of Sam' killer David Berkowitz."

TV's unofficial Hall of Shame had become a recurrent topic in American newspapers and trade journals as I read my way across the country and back again. Friends and colleagues in the business talked about it constantly. "Wait'll you hear *this*," they'd say, as yet another magazine-show caper was disclosed. Programs employed private detectives to flush out footage and facts that mere journalists, supposedly, couldn't produce. Checkbooks replaced legwork as interview subjects were bought and sold. And, not surprisingly, word from a friend still toiling at "Dateline NBC" indicated that the show had scored another real coup: two whole exclusive segments about the life and times of the Milwaukee cannibal killer, Jeffrey Dahmer, featuring an interview with his father. Who had a book to sell...

As our legal team prepared for the next round of depositions, influential voices in and around the television industry were arguing that in terms of PR, the tabloid programmers weren't just on the defensive; they were profiting on the indefensible. This was a situation, we realized, that could be turned to our advantage in court. How would NBC's top executives appear in the mirror of evidence we would hold up before the jury? Andy Coombs got a pretty fair idea when he paid a visit, on the record, to NBC's Entertainment czars in Burbank.

The depositions he took there were like pulling teeth with no anaesthetic. With the new wave of criticism fanning the firestorm of damning publicity still burning over "Dateline's" GM truck story, we were probing sore spots that promised to yield surprising evidence–not least when Andy brought my case directly to the door of Warren Littlefield, president of NBC Entertainment.

This was, indeed, a big fish, despite his checkered career at the network. Warren Littlefield had presided over a ratings slide at NBC from first to third place, losing titles like "Cosby," "Cheers" and "Letterman." Eight months prior to his deposition in Kent v. NBC, Littlefield had been effectively demoted when Bob Wright appointed Donald Ohlmeyer to the newly created post of president, NBC West Coast. Ohlmeyer, not Wright, was now Littlefield's direct boss; Ohlmeyer now controlled

Entertainment. Still, Warren Littlefield was a day-to-day, clued-in and connected member of the GE/NBC hierarchy, and a key link in the executive chain we wanted to rattle.

As the deposition proceeded, Andy Coombs showed Mr. Littlefield a clipping from the *New York Post* that dated from the height of the GM controversy. Mr. Littlefield had been addressing an industry gathering.

"'NBC Entertainment President Warren Littlefield raised eyebrows when he said that his division suggests story ideas for 'Dateline.' Do you see that?"

"No. Where are you? Oh, right."

The NBC in-house lawyer representing Littlefield, Marjorie Neufeld, cut in. "Yeah. Do you have a question?"

"You do see that. Did you say that at that luncheon?"

"I don't remember. I remember there was a question about the Entertainment Division suggesting stories. I don't remember what the exact–I don't remember the exact response."

"Do you have any reason to dispute the accuracy of this report concerning your response to that question?"

"It doesn't specifically say what my answer was, so I would say that yes, I do dispute it."

"Let me ask you the question now. Did the Entertainment Division suggest story ideas for 'Dateline' at any time before February 22 of '93?"

"Before February?"

"22nd, '93."

"Occasionally we would suggest stories for 'Dateline.'"

Andy wanted specifics, remembering Jeff Gaspin's testimony.

"If you are asking me to recall a specific story from 1992 that I think jumps out and should be told," Mr. Littlefield said, "I really have no recollection of specific stories."

"Do you recall specifically recommending an interview with Amy Fisher, for example?"

"Yes, I think I do recall."

"Do you recall proposing that as a full hour-long 'Dateline' special?"

"I don't recall that."

"To whom did you make that suggestion? Mr. Gartner?"

"You mean the Amy Fisher story?"

"That's correct."

"To the best of my knowledge, yes, I probably recommended that to Mr. Gartner."

Andy asked Mr. Littlefield about his working background in journalism. He didn't have one. His college degree was in psychology; his career was in fictional programming.

"I would have discussions with Mr. Gartner about finding the strongest, most compelling human stories. And those discussions would be more in a general sense as opposed to a specific sense. But that seemed to me to be the key to having a successful news hour, that the success is based on real stories about real people in the world who had compelling human dramas, that news magazines work best when they told good stories."

He testified that he had never been in a discussion about "foreign content versus national content."

"So in terms of your discussions with Mr. Gartner where you sought compelling human dramas, the issue of whether those dramas were foreign or domestic in nature did not come up?"

"The familiar human dramas would come up."

"What do you mean by 'familiar'?"

"Within the consciousness of the American public, our viewing audience."

Reflecting on this, I thought we couldn't have a clearer admission on the record that "Dateline" was not a real news program. Real news is not constrained by what the public already knows. It's not limited to places the public is already familiar with. Quite the contrary: news is what you didn't know before.

Andy's examination was producing a good profile of Mr. Littlefield's mindset. It was just as effective on the topic of the General Electric Company.

"Has Bob Wright ever expressed to you an interest in breaking down the divisions within the NBC corporate structure?"

"Objection," Ms. Neufeld cut in. "Vague and ambiguous."

Andy persevered. "Do you understand the question?"

"I don't understand what 'breaking down' means."

"Removing barriers between divisions," Andy said.

"'Removing barriers' is the term I am familiar with."

"Can you tell me what you understand by that term?"

"That means we are the same company and that we should

communicate as members of the same company, not as though we are working for different companies."

"Is the company NBC?"

"Yes."

Initially, Littlefield excluded GE from the equation. Then Andy asked: "And who has expressed that desire or objective to you?"

"Bob Wright."

"Anyone else?"

"It is part of the GE strategy and philosophy."

"When Mr. Wright has expressed this objective to you, he has expressed it to you in terms of a general GE philosophy?"

"Yes. And so has Jack Welch."

"Who is Jack Welch?"

"He's the chairman of GE."

Andy's persistence had won us a valuable link between the parent company and Entertainment's expanding influence over news. But a key issue still had to be nailed down: how had Entertainment's promoters interpreted the GE diktat? Examining Vince Manze, the Burbank-based vice-president of promotion, Andy returned to the issues raised by Jeff Gaspin, with mixed results.

"Do you recall any discussions that you had with Mr. Gaspin about 'Dateline' during those visits?"

"I do not recall any specific discussions about 'Dateline' with Jeff Gaspin."

This was odd–Gaspin had told us that he recalled frequent discussions with Manze. Andy probed further, but Mr. Manze said he could not recall any discussions with either Gaspin or Jeff Diamond about "Dateline" segments.

"If I were to tell you Mr. Gaspin had testified that you spoke repeatedly on the subject of foreign coverage, would you disagree with that testimony?"

"I would say that I don't remember such conversations."

"Did you at any time during 1992 have any views concerning the proper amount of foreign coverage on 'Dateline'?"

"None. No, I did not."

"You had no views whatsoever?"

"I had no views."

Once again, a clash. Andy had examined Gaspin on Burbank's dislike of foreign stories, and Jeff had replied that "the loudest thing came from Vince Manze." So Andy probed Manze on related subjects. "Did you have, at any time, any opinion concerning the amount of crime and sex which was appropriate for broadcast on the 'Dateline' show?"

"I do not recall having any opinion or stating that he [Diamond] should have more crime or sex in his stories."

Andy brought up the Guatemala piece. Did Mr. Manze recall the segment?

"Vaguely."

"Did you see that segment?"

"I did not, sir."

"If I were to tell you that Mr. Gaspin has testified that you specifically critiqued that segment to him the following day, would you have any basis to agree or disagree with that?"

"I would say to you that I do not recall any such conversation."

After his deposition, I combed back and forth over Mr. Manze's transcript. It was odd that he was certain he hadn't seen the Guatemala piece, and yet he simply "couldn't recall" the conversation about it with Gaspin.

Andy agreed, and wondered if we shouldn't find out something more about Vince Manze. With him and others, there was a name we had come across a couple of times in testimony about the Entertainment Division: Miller, Tim Miller. We decided to take his deposition.

* * *

"There seemed to be a triad here with Jeff Diamond and Mr. Manze and myself."

Timothy Wade Miller, ex-NBC vice-president of advertising and promotion, East Coast, started strong and got better as his testimony went on.

"That was kind of the information-flow triangle. And then back to the Entertainment side it would continue on to Preston Beckman, Warren Littlefield and some key players back there."

Andy wanted to know more about Mr. Manze and "Dateline." Much more.

"The Entertainment Division primarily on the arrival of Vince Manze took a great deal of a more active role in kind of total network picture promotion," Tim Miller testified. "Whereas the first three years under the Grossman/Russert era, the relationship and the work was primarily managed and directed out of the News Division. It was kind of a philosophical change."

Andy wanted that down on record again. "Were those changes attributable to the arrival of Mr. Manze?"

"Don't speculate," Mark Helm told Tim. "If you know, only."

"Only that his personality lent itself to being much more involved, as well as his sense of knowing what was the right way to position a show. He was a much more aggressive leader and he was very concerned about the performance of NBC News programs in prime time."

Well, I thought: Mr. Manze in a whole different light. I watched Mark Helm's face contort with discomfort as Tim Miller calmly answered Andy's questions.

"You mentioned some other names, Mr. Beckman, Mr. Littlefield. Was it your responsibility to deal with them with respect to the promotion of 'Dateline' or did Mr. Manze—"

Smiling, shaking his head, Tim cut in: "Mr. Manze usually communicated it in a very brash and bold way because he would most certainly tell us exactly what he thought about a topic, so I think he personally injected a great deal of his belief in its promotability.

"There was always an effort made to find celebrities to appear on the show—David Letterman and Ted Danson—and to try to find the angle that seemed to make them fit. There seemed to always be an ongoing dialogue between News and Entertainment about, you know, who is hot, and celebrities. I don't only mean movies and television, but Nancy Kerrigan, John Wayne Bobbitt, the attempt to book the newsmaker of the week, of the day, of the month, and then the Entertainment Division did try to pull in and book and help book entertainment."

Andy and I smiled at each other with satisfaction. I'd never met Tim Miller before. Until his departure from NBC eight months prior to this deposition, he had supervised up to twenty-five people in preparing promotional materials for "Dateline NBC." Now his words were flowing through the court reporter's fingertips and on to the record like pennies from heaven.

"There were times that the format of the show was not locked in, that there was some discussion as to would this segment play better with that segment, and my sense was that Vince had an ongoing dialogue with Jeff about this... The celebrity or personality aspect of the show was promotable and important and would have played high on the Vince Manze barometer."

Andy asked: "Amy Fisher is a celebrity that appeared on 'Dateline'?"

"Amy Fisher, Arlene Wuornos, the first lesbian serial killer...she had a lot of titles that preceded her name." Tim said that he thought that NBC's executives in charge of "Dateline" "wouldn't take on some of the serious social issues because of the kind of perception of them being too heavy."

The names of other Entertainment executives came up over the issue of "Dateline's" program research. "Do you recall," asked Andy, "whether Mr. Beckman drew any conclusions from this research as to the kind of programming which should air on 'Dateline'?"

"Generally, and it seemed like this kind of changed throughout the run of the show, the beginning segments should have been useful, have a positive upswing, not be depressing. And there was a real concern about showing burnt bodies, dying children, starving children, abused children, unless there was some kind of answer or resolution. That seemed to be a real important aspect particularly in Vince's mind. He didn't want to see AIDS victims and he didn't want to see the children in Somalia."

I cringed as Tim told us that the Entertainment Division's promos of "Dateline" would "shift focus" in order to "kind of eliminate the bad part of the story, try to come up with the good side of the story." Did Burbank really think news was an elastic commodity, just another script to be bent and stretched and shaped? Apparently, according to Tim Miller's description of what happened each time he came out of a "Dateline" screening.

"We would return to our offices and have a discussion and my first discussion would be with probably Vince Manze, who on many occasions was irate once I told him—once we went through the topics. He might say that it was not promotable and it has very limited interest and he would then probably call Jeff Gaspin and in a few choice words he would tell him nothing was promotable.

"I think Jeff Diamond soon learned how Vince would react to

certain things, so Vince really set up this—put everybody on guard because he really held the key to promotion inventory."

Andy asked: "Did Mr. Manze convince Mr. Diamond or how did it work?"

"There was a compromise struck. My sense is that Vince probably won more than Jeff did."

So, I thought, making notes. Now we could show a jury what Mr. Diamond meant by his testimony that Entertainment was "much more involved" at NBC News. And little wonder Jeff had run into a stone wall over promoting pieces like our Afghan or Guatemala stories.

"My sense," Tim testified, "was that only foreign stories that had some kind of impact back in the States [were promoted]." He said that when it came to a story like the huge BCCI banking scandal, "they don't want to hear about it."

"Do you have a sense," Andy asked, "as to whether the number of foreign segments increased or decreased during 'Dateline's' first year?"

"Decreased," Tim said. He could only vaguely remember discussing whether to promote a segment I had done on "Dateline," the piece about civilian victims of UN sanctions in Iraq. "I do vaguely remember that and I also remember that it was a lot of pictures of despair and that was the taboo."

Tim said that he had tried, on occasion, to broaden Entertainment's concept of what kind of stories were promotable.

"Unfortunately the decisions that I made and the information I carried back was not always respected in the mix. I also started to live in Vince Manze's vision because it was easier for me to try to make certain assumptions than fight with him every time, because that is just the way that he—you know, I got tired of him, you know, calling me different names and—"

"We all like the path of least resistance sometimes," Andy said.

"Yes. I was constantly concerned about this issue and about the non-involvement of news management in all of this. Very rarely was there a battle that involved Michael Gartner. There might have been, and if there was, it was broad and quiet."

Tim testified that at least two Entertainment executives, one of them Vince Manze, had said that "Arthur could be a key player in whatever show he was involved in." After the Gulf War, Tim explained, "[Arthur] was very hot...and there was a gap between the end of the war and Arthur's appearance–regular appearance on any show–and in my mind that was problematic. I felt like they missed an opportunity."

"Who missed the opportunity?"

"I think the News Division directly; Entertainment Division indirectly, in that they could capitalize on him whether he was part of a News show or Entertainment/News product."

"Did anyone express to you an opinion as to, you know, why it was that there had been that failure?"

"No."

"Did anyone say it was Arthur Kent's fault?"

"No."

"No one blamed Mr. Kent for his lack of visibility after the war?"

"No...the blame was not on Arthur Kent."

* * *

When it came to "blame"–responsibility for everything from the "Dateline" debacle to the Bosnia fraud–the witness we most longed to hear from was my former partner from NBC Rome, Joe Alicastro. We had worked out of each other's hip pockets for three years, from Berlin through Kuwait City. Joe would be able to corroborate almost every point of my case. But would he? Could he?

For more than a year our working relationship had been put into suspended animation, with Joe staying on at NBC News and me getting on with life in the outside world. But what about our friendship? Joe's testimony would say a lot about that, and about honor and courage. We met in NBC's legal offices in New York in mid-November 1993, fifteen months after the phone call in the night that brought our partnership to an end. Joe recalled for Andy, and the record, David Miller's words that night:

"He said, 'Joe, I'm sorry to tell you that you are suspended from NBC News without pay. You are off the computer. You are not allowed into the bureau. We are changing the locks. You are not to enter the bureau. You are not to speak to the people in the bureau, and your medical benefits, however, will remain in place'–in case I had a heart attack, I guess."

"Anything else he said during that telephone conversation?"

"That was basically it."

"Did you have any response during that telephone conversation to what he said?"

"Well, I said–I just basically took it all in and said, 'Well, I'm sure you know, David, that I think this is wrong, and that I hope we resolve this situation,' and that was basically it."

"What did you do after the telephone conversation in relation to the news Mr. Miller had conveyed to you?"

"I think the first thing I did was wipe the tears off my wife's eyes."

Listening to this, I stared hard at counsel for NBC. Mr. Helm was having a bad day, and his face showed it. Joe's deposition amounted to a step-by-step corroboration of my story, especially regarding "Dateline."

"The disagreements that we had editorially over the [Afghan] story and whether or not it should have aired led to the request for Arthur and I to fly to New York for another series of meetings," Joe testified. "It was during that first meeting with Jeff Diamond in his office where Jeff said basically, 'I can't keep any of the promises I made to you guys back in February, March. I can't put as many foreign stories on the air as I said I was going to do back then.'"

"Did he explain why?" Andy asked.

"He did not explain in detail why. He did not."

"Someone else did?"

"David Rummel, who is the senior producer on the show, told me that Jeff was under an extreme amount of pressure from Burbank about foreign stories."

Joe testified that David Verdi and David Miller conveyed the news that we were to be reassigned, and that he had objected on the grounds that his contract was being violated.

"Did they respond to that statement on your part?" Andy asked.

"David Verdi said, 'I read your contract and it's not in violation of your contract. We can do whatever we want with you.'"

Joe's testimony on the Bosnia assignment was vivid and

unequivocal. As our contract dispute had dragged on in August 1992, the Rome team had been taping a story about the Mafia's activities in Germany. David Verdi had called our cellphone from New York.

"He's calling me to tell me that he has an assignment that he wishes us to undertake almost immediately, and the assignment as he lays it out is to go to Zagreb to meet the UN people there and then to go into Bosnia, into the detention camps."

"The breaking story was these detention camps in Bosnia that were run by the Serbs?"

"That's right."

"In that telephone conversation, did Mr. Verdi say to you to go to—"

"Zagreb was a staging area. It was to meet the UN there and then to go with them to the camps."

"So Mr. Verdi said it was to go to the camps?"

"Very specifically."

Again I looked at Mr. Helm, wondering how his clients' case appeared to him now.

"Bosnia was something that anybody who lived in Europe and worked in the news business had to consider at that time," Joe continued. "Particularly since we had been to a lot of war zones...it came up in family discussion, meaning me and my wife. So when he told me what the assignment was, I said to him, 'Okay,' the usual thing that I would say, Okay, David, can you tell me, where are the camps in Bosnia? Which part of Bosnia? How will the UN be going there? Will there be a convoy? Where will be the flak jackets, the helmets, the clean syringes, the blood plasma kits, all of the things that we normally had in the Rome bureau to travel on dangerous stories, that kind of thing. I wanted to know as much as I possibly could know... He didn't know about equipment and about contacts and about translators and camps or syringes or any of the things that you would need to know to go into a war zone."

Joe testified that he had then consulted with each member of our team individually. Max and Stefano declined the assignment since Italians had been treated with particular hostility in the former Yugoslavia at that time. Joe and I agreed that the operation hadn't been properly planned and that Verdi's lack of knowledge was potentially dangerous. So all four of us, individually, chose to decline in accordance with NBC company policy that service in hazardous areas is purely voluntary.

David Verdi, Joe testified, countered the refusal with the suggestion that the team travel only as far as Zagreb. But, Joe said, "The assignment was to use Zagreb as a staging area to go onward. There was no story in Zagreb. Zagreb was outside, not only the story, but outside of Bosnia. It remained a staging area for stories in Bosnia...throughout the war. That was clearly based on my experience throughout Europe with the way everyone was covering the story and all the different war zones I had covered. That was the assignment. By Mr. Verdi telling us to go to Zagreb, in my mind, it didn't change the assignment at all."

Joe said he relayed Verdi's position to each member of the team, and each man declined the assignment. Andy asked how Verdi had taken this.

"He disagreed vehemently with me, and we went round and round on it in the same way you would about an editorial disagreement. I tried to convey to him that clearly we were not prepared to go beyond Zagreb and that it would be a disservice to NBC News for us to get there and to not undertake an assignment. This was based on three years of covering war zones, et cetera and so on, and you have to be prepared to go when you go. This was one that we were not going to undertake."

"Did Mr. Verdi have any more information concerning the preparations which had been made or information concerning the story than he had during the previous two telephone conversations?"

"No, he did not."

"There was still no information on any preparations that had been made on the ground?"

"No."

"There was still no information on the location of the camps?"

"No."

Joe testified that Verdi angrily said he would take the matter "to a higher level."

Then the suspension. Word in the New York press that it was over an assignment to "peaceful" Zagreb. No mention of the camps in management's statements. Joe testified that one week later he learned that the Rome bureau would be closed. He was in New York meeting with NBC News executives, including Bob MacFarland, a Gartner aide, and David Miller.

"Basically Bob MacFarland and David Miller laid out what the company's opinion was up to that point, but they also wanted to hear my side of the story.

"After I completed my side of the story, David Miller said to me, 'Joe, you don't seem like a person who has any remorse for this, that you have done anything wrong.' I said, 'David, you're damn right. I haven't.'"

Joe went on that day to testify that I had not been a difficult colleague. That he did not agree with management's published accusations against me. That alterations made by Jeff Diamond and his staff to our final "Dateline" story–a story that aired three months before the GM truck segment–amounted to "a bad mistake. It was sloppy."

As Andy and I left the GE building after Joe's deposition, I felt a huge weight off my shoulders. Under the greatest pressure, Joe had told the whole truth. To me, this meant more than mere evidence. It meant that the good times together in Rome hadn't been a lie. And that my case against NBC management was looking a lot like our old bureau in its heyday: unbeatable.

CHAPTER SIXTEEN

Eyes on the Prize

An NBC employee explains... "It is not enough to be ambitious and smart and talented and experienced anymore at NBC. You have to be willing to kill people as you advance."

—Esquire, *February 1993*

NBC is just not a happy place... My superior literally said to me, "I can't help your career, but I can destroy you."

—Esquire, *February 1993*

DES MOINES, IOWA, was not a place I ever imagined spending the eve of my fortieth birthday. But I was pleased to be there in early December 1993. The case of Kent v. NBC, after fourteen months of slow progress through the U.S. justice system, had finally caught up to the man who had dismantled NBC's foreign news apparatus, presided over "Dateline's" disgrace in the GM affair, and brought my own career in U.S. network television news to a sudden stop.

It was particularly satisfying to see Mr. Gartner arrive at the court reporter's office for his deposition, wearing his signature bow-tie and suspenders. Des Moines was Michael's turf; his past had followed him home. I shook hands agreeably with Michael, and Andy and Mark Helm ushered him to his seat before the camera.

I marveled at the spectacle. The newspaperman who had never really been comfortable with the trappings of television now put on a brave face and tried, unsuccessfully, not to look uneasy about the TV technology pointed his way. Mr. Helm, representing him here, had obviously warned him about the electronic record we had insisted on taking. Given Mr. Gartner's separation from NBC, my lawyers couldn't be certain they could force him to appear at the trial, so we were exercising our right to put his deposition on videotape. That way, the jury could have a good long look at him in court.

Michael had aged considerably, and I felt a twinge of sadness. The man had hired me and given me the Rome posting, one of the best reporting jobs I'd ever had. But any sympathy I felt for him drained away as Andy tried to find out how and why he'd blown our bureau team off the map.

"I don't recall," Michael said. Andy had asked if he recognized the quote attributed to Michael Gartner in NBC's announcement of my signing to "Dateline"; did he write or approve the statement? "I don't recall," Michael repeated. Did he remember the first time he'd met me? "I don't recall."

Andy showed Michael a copy of Bruce Lilliston's July 31, 1992, letter written on my behalf.

"Do you recall ever receiving a copy of that letter from Mr. Browne?" Andy asked.

"No, sir."

"Do you recall ever preparing a response to that letter."

"No, sir."

"Do you recall undertaking any action whatsoever in connection with this letter?"

"I don't recall."

Mr. Helm, looking concerned, cut in: "Could we go off the record for a second?" He ushered Michael into the next room. When the two returned a few minutes later, Mr. Helm said, "The witness has a—has a clarification to make."

Andy and I exchanged a glance.

"I was somewhat—there were several letters apparently from this gentleman. I recall Mr. Browne walking in my—walking in my office and leaving me this letter at one point."

Strange—what had jogged Michael's memory? Andy zeroed in on the passage in Bruce's letter stating that I wouldn't undertake war-zone duty until the "Dateline" matter was resolved.

"Did that play any part in the decision to post Mr. Kent to Yugoslavia during the summer of 1992?"

"Well, that sounds ridiculous, no," Michael said, looking flustered. "Let me—let me ask you if I understood the question correctly because there must be something I don't— Are you asking me that because Mr. Lilliston and Mr. Kent would refuse some assignments, that we assigned—that we, therefore, made the assignment based on that?"

"Do you know what date he was assigned to Yugoslavia?" Andy said, challenging his witness to continue in detail.

"No, sir," Michael said, backing off. This was clearly cutting too close to the bone. But Michael had acknowledged the key fact that both he and Don Browne had known full well prior to the Bosnia marching order that I would refuse the assignment.

"When was the first time that you learned about Mr. Kent's assignment to Yugoslavia?" Andy asked.

"I just don't know."

"Was it before or after the assignment was made?"

"I just don't know."

"Do you recall any discussions with Mr. Verdi concerning Mr. Kent's assignment to Yugoslavia?"

"Not specifically, no, sir."

I shook my head with pity for Michael, but with satisfaction for our case. Verdi had testified that Michael Gartner was the only NBC News executive he was reporting to at the time of the assignment. That Michael had been the person who first revealed to him a copy of the Lilliston letter. And that Michael Gartner had directed him to write details of the Yugoslav assignment in the form of a memo. "I recall Michael showing me a number of letters both coming and going," Verdi stated, adding that Gartner showed him the letter suspending me before it was sent to my attorney.

Michael claimed he could not recall that letter either.

"Do you recall having any part in the drafting or transmission of the Exhibit 2 letter?"

"No, sir."

"Did you approve the contents of the letter before it was sent?"

"I just don't recall, sir."

"Is it reasonable for me to conclude because of your signature on the bottom of the second page that you, in fact, approved the contents of the letter?"

"You can conclude whatever you want, sir."

It was astonishing. Mr. Gartner used the reply "I simply don't recall" or words to that effect some 206 times during the approximately three hours of his testimony delivered under oath. No other witness in the case displayed such a pervasive lack of recall. Andy, struggling to pin him down, was frustrated. As Helm and Gartner conferred, I put a hand on my lawyer's shoulder and encouraged him to persevere.

"As part of turning NBC News around during your tenure as NBC News president," Andy continued, "NBC News laid off about 18 per cent of its employees?"

"Is that a question?"

"Yes."

"I don't know what the percentage was."

Really, I thought. Michael was quoted extensively in a *Washington Post* story April 3, 1991, that reported "GE-mandated layoffs have shrunk the NBC work force from 8,000 to 5,700."

"Do you have an estimate as to the number of employees?" Andy pressed.

"No, sir."

I can help Michael, I thought to myself mischievously: there were about 1,400 NBC News staffers when you came and about 950 when you left.

"Do you have a range that you can testify to?"

"No, sir. It's been quite some time, and I've gone on to other things, and I just don't have that in my head at the moment."

"Was it more than 100 employees?" Andy asked.

"Oh, I'm sure it was, but— Well, I don't know. No. I can't say layoff of more than 100 in employment. Whether they were laid off or quit or there was attrition, I would—I just don't have those facts at my fingertip."

Andy asked him if he'd closed any overseas bureaus.

"I would have to check the records. I don't know. I suspect there was, but I don't—I don't know for sure."

Oh really, Michael, I thought. What about Paris, Amman, Manila, Budapest, Tokyo, Johannesburg, Berlin, Frankfurt and Cairo? All closed during Michael's tenure. As well, he had presided over deep cuts in budget and staff at the London, Moscow and Hong Kong bureaus.

"Do you know whether the Rome bureau closed during the time you were president of NBC News?"

"I don't know that there—if there's a Rome bureau today or

there is not a Rome bureau today. So I can't answer that question."

That'd sound great in a courtroom. The Rome bureau was closed in the autumn of 1992, months before Michael Gartner was forced to resign, and it remains closed to this day.

On the libel issue, Andy focused on Mr. Gartner's publicity campaign against me. He passed Michael a clipping from the *New York Daily News*.

"Could you read into the record the first full paragraph appearing in the second column, which reads, 'Kaplan's death'?"

"Kaplan's death came as NBC News suspended correspondent Arthur Kent for refusing an assignment to the region. The handsome Kent won the nickname 'SCUD Stud' for his live reports during the Gulf War."

"Do you see anything in the article which–by which Mr. Kent is the cause for connecting his suspension and David Kaplan's death?"

Mr. Helm objected. He advised Michael not to answer. His florid complexion became damp, agitated.

"The document speaks for itself," he said angrily. "Why don't you ask him a question that he knows something about."

The story did speak for itself. I was nowhere in it. All the information was attributed to Peggy Hubble, Mr. Gartner's spokeswoman. Contrary to the spurious accusations of a number of Mr. Gartner's management associates, the evidence proved that I had done nothing to link my circumstances to David's tragic death.

After the deposition ended, there was just one thing left for me to do: say a formal goodbye to Michael Gartner. I approached the figure pulling on his coat and scarf. I held out my hand. Michael took it into his own. Then I quietly spoke to him, not just for myself but for all the others, the hundreds of overseas staff and their families who have been hurt by his policies.

"Thank you for displaying here today," I told him, "the unique kind of honesty and integrity that so distinguished your administration of our company."

The sad grey eyes stared back at me as he stood there speechless at Helm's side. Andy and I got out of there quickly and went for a beer, wondering how NBC could ever afford to go to trial with a videotape like that in existence.

* * *

"I think that he felt, with Arthur being suspended, that it was bound to get sticky either internally or externally and that he wanted me there."

Peggy Hubble was calmly testifying about Michael Gartner's instructions to her on or about August 11, 1992. The man who just couldn't recall was everywhere in the corridors of Peggy's memory.

"And when you say 'get sticky,' what do you mean by that?" Andy Coombs asked.

"You suspend one of your top correspondents and things like that kind of go like wildfire through the company and through the industry. And there's not a time I can recall that anything controversial happened inside NBC News that it wasn't a matter of hours or days before the press was informed about it."

Listening to this with the court reporter's video camera humming at my shoulder, I marveled at Peggy's dispassionate recitation of how she had prepared to tell the nation's media that I had allegedly shirked assignments and breached my contract. We'd been good friends, I had thought, at NBC–even shared lunches and dinners when I'd been in New York. Always immaculately dressed, with her hair carefully coifed in a storm of curls, Peggy had presented herself to her colleagues as a PR operative we could trust. How wrong I'd been about her, I thought, as she threw me a hostile glare from the far end of the conference table.

"So you anticipated some controversy concerning the suspension?"

"Yes."

"And you say that you then proceeded to do what you always do, which is get as many of the facts as possible in order to give appropriate advice as to what NBC News' response should be; is that correct?"

"Yes."

"And what did you do at this time in terms of attempting to obtain facts concerning Mr. Kent's suspension?"

"As I recall, I talked to Michael Gartner, I talked to Don Browne, I talked to Bob MacFarland. I think that was the time I got the memo from David Verdi outlining his view of what had happened. It was obvious no one had the say, it wasn't the kind of thing we were going to put a press release out about. It was the kind of thing that we would like to keep internal as much as possible but it wasn't likely that was going to happen."

"Did you talk to anyone other than those you've identified, in terms of getting as much of the facts in anticipation of NBC's response to the suspension?"

"I don't recall."

"Did you speak to Mr. Kent?"

"No."

"Did you attempt to reach Mr. Kent?"

"No."

"Did you talk to Mr. Witt?"

"I don't think at that time I did."

"Did you attempt to reach Mr. Witt at that time?"

"No."

"Did you talk to Joe Alicastro?"

"No."

"Did you attempt to talk to Mr. Alicastro?"

"No."

Terrific, I thought. Armed with one side of the story–management's–Peggy prepared to disinform the nation's media. Mr. Gartner, in the end, hadn't needed to put out a release. A leak about Kent and Alicastro would provoke a flood of reporters' calls to Peggy, who was ready with verbal confirmation–ready, because Peggy found out about our suspension, she testified, "one or two days" before we did. Michael Gartner had told her what he was going to do, and his reasons why.

"Was it your understanding that Mr. Kent had announced he was going to not accept assignments?"

"I was told that."

"Of any kind?"

"I believe that's the way it was related to me: that Arthur Kent said until this was resolved, that he refused to take on any further assignment."

On this point, we could prove that Peggy had been lied to. Not just with Bruce's initial letter, which clearly stated that only high-risk assignments would be declined during negotiations– we also had tapes of my "Nightly News" stories running right up to the day of my suspension. We had copies of computer messages to Joe and me from Don Browne congratulating us for the quality of stories we had filed from mid-July to mid-August, and documents showing that all these assignments were done in complete compliance with NBC News operating practice, and with the full knowledge and authority of the news desk in New York.

Peggy's misinformation from Mr. Gartner and his associates ran deeper still. Management had briefed her in a peculiar and selective way, withholding key facts and explanations. Andy began his examination on this front by asking: "Did Don Browne at any time tell you that Arthur Kent had offered to resign from NBC as a way of resolving his differences concerning the 'Dateline' production?"

"Not that I recall," Peggy said.

Andy showed her a copy of the release she had prepared to announce my termination. "The middle of the first paragraph, it refers to Arthur's repeated breaches of his agreement with NBC. What were you referring to in that passage?"

"You know, I think on all of these things with repeated breaches of contracts you have to be aware that I didn't write this in a vacuum and that meeting with lawyers and executives and other people involved in this decision, a lot of this information I got from them."

I smiled. That piece of testimony would help my lawyers secure depositions from NBC's lawyers. And a memo Peggy had written herself at the time of the suspension, a kind of briefing note she used to guide her confirmation statements to reporters, proved that she had been completely misinformed about the Bosnia assignment. Gartner, Verdi and the others told her Zagreb was the only destination. There had been no mention at all that the mission had been to the Bosnian detention camps, as Joe's letter to Michael the previous week had confirmed.

Peggy testified that she wasn't shown or made aware of correspondence from my lawyer, Bruce Lilliston, until a week after the suspension–a full week after she'd begun briefing writers and putting out news releases. Andy showed her Bruce's first letter, a portion of which spoke about the possibility of legal action.

"Had you been aware of the contents of that paragraph, would it have made any difference to the content of your

Exhibit 441 talking-points memo?"

"I can't really say, honestly. First of all, it probably wouldn't have made a difference because it wasn't my decision. The decision was made to suspend Arthur. And once the decision was made, it was my responsibility to answer press requests with the best information that I had under the circumstances. It wasn't my responsibility to interpret letters from attorneys."

But the evidence showed that it was indeed Peggy's responsibility to do so. In fact, it was company policy. And Peggy had spelled it out in a memo she'd circulated to executives about the time that the publicity storm was getting out of control. Andy pulled a copy from his case and confronted Peggy with it.

"It is NBC policy not to comment on matters involved in litigation or a threat of litigation."

"Yes."

"Is that an accurate statement of NBC policy?"

"Yes. It's a comment that was commonly made if there was a lawsuit under discussion or—"

"Is that policy reduced to writing anywhere?"

"I'm not sure if it's reduced to writing. It's something that was fairly standard. And it was our policy. There were times that we veered from that policy, depending on the situation, but— depending on if there was information that we felt required a response. But in general we felt that if we could keep legal matters or personnel matters internal, that was our preference. And of course, with matters involved in litigation, you never know where it's going. So this is fairly standard."

So Peggy, acting on disinformation from Mr. Gartner and his associates, had broken one of her department's key policies. She'd commented freely, filled scores of newspaper columns with management's claims. And she'd done so while I was cut out of the communications loop in Rome.

One huge question was: who had sprung the leak that brought all the calls flooding in to Peggy immediately after the suspension? Peggy testified that the "whole thing happened on the 13th and I started getting press calls and the press started asking me how to reach Arthur."

Whoever had tipped off the press clearly had no knowledge of my whereabouts, much less my position on the story. And the scores of newspaper clippings we planned to exhibit at trial revealed a complete absence of any comment from me or my representatives in the first day of coverage by U.S., Canadian and British reporters. Ms. Hubble and other "unnamed" NBC management sources quoted by reporters enjoyed twenty-four to forty-eight hours' head start in the publicity battle.

The *Philadelphia Enquirer*, for example, ran a nine-paragraph story about my suspension on Friday, August 14. All of it was based on information from Peggy, except the final sentence: "Kent could not be reached for comment." Without any information to balance NBC's false claims, the *Enquirer* had even published a claim by unnamed "NBC insiders" that this "was not the first assignment Kent has turned down." Even hostile management witnesses could never substantiate that claim. It was a lie. Without attribution, the *Enquirer* stated as fact in the second paragraph of its story that Joe and I had been suspended for "refusing last week to go to Zagreb, Croatia..."

The damaging effect of the *Enquirer*'s treatment of the story was multiplied when papers as far afield as the *Arizona Republic* and the *Toronto Star* reprinted it from the wires—in the *Republic*'s case, without even including the disclaimer that I could not be reached for comment. Papers like the *Chicago Tribune* printed only NBC's comments that first Friday—a disappointment since clippings from the *Atlanta Constitution* and the Associated Press, among others, included quotes from me disclaiming management's version of events.

Andy wanted to know more about Peggy Hubble's skill in tilting coverage to NBC's liking. Had she, for example, tried to color the views of the reporter from GQ magazine when she spoke with him?

"Do you recall whether, during that conversation at any time, you asked to remain unidentified in any piece he was preparing?"

"I might have."

Andy asked why.

"It's not uncommon for me to make that kind of request when talking to the press. I think that if he's doing a piece on Arthur and Arthur is being aggressive with someone in the press and presenting his point of view, that I would likely, on background, give him my understanding of the situation and my picture of Arthur and not want to be quoted directly on that."

The jury would love that, I thought. If the picture Peggy gave was the true one, why didn't she want to be quoted?

Taking all this testimony, Andy and I concluded that the mishandling of my situation had been part of the reason Peggy had left NBC News not long after the forced resignation of her patron, Mr. Gartner. Her fingerprints were all over the libel side of NBC's liability in the lawsuit. A jury would see that in our evidence, we felt, along with the picture we would reveal of the conflicting personae of Ms. Peggy Hubble.

First, the caring professional who helped present Arthur Kent to the public during and after the Gulf War. "I recall Arthur thanking me," Peggy's videotaped image would say, "for handling things well for him and not exploiting him and him being concerned that he be perceived as a serious journalist and wasn't comfortable or interested in sort of the SCUD Stud image that became part of the headlines. And I was concerned about that, too. And I appreciated that he appreciated that I worked on his behalf for that."

Then cut to the woman who was just following orders as she helped Michael Gartner erase me from NBC's honor roll. A boss, surprisingly, whom she really didn't feel comfortable with in many ways. "I disagreed with [Michael] naming the rape victim in the William Kennedy Smith trial. I disagreed with him making Deborah Norville the anchor of the 'Today Show'... I disagreed with him canceling Ken Auletta on the 'Today Show' to discuss his book *Three Blind Mice*... And I disagreed with him on defending the General Motors segment on 'Dateline' when he first came out with a statement that he defended the story in its entirety and its detail."

But Peggy hadn't disagreed with Michael's tactics in cracking down on the Rome bureau. She hadn't even cared enough to pick up a phone to find out from any of us what was really going on. But then she'd just been following orders at GE's NBC.

This ruthless adherence to arbitrary management policies had emerged as a prominent theme in our evidence. And now that we had Michael and Peggy on videotape, any courtroom exploration of the rampant intrigue and hypocrisy within the NBC hierarchy would lead naturally into the darker compartments of the company's parent. At GE, the inconsistencies of corporate culture were even more glaring.

For instance, Chairman Jack Welch proclaimed in his 1991 annual report to shareholders that "we cannot afford management styles that suppress and intimidate." This was more than just an embarrassing quote that we could hold up for examination in court. It would enable us to plant the question in the jurors' minds: what kind of chief executive talks peace, then lets his division heads make war on individual employees?

Some damning vital statistics would be on hand to help answer that one. Mr. Welch had slashed 100,000 jobs from his overall workforce during his tenure, leaving some 284,000 worldwide. GE had profited immensely, and "Neutron Jack" had virtually institutionalized the slash-and-profit psychology throughout his empire. In 1993 second-quarter profits jumped by 10 per cent to record levels; simultaneously, Mr. Welch wiped out 1,600 jobs because of reduced defense-budget work and a slump in orders for domestic airliners.

While that kind of zeal is celebrated by some business specialists, evidence was beginning to emerge in the U.S. economy by 1994 that doctrinaire downsizing was eating the hearts out of many companies. Secretary of Labor Robert B. Reich, writing in the *New York Times*, pointed to a study of 531 large firms conducted in 1993. Although three-quarters of the companies had cut their payrolls, most reported that the cuts had failed to achieve their expected results. "Of the companies surveyed," he wrote, "earnings increased for just 46 percent of them; while 58 percent expected higher productivity, only 34 percent experienced it ... "

Yes, GE was one enterprise that had profited with cut-and-cash-in tactics. But at what cost—that was the question my lawyers and I could pose to the jury, using both our own evidence and the growing unease in the United States that America's business elite, the managerial overclass, was failing to inspire the nation's workforce. It was too often just scaring the daylights out of it.

* * *

There were many empty hotel rooms and a lot of solitary,

pre-dawn cab rides to cheerless airports on the road with Kent v. NBC. The pursuit sometimes got me down, reminding me that this was not the life I'd trained and worked so hard for. During the lonely hours, the in-between times when road weariness cast a pall over my mind, the $25-million question that banged around in my brain was how long this fight would go on. We had scored some major body-blows in terms of evidence, sure. But it was winter 1994, more than fifteen months since Mr. Gartner and his associates had blown me off the air. It had been a long time to keep motivated, to stay up. And I couldn't help wondering, even as we revealed the seedy, undignified behavior of Michael and his intimates, just how much dirt we could belt out of them before we too choked on the smell and the funk of it all.

It wasn't a pretty place to be, the inner sanctum of GE management culture. Could I avoid the trap good cops find themselves tripping into from time to time? Because getting down and dirty with the bad guys can spoil a professional's code of ethics in a hurry–if you take short cuts, or if you cheat to nail the competition.

I had to remind myself constantly of my one big advantage: the cleaner we kept our case, the better it looked. We were the diggers; we loved the facts, while our opponents were anxious only to conceal, to deny. We believed that any chance discovery of a scrap of evidence we didn't know before could only help us. NBC's lawyers heard only skeletons rattling away in their clients' closet. Compared to them, I could be as relaxed and diligent as I would be on a news assignment.

"He who digs wisely succeeds," I had heard CBS correspondent Daniel Schorr say on TV not long after he'd found his name on Richard Nixon's "enemies list" during the Watergate hearings. Schorr was a hard-driving, radical newshound who was not afraid of rattling the executive chain–both at the White House and within his own company. He had weathered his share of controversy. Watching him and other committed journalists taught me that being a good reporter sometimes meant working beyond the confines of your story. As in medicine or law, the ethical dilemmas that we encounter in our craft need to be addressed forthrightly from time to time, whatever the consequences.

It's a profession that cries out for new challenges, for healthy doses of confrontation. "All governments are liars," Isador Franklin Stone said, "and we shouldn't believe a damned word they say." Some critics would call Stone a journalistic absolutist, an iconoclast. But as a student I thought his Washington news-letter was everything good reporting and analysis should be–not least because I.F. Stone believed in the truth of what he was doing, not just the profitability of it.

I was lucky that I had some heroes to summon down from my memory and on to the empty barstool beside me, or into the back of a beat-up cab heading God knows where. Ironically, I'd dis-covered many of these great men and women while reporting for NBC News. They were inspirational figures who put everything on the line for the causes they championed. People who came through all the cynicism and shallow doubts of our times to prove that true heroes do, in fact, live and work among us every-where, every day. People like Giovanni Falcone, the anti-Mafia investigator who sacrificed everything for his work, even when he knew that he personally was doomed, condemned to a violent death because of his faith and his diligence.

Covering Falcone's murder in Sicily in May 1992 had deeply moved all of us in the Rome bureau. It was an epic tragedy: Judge Falcone had dedicated his life to understanding and defeating "La Piovra," or The Octopus–the brutal network of crime families in southern Italy. But even as he inched closer to bringing the Godfathers to justice, the politicians Falcone served were taking bribes from the Mafiosi, and shielding them from prosecution. Finally, a bomb placed beneath Palermo's airport road dispensed with the troublesome judge once and for all: Falcone, his lovely wife, also a magistrate, and their bodyguards were killed when their motorcade disintegrated in a fiery blast.

Falcone had written about his lonely, dangerous work chasing down criminals while corrupt government officials, his bosses, peered over his shoulder. Perversely, he sometimes found more honor among Mafiosi than within the government he served. Today, I still keep in my briefcase a newspaper clipping quoting Falcone's thoughts about his work:

Knowing and working with these Mafiosi has pro-foundly affected my attitudes towards people, and even my beliefs. I have learnt that whatever happens, you have to behave decently–to show real respect for what you believe in and not just make meaningless gestures. This harmony between one's beliefs and one's actions is crucial to our physical and mental well-being.

I have learnt that every compromise–every betrayal, every time you fail to face up to something–provokes a feeling of guilt, a disturbance of the soul, an unpleasant sensation of loss and discomfort with oneself.

Considering the odds that Falcone had stacked against him, if he could put everything on the line for what he believed was right, how could someone like me do anything less? What did I have to lose? Nothing by comparison.

The dark thoughts, the temptation to despair...these were threats I could overcome.

* * *

My lawyers and I flew into New York many times during the pre-trial process, but the meeting Andy and I attended in late autumn 1993 represented a new twist in the proceedings. And a breakthrough: our host was none other than Richard Cotton, NBC's vice-president of legal affairs–the boss of the network's law department, and Bob Wright's legal right hand. Through his litigator, Mark Helm, Cotton had invited me to a suite in my hotel where we could talk, over breakfast, about settling the lawsuit out of court.

When Andy Coombs and I rode up the elevator just after eight o'clock, we found Bill Wheatley at Cotton's side. This was supposed to impress me–and it did, because I remembered Bill Wheatley as one of the more honorable news professionals at NBC. We shook hands, warmly and sincerely, I thought at the time. Over coffee and bran muffins, Mr. Cotton got down to business.

"We'd like to present you with a package to put this whole thing away, once and for all." Richard Cotton spoke as smoothly as he dressed. No wrinkles, no stains. Just flawless, expensive pinstripe beneath a carefully groomed executive haircut. "The package," he told us, "is worth one million dollars."

Andy and I didn't flinch. Didn't telegraph any response, one way or another. Mr. Cotton went on to explain that his "package" would mean my return to employment at NBC News, and the money would be paid out as salary over three years.

"Of course there's no question," Bill Wheatley said, "of NBC making any kind of elaborate apology like we did in the GM case. That just isn't going to happen."

This wouldn't have surprised me coming from Mr. Cotton. He was the company lawyer trying to put the best spin on things. But Bill Wheatley was a journalist, one I had been willing to take a lot of risks for. I'd done some of my best reporting for "Nightly News" when Bill had been executive producer there. He too had been treated crudely by Michael Gartner: he had suffered the indignity of watching Steve Friedman take his job at "Nightly" while he had been shunted aside and exiled to special projects.

Now, years later, at the urging of his friend Tom Brokaw, Bill had been rehabilitated by Gartner's successor, Andy Lack, and named vice-president of the News Division, succeeding the disgraced Gartner confederate Don Browne. So I had to wonder: since Bill Wheatley understood GE culture as only a survivor can, why couldn't he recognize the wrongs that had been done in my own case and face them openly? I told him: "If the company can make a retraction for a corporation, it can tell the truth about an individual journalist too."

It was immediately clear to Andy and me that this was not Mr. Cotton's mandate. He wasn't there to correct injustice, just to bury Kent v. NBC. His package fell far short of what we felt the evidence proved we deserved—particularly with respect to reversing the lies of Mr. Wright's previous management team.

"But we've broken the magic barrier," Andy said, as we left for our next deposition. He grinned and shook his head. "They wanted to dazzle you with the million-dollar figure."

"Welcome to GE," I told him, "where they think that everybody's got his price."

Not long after the breakfast meeting Bill Wheatley was instructed to try again. The Gartner and Hubble depositions had clearly stirred a new level of concern within NBC management, and Bill was eager to try to fit a meeting into my travels. He reached me in Los Angeles, where Mr. Helm was continuing my own deposition. I told him I had the coming Sunday free but that I would have to be on base in Toronto for my "Man Alive" hosting duties at the CBC. Bill said he would happily fly up from New York for the day.

Stunned by the turnaround, I agreed to see him. NBC had tried to eliminate me, then had stonewalled me. Now the company was using shuttle diplomacy to try to woo me. It was certainly a friendlier approach, but no less desperate: Bill Wheatley and his bosses at GE wanted something very, very badly. Not a good time to lower my defenses, I realized. Even with my lawyers' assurances that we had nothing to lose just by talking with our adversaries.

I tried to make the most of Bill's visit. I picked him up at the airport, and we chatted warmly about old times at NBC News as the shore of Lake Ontario slipped by, ushering us towards Toronto's cold November skyline. I had booked a table for us at the Skydome, always an impressive building, even when ball players or evangelists or trapeze artists are not summoning up shock-waves of appreciation from the crowd.

We looked out from our booth in the restaurant high above the empty ballpark and admired the Blue Jays' 1992 and '93 World Series pennants. We talked some baseball. But by the second drink our conversation had a lot in common with that vast empty ballpark, lights dimmed now, weeks after Joe Carter's glorious homer in the bottom of the ninth against the Phillies.

Bill pitched, but there was nothing to swing at. Management sincerely wanted me to come back to NBC, he said. I could name my position. But it was clear that he and his superiors wanted to be less than frank in their acknowledgment of the lies Mr. Gartner had told about me. Lies that Mr. Wright's lawyers and executives had covered up and done nothing to remedy for more than a year.

I gazed out into the man-made cavern of the Skydome as Bill went over the offer again. My mind wandered a bit: inside the dome, I thought, any kind of show at all could be staged. It was a place where a promoter's fantasy could become reality, for the right price. Had the business of television journalism become just another convertible arena like this one, an abyss where games and light and magic could be manipulated by corporate ringmasters–the doomed black hole of greed prophesied in Paddy Chayevsky's brilliant filmscript *Network*? When I had worked for Bill Wheatley at "Nightly" it had been for a man who wanted the truth, all the truth we could write and shoot and feed into his newscast. Now he was talking spin, damage control and suppression of the facts.

I dropped Bill at the airport for his flight back to New York, and we agreed that we would keep talking by phone. But any hopes I had of speaking to the old Bill Wheatley, to a keeper of the traditions and conscience of NBC News, had dimmed forever. Bill was part of Mr. Wright's team now, and his pitches were being called in from the GE dugout.

* * *

My own lawyers, fortunately, have the kind of poise on the mound that any adversary should respect.

Just before New Year's Day 1994 Andy formally put the network's lawyers on notice that we wished to depose another group of witnesses, namely those NBC personnel who could testify on legal and computer-filing matters, plus four or five character witnesses, colleagues of mine, several of them based in London, who could speak about my behavior and work habits in foreign news. And there was one other demand: we would depose Mr. Robert C. Wright, president of NBC.

No way, declared Marjorie Neufeld, NBC's in-house lawyer; Bob Wright was off limits. For five days angry phone calls went back and forth between NBC and my lawyers. Then, on January 11, Mark Helm proposed what he called a compromise. NBC would go along with a selected few of the depositions, with the witnesses NBC felt were pertinent to the case, as long as they were conducted "without the expense and burden of a trip to London." But there would be no session with Bob Wright. And with an awkward dash of impertinence, Mr. Helm stated the obvious by suggesting that NBC would not call the network president as a witness at trial. Some favor, if they prevented us from deposing him.

Brian Lysaght's response was brief and to the point. "This is in reply to your letter of January 11 in which you attempt to concoct a position," he wrote. "Thanks, but no thanks."

Then Brian filed an application to the court requesting a ruling on the matter. "During the depositions of Peggy Hubble and Michael Gartner," he wrote, "it became clear that Mr. Wright was kept advised at each stage of NBC's conduct towards plaintiff. During Mr. Littlefield's deposition...it became apparent that Mr. Wright played an active role in the formulation and development of 'Dateline.' It was the tabloid and insubstantial nature of 'Dateline' (in contradiction of the promises and representations made to plaintiff when he was recruited to join the program) which constitutes a central allegation of the plaintiff's case."

Mr. Helm filed his own application in response. "So serious are Defendants' objections that, should the Court nonetheless be inclined to authorize these depositions...Defendants request that such an order be without prejudice to Defendants' filing a fully briefed motion for protective order." In other words, NBC was serving notice that it would fight on, regardless of the judge's initial ruling, to protect Mr. Wright.

Mr. Helm must have sensed what was coming. The judge ruled in our favor, clearing the way for us to depose all the witnesses we had requested prior to our discovery cutoff of January 31st– which was now just over two weeks away.

"Do you believe these guys," I laughed down the phone during a conference call with Brian, Andy and Fred. "They lost on venue, they lost on trial date, they had to cough up evidence like the Alicastro letter, and we've got Gartner exposed on tape. Now we've given them another black eye, and they still don't get the picture. They're going to lose, and lose big."

"Yeah, but not without putting you through your paces, Arthur," Brian cut in. He told me that Mark Helm had called to say that NBC would pull out all the stops to block our grasp at Wright. "They could seriously delay things," Brian warned. "Maybe even push the trial back."

Judge Pfaelzer's decision to put the case in front of a jury April 12 had been an enormous boost for my case. An early court date helped keep my costs down and the pressure up on NBC. The last thing we wanted was a delay.

"What are you saying?" I asked.

"I'm saying we might be able to make a little deal with Mr. Helm." It was Brian's vampire inflection again. He told me what he had in mind. I liked it a lot. He called Helm and got back to me within an hour with the good news.

"I told Mark," Brian said, "that by virtue of Mr. Kent's great respect for the office of the president of NBC, we were willing to desist on the demand for Wright. As long as we get everything else we want, without delay. He went for it."

And so we celebrated another victory. Helm would follow us to London for depositions with four character witnesses. He would come back to New York for depositions with Gordon Manning, the respected former vice-president of special projects at NBC News, and Tim Miller, the ex-promotions executive whose testimony would prove so useful on the "Dateline" issue. And Mr. Helm would produce witnesses from the NBC law department, a big gain for us. We would put Richard Cotton's own little empire under the microscope.

"Brian," I said, "I like the way 1994 is getting underway."

"Arthur," he replied, "I hope you know where we can get a good pint of Guinness in London."

* * *

Time was short now, and we had an enormous amount of preparation to do for this next critical round of testimony. In less than two weeks, on January 25, we'd be on our way to London. I felt excited, anxious: the thrill of beating NBC on another procedural debate was tempered by the queasy feeling in the pit of my stomach that some unexpected factor might throw our legal road show off the rails. We couldn't afford any delays, any hiccups. Most especially, we had made no provision for what happened in Los Angeles at 4:31 a.m., January 17, 1994.

I heard the first report about the earthquake on TV as I was getting ready for work in the apartment in Toronto. I flipped over to CNN in time to hear Larry King describe how he'd been jolted out of bed in his L.A. hotel room. No reports of casualties, but early pictures showed a lot of destruction. I looked at my watch–it was 7:45 in Toronto. I thought about our team and their families three time zones to the west–Brian, Fred and Andy; Pam, their assistant...and all the people in their office who had done much more than simply bring my case to life. They had become friends, trusted and good friends. Had anybody been hurt? What about their homes, their children?

When word came that the San Fernando Valley had been worst hit, I grabbed at the phone. Encino, straddling the south valley wall, is home to Bruce Lilliston and his family. I dialed the cellphone in Bruce's Jag; land lines were down. A woman's voice answered with a tentative "Hello..."

As she spoke, Katie, Bruce's wife, sounded more exhausted than fearful. But I could tell that her nervous laughter teetered on the edge of despair. The house, she said, had been badly damaged. Walls shattered, back yard fallen away into the darkness. But she and Bruce and their young daughter were all right, and thankfully their son, Roger, was on the east coast at school. Katie explained that Bruce couldn't come to the phone right now—he was searching for water.

Searching for water. My friend, one of Hollywood's hottest film-finance attorneys, was picking through the wreckage of the city just to keep his family alive and well. Along with millions of other men and women... I tried to reassure Katie, but at such a comfortable distance I felt useless, an intruder into their emergency.

It was hours before Bruce got through to me. By then, the voice I knew so well from the hundreds of calls we'd exchanged in recent months sounded relaxed and not entirely devoid of his familiar lawyerly irony. We're coping, he said, as if the Lillistons were merely adjusting to another twist in the L.A. experience. But ominously, Bruce had no word on how parts of the city had been affected, places like Santa Monica, Brentwood or Malibu—home to the other members of our team and their families.

After hours of trying everyone's numbers without success, I finally reached Andy Coombs in Malibu. To me his voice had a strangely disturbing quality. It was calm and even, without a trace of panic. He explained that his wife Klara was out of town—a stroke of luck, since Klara's office at Cal State in Northridge had been completely destroyed. Andy said he was marooned at home because the road along the coast to the office in Santa Monica was blocked by landslides. I asked him what he was going to do.

"Keep working," he told me. "I've got all the background papers for the witness briefs with me here."

When I spoke with Brian and Fred I learned that their offices on the seventh floor of a statuesque tower block overlooking the cliffs at Santa Monica had been rattled and rolled by the tremors. All day long as I got through to each member of the team I pleaded with them to realize that work could wait till life returned to something like normality. And all day long they thanked me and didn't take a word of that advice.

Buildings all around Santa Monica had been evacuated and condemned, including the apartment tower sandwiched directly between Brian's and Bruce's office blocks. Their kids had been thrown out of bed; back yards had turned to crevasses; filing cabinets now perched on top of fax machines, and glass-topped desks had disintegrated. But the combined loss of man- and woman-hours among our legal team amounted to no more than one half of a single day. There was not a whisper about delaying discovery, and no suggestion that the trial date of April 12 might be delayed. Brian correctly predicted that the U.S. District Court House would be closed for the remainder of the week, but that lost time in current cases would quickly be made up.

In the news business we often talk about showing grace under pressure. But during those uneasy days in January 1994 our legal team gave me a lesson in fortitude and faith, and a demonstration of that basic, awesome human capacity to cope with the unexpected and get on with it. I told Brian how proud I was to have the people in his firm as my friends. He said thanks—and that he'd be pleased to let me buy the first pint when next we met, as scheduled, over a hot deposition on the other side of the Atlantic.

* * *

Since London had become my overseas base after Rome, I did, in fact, have knowledge of the pubs. The Guinness flowed as freely as the testimony.

"He is extremely pleasant to work with as a colleague," Peter Sansun said of me, "and over the years that we worked together I think that I could say, in addition to being a colleague, that he was a friend."

Peter had been one of NBC London's top soundmen—and by recording the very first pictures of East Germans pouring through the Berlin Wall, a pretty good hand with a camera, too.

Brian asked Peter about my reputation among the crews.

"We liked working with him, and whenever I had the opportunity to do so, I was glad to do so. I would like to think that I would speak for my colleagues on the technical side. I think I do speak for them to say that we all enjoyed working with him."

Mr. Helm, visibly worn by the eight-hour time difference between Los Angeles and London, listened to this and grimaced. In addition to Peter, he had three more of our character witnesses ahead of him, all telling a dramatically different story from the one his management clients had supplied.

For example, about my alleged recklessness, the focus of many questions during my own deposition, Peter testified that in his view I had never unnecessarily exposed myself or my co-workers to danger. And during the Gulf War, as rockets and publicity had fallen upon me—and him—he said that I conducted myself "admirably under that pressure." Of a disagreement over air-time with another correspondent, a dispute Mr. Helm implied was a major confrontation, Peter said: "I don't think it was any more than a spat."

Most important, Peter echoed the view of all field personnel that we deposed: at NBC, war assignments were purely voluntary. He believed this was the case throughout the industry. Some months after being laid off in Mr. Gartner's 1991 staff cutback, Peter had turned down a request from another network to travel to the Balkans.

"I feel that the whole of the former Yugoslavia is a dangerous place and that is why I turned down a job as a freelancer to go."

"When you say the whole of Yugoslavia is a dangerous place and you have turned down those jobs," Brian asked, "I take it, for the precision of the record, that you would include Zagreb in that category?"

"You are right, that is correct."

"And you would turn down an assignment to Zagreb for exactly those same reasons?"

"Were it to be offered to me today I would turn it down."

Our other London witnesses answered Brian with page after page of testimony on the hazardous-assignment issue. Tony McGrath is a veteran war-zone stills photographer, and was assistant editor, pictures, at the *Observer* during my time there. Brian asked him about his assignment practice. "The first thing you do is ask if they want to go. If they said no, what would you do?"

"We would go to someone else."

"Would you regard that as in any way subjecting them to discipline within the organization?"

"Come on," Tony groaned. "I mean the only person you can send to war is a soldier. You are asking someone to risk their lives."

"In Yugoslavia, for example—what is the former Yugoslavia—would the same rule apply, namely that you would ask the journalist whether he wanted to go before you sent them?"

"Yes."

"And would that apply to Zagreb?"

"Anywhere."

"Any place else in Yugoslavia?"

"Anywhere that is remotely connected with the conflict."

That was backed up by Nicholas Guthrie, one of the BBC's top assignment editors, and the supervisor of stories I produced for the network from Afghanistan to Bosnia.

"It is very difficult to say that one area is particularly bad or worse than another," Nick testified of the former Yugoslavia. "The fact of the matter is that the whole thing is a stinking pot from one end of it to the other." About refusals of dangerous assignments: "If you say for family reasons, for whatever reasons, 'frankly, I don't fancy it,' then, you know, we don't push that. It isn't seen as something nasty on your record." And Nick was mystified why a correspondent would be sent to a war zone during a contract dispute.

"It seems to me if you are going to say to that person at the same time you are in dispute with them, go and do something for me, then there is clearly something wrong with the management system. How can that happen?"

Nick was asked about the importance of knowledge and expertise on the part of senior staff directing news coverage. "I would answer that by saying inexperience and incompetence is the scourge of our business."

Recalling the Verdi deposition, Brian asked Tony McGrath: "Would it be appropriate to have someone at the home desk, as far as Yugoslavia is concerned, for example, who couldn't even tell you the geography of Yugoslavia, would that be appropriate?"

"They would never get to that position in the *Observer*, it wouldn't happen. It would be foolish."

Finally, Garrick Utley, a thirty-year veteran of NBC News and one of America's foremost foreign correspondents, said the decision to accept an assignment was solely up to "the person who is putting his or her life, body on the line." Acknowledgment of that right, Garrick told us, went all the way back to Vietnam and before. "I remember sitting up in Da Nang in a restaurant, some colleagues and Dan Rather were there, Dan Rather for CBS News, and the conversation was about this very topic and various people said: 'How do you handle it?' I remember distinctly that he said: 'The correspondent has the right to say yes or no to any assignment.' And that is, of course, how it happens. The network can say if you don't want to go into an area, we can have somebody else who wants to go into this battle situation but that should not be in any way prejudicial to the journalist involved who was on the scene..."

Mr. Helm's face became flushed and long as the mountain of testimony grew higher. During his cross-examination of the witnesses he tried desperately to turn some of the testimony in his favor. He got Nick Guthrie, for example, to admit that Zagreb was in some ways less dangerous than other parts of Yugoslavia.

But then Brian took back the initiative with his redirect. He wanted to confirm that Zagreb had been, after all, just a smoke-screen thrown up by management. "In the summer of 1992," Brian said, "there was a lot of press coverage and conversation about Serbian detention camps. Do you remember that?"

"I do," Nick answered.

"Could you cover a story on Serbian detention camps from Zagreb?"

"No."

"The places where the Serbian detention camps are, or were, are those dangerous locations?"

"Oh yes, yes."

On a different point, Brian was able to expose a clumsy piece of behind-the-scenes maneuvering by the NBC attorney and make it backfire on him. Garrick Utley had mentioned to me as he arrived for his deposition that Mr. Helm had telephoned him the previous day. I passed this little nugget on to Brian.

"You and I have never met before today, correct, just for the record?" Brian asked Garrick.

"No."

"Have you had occasion to chat with Mr. Helm from NBC at all?"

"Briefly by telephone for a couple of minutes yesterday."

"Can you tell us, in general, the substance of that conversation?"

"Well, I told him that—he asked when I would be in London, would I be free to meet to have lunch, and I said I couldn't because I would just come in in the morning and I was tied up, and that phone call didn't last very long because I had to get off to an appointment and so the conversation was not very long."

Mark's face was blushing brightly now. He'd been caught out. Why, exactly, had he wanted to meet with Garrick? To find out why one of the all-time network greats had agreed to my request to testify? My own lawyer hadn't spoken to the witness before the deposition. Why did NBC's attorney feel that he had to?

Of course the answers, whatever they were, had everything to do with Garrick's stature and reputation. All the London depos were recorded on videotape, and at trial the jury would recognize Garrick as one of the most trustworthy professionals in network news. His testimony about me would constitute a hammer-blow against NBC's case.

"In connection with your dealings with Mr. Kent during the time when you were both at NBC," Brian asked, "did you have occasion to form any opinion as to his journalistic competence?"

"I would say very high. Highly professional journalist and experienced journalist."

Brian asked Garrick his views on my suspension and firing.

"My personal judgment as a journalist, he certainly had the credentials which should not justify termination. I do not know the particulars as to what happened at that time. Knowing his record in past experiences and past situations, to wit, the Gulf War, to wit Afghanistan completely, there is nothing in his journalistic performance that showed that he was afraid of going into a combat situation, that he would do other than make a judgment based on his own journalistic experience."

During my own deposition, Mr. Helm's questions had implied that I had become a prima donna after the Gulf War. Brian explored that with Garrick, who anchored programs I had appeared on throughout my time at NBC.

"And I take it your view of his first-rate journalism was the same throughout the period of time that you were dealing with him, even after the Gulf War?"

"Yes. Yes. As far as–there is nothing to change that opinion."

With the other witnesses too, character evidence expanded by the page. Tony McGrath said I'd shown a unique ability to produce both words and pictures.

"I had complete confidence in him. I was happy that any assignment he was given, he would go and deliver the goods at the end of the day... He was very quick to sort out our operating procedure and adhered to it religiously. He was one of the many people that worked for us that we never worried when he was out of our sight."

"Arthur has never been a death-or-glory boy," Nick Guthrie testified. "He has never wanted to be that. I don't honestly think he could have got half the things he has got if he had been a death-or-glory boy."

Specifically, Brian wanted to know how the Bosnia film project, in part Nick's baby, had turned out.

"I believe now the Imperial War Museum have taken the film as part of a national record, an international record of events. So, what you have got with Arthur now is one of the great war cameramen, no question about it, whose pictures are lodged in perpetuity in the Imperial War Museum here in London. That has got to be some accolade."

I directed a confident smile at Mr. Helm. Nick's rather extravagant praise was more than just gloss and flattery. We were now in a position to demonstrate that good tradecraft produces good stories.

Still, Mr. Helm tried to show Brian and me that he wasn't flustered as the depositions concluded. "Think I'll go out and find a good blues bar," he said casually.

Brian and I just grinned at each other.

"I hope you have better luck with that," I told him, "than you had getting lunch."

* * *

If Mr. Helm hadn't had enough of the blues by the time our traveling show reached New York five days later, then Andy Coombs had just the thing for him—an even more bruising round of depos. Andy had flown in fresh from the west coast, ready to take up where Brian had left off in London. The first witness Mr. Helm regarded through eyes red with jet lag was a crusty network news veteran, who stoked the character fires even higher.

"I was very impressed with his bravery and his stick-to-it-iveness in Afghanistan," Gordon Manning testified about me. "He was a singularly brave and resourceful correspondent there."

Gordon was a voice from within NBC News management itself—he had been Michael Gartner's vice-president in charge of political programs and special projects. An elder statesman of American broadcast journalism, Gordon had been at NBC for eighteen years and at CBS for a decade before that.

He had watched me work in Tiananmen Square, Moscow, and at 30 Rock in New York. He dismissed suggestions that I had been party to any unusual disputes with colleagues at NBC prior to "Dateline." And he put the Sixth Avenue incident— my response to the smear campaign—into context. "I think that there was a drumfire of criticism appearing in the press... They had the whole apparatus of the NBC armament and management [and] communications, and I think he felt abandoned and estranged from the organization."

As vice-president, Gordon had been uniquely placed to form opinions of Michael Gartner. Andy asked him to assess Gartner's management skills. "I must say I was disappointed over the periods of his career of his inability to direct and manage his division."

"What was the basis for your disappointment?" Andy asked.

"He was reclusive, secretive. He was not involved in the product. I mean he didn't—the president of the News Division in my judgment has to know the people and know the stories and be directly involved in the whole procedure, in the apparatus, and he was removed from them."

"Was Mr. Gartner collaborative with management?"

"Was he collaborative? That is what I was talking about. He

was not."

But on one issue at least Michael Gartner had been very successful in drawing his management circle tightly together–the suspension and termination of Arthur Kent. The testimony of senior NBC lawyer Roberta Brackman broke a lot of fresh ground on that score, and revealed widespread complicity of senior management throughout NBC.

As primary attorney for NBC News reporting directly to Richard Cotton, Roberta had been named in the official investigation of the "Dateline" GM truck controversy. Along with members of the "Dateline" production team, she was criticized for not inquiring more carefully into the segment's description of "unscientific crash demonstrations."

"At least in hindsight," the investigators reported, "she could have inquired more thoroughly...and perhaps that inquiry would have ferreted out the igniter issue for more discussion."

So now, examining Roberta Brackman in her own boardroom at 30 Rock's legal department, Andy and I wanted to know exactly what standards and practices she had employed in my case. A small, dark-haired woman in her late thirties, Roberta looked nervous as she reread the August 6, 1992, letter from Michael Gartner to Bruce Lilliston, my attorney.

"As best as I can recall," she testified, "I drafted the original version or draft of this letter and probably shepherded other people's comments and my own changes through."

"What was the stimulus that led you to draft the initial draft of this letter?" Andy asked.

"I will instruct her not to answer," Mr. Helm cut in. To me, Mark looked even more uncomfortable than did Roberta. But then NBC's legal eagles had tried very hard to prevent this or any other examination of the company's lawyers.

"Why did you write a draft of the Exhibit 2 letter?" Andy persisted.

"Same instruction," Helm told her.

Of course we really didn't expect much candor on the Gartner letter. It was full of damaging inconsistencies that had been acknowledged in the testimony of Don Browne, Gartner's vice-president. For example, the letter stated, "Mr. Kent was removed as a full-time contributing correspondent in favor of part-time." That kind of assignment change was against the terms of my employment contract. But the most glaring error in the Gartner letter was the claim "NBC did in fact designate Mr. Kent the Senior European Correspondent." That designation, of course, had never happened. The company hadn't been able to produce a single piece of evidence to back that statement.

Andy tried again. "Could you tell me with whom you spoke at NBC News concerning the substance or subject matter of the August 6th letter?"

"You may answer that," Mr. Helm said.

"The best I can recall, Michael Gartner, Bob MacFarland, David Verdi, Pat Langer, and I believe I spoke to Don as well." Pat Langer, Roberta explained, was another NBC lawyer. She added: "Peggy was probably around, Peggy Hubble."

After drafting the letter, Roberta said, she passed it around for comments.

"From whom did you solicit those comments?" Andy asked.

"Pat Langer, Michael Gartner, and I didn't specifically solicit comments. What we did, I believe, is that the draft was handed to people sitting in the room."

Then Roberta appeared to remember something. She and Helm whispered a while off the record.

"The witness has an addition she would like to make to a prior answer," Helm announced.

"When you asked me those people who I solicited comments from on the draft of the August 6th letter," Roberta said, "I neglected to mention either Anne Egerton, and Margie Neufeld, who are litigators in the NBC law department in Burbank."

Andy and I looked at each other. Up to that point we had thought that Anne and Margie had become involved much later, blocking my appearance on the Jay Leno show a week after my suspension, and ultimately representing NBC with Mark Helm in court in Los Angeles. But now we knew that the Burbank Entertainment litigators had been consulted prior to my suspension. And all these lawyers had something in common: they all reported to one Richard Cotton, who reported directly to Robert C. Wright. Michael Gartner's actions and words might have been rash, but now we had evidence of a situation not unlike the "lapses" cited in the GM inquiry. And on a much broader scale.

Roberta Brackman went on to corroborate our claim that my lawyer, Bruce, had spoken with her soon after Gartner's receipt of our first letter. During their conversation Bruce had agreed to her request to extend the time limit we had set on management to resolve the "Dateline" dispute. Sadly, this concession, made in good faith, was used by NBC management to formulate its action against me.

Andy asked if Roberta had sought information from Bruce or my agent prior to sending the August 6 letter. No, she testified. Remarkable, we thought, since the actions contemplated were so extreme, and wholly unprecedented.

"Had you at any time in the past been involved in a situation where an NBC News correspondent had been suspended?" Andy asked.

"Not that I recall."

"Have you been involved in any situation where an NBC News correspondent had been terminated?"

"Not that I can recall."

"Do you recall any past disputes with an NBC correspondent concerning a refusal to accept an assignment from the foreign news desk?"

"Not that I can recall."

Andy pressed the NBC lawyer on this issue of adequate preparation. "You were satisfied at the time that you wrote the August 6th letter that you talked to everybody you needed to talk with in order to prepare that response?"

Again, Mr. Helm interrupted. "I will instruct her not to answer."

But for NBC, it was too late. The cat—a straggly black one—was out of the bag. The law department's fingerprints were all over my case; Michael Gartner and his associates hadn't acted alone.

"No wonder they've fought us so hard," I told Andy over a beer. "The cover-up goes all the way to the top."

"It would have been nice to get Mr. Wright on all of this," Andy said with a smile. "But now, I don't think we really need him."

"Not him, maybe," I said. "Just his checkbook."

CHAPTER SEVENTEEN

Justice and Champagne

Already racked by years of staff cutbacks and retrenchment in news and sports, NBC's free-fall into third place in prime-time ratings after a remarkable seven-year winning streak has rattled the nerves of once-confident executives and depressed morale. Wright, who championed NBC's failed strategy to focus on a younger audience, held himself responsible for the programming miscalculations that have dragged down the network.

–Los Angeles Times, *February 4, 1993*

WITH LESS THAN two months to go until trial on April 12, 1994, NBC continued to show a brave face–regardless of ongoing criticism in the press and the evidence mounting against them in Kent v. NBC. Bill Wheatley and News Division president Andrew Lack phoned me at home from time to time, embroidering their offer to reinstate me. But they rejected any suggestion of pulling back the veil on senior management's continuing cover-up of the past regime's deceit and defamation. Meanwhile, NBC's attorneys told us, "We're not afraid to defend ourselves in public with all of this."

Then why, I had to wonder, did Mr. Helm ask to talk settlement directly with me, the plaintiff, as he wound up the fourth and final day of my own pre-trial examination?

"Try to think ahead to the trial," he told me after the court reporter had left the room. "All the publicity, everything out in the open..."

"That's fine with us," I said. "Everyone will benefit. Think of it–my reputation restored, NBC facing up to dishonest management practices."

"But try to think of your life after the trial..."

"I do, every day. You don't seem to understand, Mr. Helm. I

long for the truth to be out in the open."

"But things can happen at trial. Unexpected things..."

"Mr. Helm, if you're trying to frighten me, you're wasting your time. You should be explaining the facts of life to your own clients. They're guilty as hell, and the record proves it."

"You just don't listen!" Helm exploded, his face suddenly flushed and damp. Andy, at my side, shook his head in disbelief. I stood, turned for the door.

"I'll listen to you," I told Mr. Helm, "just as soon as your clients come clean about what they did to me."

Inwardly, I suspected that NBC management would eventually do just that. How could they afford to be exposed in open court? To be placed under a microscope and probed and gutted in full view of the public and the industry? My lawyers and I realized that it was only this threat of exposure and punishment that would keep the momentum moving in our favor. So we decided to adopt a trial psychology–to prepare single-mindedly for a court-room showdown–to turn up the heat on NBC's top executives.

Fred Friedman, Andy Coombs and I reviewed and organized all the evidence, they in their offices in Santa Monica, I toiling in the cold pre-dawn hours back in Toronto. When the alarm sounded at 4 a.m., there would be a lengthy fax waiting for me in the machine in the kitchen. I would drink my coffee over by the tall broad balcony windows, glazed with frost, and there I could read my lawyers' overnight messages while listening to the news, glancing up from time to time to watch the ice-breaker struggling to clear a path for the Toronto Island ferry in the harbor. By the time my dual careers as litigant and broadcaster normally wound down around eight o'clock in the evening, Debs would have to coax my comatose form from the couch (at the end of another "Star Trek" episode I had slept through) and beam me up the stairs and into bed. Managing the lawsuit by night and staying on the air with the CBC by day–with just enough sleep and exercise squeezed in between–I had reached another peak, another extreme. And I would toughen up still further. I would have to: the big climb, the trial, lay just ahead.

Meanwhile, Brian Lysaght was already trying out his approach. Keeping one ear open for further settlement offers from NBC, he had shifted attention to the presentation of all the witnesses and documents and videotape evidence to the jury. There could be no distractions.

Brian suggested that we hold a mock trial just prior to jury selection, a dry-run where we could try out the opposing arguments and personalities of the case in front of sample juries. It seemed like a good idea: Brian would get a feel for how best to present the evidence and the kind of juror who would be most influenced by it, thus strengthening our chances for success. The only snag was that a mock trial would add about $15,000 to an already hefty legal bill. The trial proper might run up $50,000 in fees and costs. On top of this, it would cost about $25,000 to fly in the more than twenty witnesses we had lined up–colleagues and industry figures from across North America and overseas.

I didn't waste a lot of time agonizing about what to do next. Fifteen months of litigation had hardened me, I guess, and I felt pretty much as I did after a long journey towards a dangerous story: eager to get the work done and get on home. So I mortgaged my house in London. Now my war chest would see me through trial. And if we won, there was always my Aaton XTR and a few other trinkets left to help finance our way through the inevitable appeal by NBC. Everything I owned in the world was on the line. Luckily, there was no time to think about that. In the few weeks remaining, I had to devote all my energy to the search for more evidence.

I wasn't the only one searching. When I contacted a colleague who had worked with me at "Dateline," publicist Tory Beilinson, she said she had received another call about my case.

"I don't remember his name. Mark Helm it is, I think. And he said he was contacting me because Peggy Hubble told him that I would be able to substantiate some of the things that she said about the case and my dealings with you. And he proceeded to tell me–he proceeded to ask me, don't you remember Arthur Kent being unco-operative and uneasy to work with, which I said to him, no, I don't remember that. Nor am I prepared to sit and answer your questions right now."

Thankfully, Tory agreed to answer questions from me–in a last-minute declaration under oath, witnessed by a notary. And she agreed to testify for me at trial. Another backfire for Helm and NBC.

Tory recalled how she had publicized my signing at "Dateline" specifically to report foreign stories. And how my stories had been rejected.

"I think there was talk about it among 'Dateline' staff. I think that whether it was for ratings or to please the West Coast Entertainment folks, whatever the reason was, I just don't think that foreign pieces were very appealing to the Entertainment folks."

About Peggy Hubble's conduct Tory said, "I can't remember an incident where we had commented on personnel issues." She said that, in her view, Peggy's characterization of my Sixth Avenue appearance as "bizarre and unfortunate" only fanned the flames of the dispute.

"I remember saying to Peggy that I couldn't believe that she was putting out a statement that called you that, to which she had the sort of nervous little laugh and said well it is not even up to me, that is just what is happening. It is the way it is and there is nothing you can do about it."

Tory stated that Peggy's statements were suspiciously one-sided.

"A lot of times in a situation like this it is not very responsible of someone to just act as a mouthpiece. I think that Peggy Hubble just took orders from her superiors, whether it was the legal department or Michael Gartner, she was doing what she was told to do. I don't think she went out on her own and just made these things up. If I were in her position, I would have wanted to know all sides of the story."

My attorneys were thrilled by the news of Tory's testimony. "Bet you'd take a mean depo," Fred joked over the phone.

I saved the best news for last: NBC had called someone else looking for dirt–a certain David Miller, the foreign-assignment director who had issued Joe and me with our suspensions. Within months of delivering that blow, David had himself been pushed out of NBC News by Michael Gartner, and had moved from New York to St. Petersburg, Florida. Now he wanted to go on the record.

"I remember talking to the Rome bureau every day," David said under oath, "and they always wanted to travel, always wanted to go everywhere, very enthusiastic, ready to move."

Like Tory, David spoke to me under oath before a court reporter. It didn't constitute a deposition, since NBC's attorney wasn't present. But the statement would help us predict what David's testimony would be in open court. And what he said was explosive.

David had been on holiday when Joe Alicastro and I were assigned to Yugoslavia. His superior, David Verdi, informed him on his return that a decision had been made to suspend us.

"The explanation was very simple. The explanation was Arthur and company refused a direct order." David described the reasoning for locking us out of the Rome bureau, and removing us from the computer without warning. Management "wanted to cut them off and then to–since they were not working, to eliminate them from the system."

But when Joe Alicastro sat down for the breakfast meeting at 30 Rock, he had told David Miller and Bob MacFarland a very different story about the Yugoslav assignment.

"He explained very carefully that they wouldn't go because no preparations had been made, and that it was–that everybody acted very sincerely and very truthfully. He said to me that going to Zagreb was merely the first step, that there was no story in Zagreb, and Zagreb was merely going to be the trip wire to go to Sarajevo. As we always say in television, you know, you are only an inch away, why don't you go into the next territory? So there never was a story in Zagreb, so the story was in Sarajevo..."

David said he informed Don Browne and David Verdi of Joe's explanation. I asked what impact this had had on management.

"I got the feeling that Don softened, that when he heard it from MacFarland and me how impressed we were with what Alicastro had said, I think he softened a little bit, I think he realized that it was not such a black and white thing."

Further proof, I realized, that even management figures outside Michael Gartner's inner court had known about the Zagreb deception almost immediately. And yet no one had pulled in the reins, tried to avoid disaster. Just the opposite. David Verdi, whose inexperience in foreign news Miller described vividly under oath, plowed forward.

"What was his suggestion?" I asked.

"Fire them all. Fire them all."

"Fire them all?"

"Fire them all. Fire them all."

"Them being?"

"Meaning the entire—everybody in Rome who wouldn't go to Yugoslavia, yes."

Listening to David, I tried to picture what effect his testimony would have on a jury. The man who had handed down the suspensions was now explaining that he had been set up—misinformed about our actions—and then prevented from trying to undo an injustice. It was a revealing first-hand account of the intricacies of NBC management.

I was happy and relieved to take David to lunch that day in St. Petersburg. Only weeks earlier, he'd been one of them, one of the enemy. As we looked over the harbor I told him that he should have asked for our side of the story before he hit us.

"I know," he said sadly. "I know."

"Never mind," I said. "The jury will understand."

* * *

As our case strengthened, NBC's tactics became more desperate. At times, they were downright absurd. The company's formal statement of defense, for example, contained fresh accusations against me that we could easily disprove. It was another backhanded gift from our adversary, because debunking NBC's claims and evidence would both support my own position and cast further doubt on the company's already strained credibility.

"And remember," Brian liked to remind me, "we're up first." My lawyers would lead off at trial, putting our case to the jury for perhaps the first ten days of the proceedings, with NBC having to play catch-up. Among our easiest and earliest home-runs, we thought, would be the Gulf War.

NBC's attorneys had contrived claims, evidently with help from Bob MacFarland, the Gartner aide who managed the Dhahran bureau in the early weeks of the war. "When Mr. Kent was angered by an instruction by Mr. MacFarland to leave a live camera location in Dhahran...Mr. Kent proceeded to lock himself in his hotel room and refused to communicate with his colleagues..."

This wild fiction was at odds with testimony from witnesses

including Joe Alicastro and Peter Sansun–both at my side throughout my reports from Dhahran–and from the body of video-tape evidence of NBC's war coverage. But management's lawyers had booby-trapped their own case with an even more outrageous string of lies.

"Through his persistent contacts with New York," NBC claimed, "Mr. Kent ultimately was able to go into combat with the First Cavalry, over the objections of Dhahran executives, who were then left with no able-bodied correspondents to cover the taking of Kuwait City. Once on assignment with the pool, Mr. Kent then refused to follow the policy of giving over the tapes to pool officials, and refused to return from the assignment when asked..."

I laughed out loud when I read this. We already had documents in our possession proving that Dhahran executives had helped to *arrange* my departure to the ground-war pool with the First Cavalry Division. Indeed, an NBC press statement by Peggy Hubble dated February 21, 1991, explained the move as "part of the rotation of reporters on pool assignments." And written messages from senior bureau staffers to our team in the desert illustrated that we were operating with management's blessing.

As to the rest of the accusations, I was able to line up three particularly well-placed army officers for rebuttal. Brigadier-General Randolph W. House, a fishing buddy of one Norman H. Schwarzkopf, had commanded the 1st Cav's Second Brigade in Iraq and Kuwait. In response to my request for his view of my performance, he wrote to me just weeks before the trial.

"It is always a pleasure to renew friendships that were forged under such difficult circumstances as Desert Storm presented. You became a real part of the Blackjack Brigade by sharing the hardships, danger and uncertainty the soldier faced.

"I appreciate the professional way in which you carried out your mission. You covered the war looking out at the enemy from the same vantage point as the soldier at the tip of the spear. And, you did this without disrupting our preparations or execution of the battles. It takes a gifted correspondent to pull that off."

As to NBC's claim that I had refused to turn over tapes to pool officials, we would produce Captain Jeff Phillips, who had

been the public affairs officer co-ordinating the pool. There
hadn't been any clashes over footage; both Jeff and I worked
hard to get as much tape as possible out of the desert and on to
the air. Jeff wrote: "Even when it was difficult, the difficulty
arose from your ardent pursuit of honesty and quality. A lot of us
saw that and respect it still. You belong in the battle, and I
would like few things more than to share one with you again."

And finally, about my alleged refusal to return from the desert
when asked, enter Captain David Francavilla, with whose
company I had traveled throughout the ground war. Both he
and Jeff would testify that no messages whatsoever reached us
from Dhahran once the sixty-four-hour "march" into Iraq had
begun. I had never refused a request to leave Charlie Company
because no request of any kind had reached us. I flew out on the
first available chopper after the ceasefire was called.

Brian relished this evidence, and the witnesses themselves—
the jury, he said, will love those uniforms. These were decent
officers, home from the war, telling our story.

Meantime, beyond our own evidence file, the background
atmosphere in the United States was getting better all the time.
TV industry theorists, practitioners and critics were vigorously
debating the sorts of editorial and management controversies
that would feature prominently in our trial. The reason: an
avalanche of dubious and frequently tasteless coverage during
the 1993-94 season, headlined by the Menendez brothers'
murder trial, the Michael Jackson controversy and Lorena
Bobbitt's mutilation of her husband.

The annual Alfred I. Dupont Forum at the Columbia
University Journalism School featured a panel entitled "Declining
Standards in News: Is It All Television's Fault?" The *New York
Times* thundered out, "Tabloid Charge Rocks Network News."
Columnist Walter Goodman wrote, "Tabloid news has always
been famous for crime and scandal, but the reach and punch of
television have given new power to its excesses." The article
slammed increased coverage of "sordid horror stories" and
decreased coverage of matters "that do not lend themselves to
hot pictures."

Then Michael Gartner made a surprise return to the
American media spotlight. "Dump On-Air TV News Reporters"

read the headline of his submission to *USA Today*. Reporters, Mr. Gartner wrote, "add clutter, not substance, so let anchors deliver the news."

I had to read Michael's piece several times before I believed that he would allow this bizarre tract to be published under his name. Yet there it was—a full-blooded call to arms to news management to fire, eliminate, get rid of absolutely all their on-air correspondents.

Brian, Fred and Andy thought it was Christmas all over again. They wrote NBC's attorneys that Gartner's statements would be introduced at trial. The man who had unjustly fired and libeled their client had gone public with his urge to slash his way through the entire combined correspondent corps of not one, not two, but all the major networks. Naturally, we weren't the only ones to think that Michael had flipped his lid.

"Gartner still feels so bad about his unfortunate exit from NBC," Rita Braver of CBS News told *USA Today*. "He should get a life."

Chris Wallace over at ABC News was more blunt in his response to claims in the Gartner article about his earlier service at NBC. "Gartner presided over a dishonest report on GM trucks and got fired for it. Now he's telling lies in the newspaper."

Of course we expected that NBC's attorneys would try to distance the disgraced former president from Andy Lack's new regime under Bob Wright. But a mysterious connection remained between Mr. Gartner and GE's NBC. In his video-taped deposition Michael had refused to answer whether he was still being paid by the network one full year after his fiery departure. And NBC's lawyers refused to say why they had advised Gartner not to answer that question under oath, and why they were resisting our attempts to have the court force them to come clean on the matter. So Michael Gartner's shadow haunted NBC; it would be simple for us to bring his apparition to life in our Los Angeles courtroom.

* * *

By late February 1994, with only five weeks to jury selection and six to trial, events were clearly troubling NBC's lawyers and management. Mark Helm was regularly on the phone talking settlement with Brian. He mentioned it in every meet-and-confer session with Andy Coombs. Serious money was now being thrown around in conversation among the lawyers, much more than I had realistically expected to secure in any settlement. But NBC was refusing to put hard wood behind a retraction.

"Why won't he settle?" Mr. Helm asked Andy at one session.

"Because money's not everything, Mark. Besides, we've got a winning case."

"Well," Mark said, "Arthur should know when to hold 'em and when to fold 'em."

Now, as bluffs go, Mark's little recitation from Kenny Rogers' "The Gambler" scored one out of ten in the scare department. But it made us laugh. And it triggered a sense of great expectation among our team. Could this be it, we wondered? Could this be the beginning of the end?

Sure enough, it was, though it would not be Mark Helm who sang the final chorus for his client. It was Richard Cotton who called Brian Lysaght one afternoon in late February. He said he wanted to talk settlement—only the second time Bob Wright's head lawyer had spoken directly to anyone from our side. But Brian had never met or spoken to Cotton. Only Andy and I had. So Brian, feeling confident, had some fun with his opposite number from NBC. He put on a formal air:

"Mr. Cotton, NBC is represented by counsel. I am not permitted to speak to anyone at NBC except a lawyer."

"Brian," Richard Cotton said in a low, impatient voice, "I am the fucking general counsel of NBC."

"Oh," Brian said. "You qualify."

Brian phoned me at my apartment in Toronto immediately after his discussion with Cotton. "Arthur, if they haven't been taking us seriously before, they are most certainly taking us seriously now."

He spelled out Cotton's offer. It had come in part from Andy Lack, who was now emerging as management's executive point-man on the case, taking over from his deputy, Bill Wheatley. Lack authorized Cotton to tell us that NBC would retract all defamatory statements by way of a joint news release agreeable to both sides.

"Wow," I said. We had broken them.

And the company, Brian continued, was ready to pay up, and pay up big. He told me how much.

"Double wow. Double-double wow." GE's payout in 1989 to settle federal charges of military-contract fraud had set a record. Now we might set one of our own.

But there were strings attached. NBC would pay me over three years, and in return I'd have to grant them complete silence. The deposition transcripts would be locked away. I would be forbidden to reveal any of the testimony. And Judge Pfaelzer would oversee the settlement and rule on any failure to comply by either party.

"Tell Mr. Lack and Mr. Cotton," I said slowly, "that the money's fine. But I'll accept it only in a single payment, up front. And there can't be a gag of any kind on the facts of the case. No censorship, ever. Otherwise the damage award is nothing but a bribe."

NBC's response came quickly. Out of the question, Richard Cotton said. Brian sighed and told him we'd see him in court.

As our team worked around the clock in early March preparing our evidence, Brian's phone would ring every couple of days with new entreaties from the NBC law department. He and Cotton worked out the wording of a news release—the retraction—just in case things worked out. And Bruce Lilliston opened a second negotiating channel, trading calls with Andy Lack. But from 30 Rock there was no movement on the gag issue. Mr. Wright's lawyers wanted a guarantee in return for cash that I would not reveal the substance of the evidence we had gathered.

Brian countered by teasing Cotton a little. He said that since I, the plaintiff, had paid my fair share of the depositions' cost, I had the right to keep them and use them as I wished. That suggestion triggered some unlawyerly language from Mr. Cotton, and a strange phone call to me in Toronto from Mr. Lack.

"Arthur," he said, "we know how painful this has been for you. We want to help relieve that pain."

"That's very kind of you Mr. Lack," I told him. "That's exactly what we've been suggesting to your company for about eighteen months now."

But Andy Lack wouldn't give in on the gag. He told me that

he couldn't have me upsetting the progress he felt he was making at NBC News with what he called "a lot of stories about what happened long ago." Patiently, I pointed out that what he viewed as mere "stories" were, in fact, libelous statements that had seriously damaged my career. The company was covering up the previous management's dishonesty and defamation. As the new president, he would have to reverse that, I told him—especially if he truly wanted to change the culture of the News Division.

Mr. Lack didn't see things that way. With a sigh of exasperation he said that he had tried, and hung up.

Next day, he pulled back the carrot and tried the stick. Cotton phoned Brian in Los Angeles and barked down the phone at him. "Don't think we aren't ready to go to court on this. I know how to protect NBC News."

Brian held his ground and laughed off Cotton's ploy. But when he had said his goodbyes, Brian immediately called me in Toronto. When the phone rang, I was frying a steak and studying a depo transcript at the same time. Brian told me he felt a responsibility to pass on Cotton's warning. Then he sounded me out: couldn't I find a way to accept the NBC offer?

No way, I told him. I explained that since I hadn't committed any misconduct, I shouldn't be made to agree to a gag order supervised by the court. I'd feel as though I was on parole, I told him. Meanwhile NBC—the guilty party—would never really have to face the music. The offer on the table was a bad deal both for me and for the journalists at NBC, and I'd never go for it.

Brian argued with me, forcefully. It was March 10, he pointed out. The next week, March 16, both sides had to file detailed pre-trial statements with the court. The accusations from each side would become public, inflaming the dispute still further and making it harder for the two opponents to disengage and avoid a trial.

Brian worked me over some more, telling me that the damage payment NBC was offering was, in his view, "terrific." He couldn't promise winning any larger amount at trial. Although he and Fred and Andy loved the evidence and believed strongly in my case, he had a responsibility to tell me there were no guarantees in a jury trial.

I heard him out and then took the precaution of taking my steak off the grill; a little speech on my part was in order, I decided, and it might take a while. I told Brian that I was grateful for his advice. That he was right to be cautious. But that he would never persuade me to back down. "I've seen you in action. I've watched you in court. You won venue for me. You won us an early trial date and as many witnesses as we wanted. You've won every-thing. And with the evidence we've got, you'll win at trial too. No gag, no payment over time—that's final."

Brian sighed and relented at last.

"You're gonna destroy them," I told him.

"Yeah," he laughed. "What choice have I got?"

And so began a very long weekend. On Saturday, March 12, I called Andy Lack at home to make sure he understood my position. But he'd already heard, and he rushed off the phone saying he didn't want to talk. Through Sunday night and into Monday morning Andy Coombs and I worked over the phone collating testimony and documents.

On Monday afternoon Brian called from Los Angeles, laughing his vampire's laugh. "Cotton's aching to settle this case," he said. "He's in pain—you can hear it over the phone."

"Then tell him to give in. Tell him to surrender."

"He says it's not his decision any more. It's higher up and they don't want the embarrassment of a retraction."

"Tell him we'll show them a whole new meaning of shame in court."

"You're not going to give?" Brian said.

"I'm going to give them hell. In court."

Which was the prospect that must have been weighing very heavily on the minds of Bob Wright and Andrew Lack and all their attorneys. Late on Monday night, Bruce Lilliston, an active and creative intermediary over the previous weeks of negotiations, called to give me the news.

"You'll never guess in a million years," he laughed. "Andy Lack doesn't need a gag any more. He says he trusts you."

"He can trust me," I said, "always to tell the truth about what happened. All of it, in every detail."

"And the money's not a problem," Bruce continued. "The

whole amount—one check, no strings. Except the amount. They want that to be strictly confidential."

I told him that wouldn't be a problem—the Kents never brag about money. Not that it had been much of a consideration till then.

"The joint news release stands as is. Lack and Cotton want to finalize tomorrow in New York."

The words echoed. I guess my end of the line went silent. After a while Bruce said: "Arthur, congratulations. You've won."

It took a while for it to sink in. A retraction. And what was it, I tried to figure it out, but couldn't: a head-spinning multiple of every dollar I'd ever earned in my life, and then some. The total combined fees I had paid my lawyers now looked small, a terrific investment. And then it hit me: from now on, work of any kind would be a choice for me, not a necessity.

"I guess we showed them when to hold 'em and when to fold 'em, huh, Bruce?"

"You showed them."

* * *

The details were worked out over dinner Tuesday night at Andy Lack's private club on Central Park. He seemed eager to get the whole thing over with. Bill Wheatley, dining with Lack, seemed morose. He suggested changing a sentence in the news release. Firmly, we told him no. The release had been painstakingly drafted by Richard Cotton and Brian Lysaght and agreed to by Lack and Kent. Wheatley relented.

So it was that on Wednesday, March 16, 1994, NBC's fax machines distributed the following joint news release:

> Arthur Kent and NBC News today announced that they had entered into a settlement of the litigation brought by Mr. Kent against NBC in connection with Mr. Kent's termination by NBC News in August of 1992. The settlement involved dismissal of the litigation in return for a fair and appropriate payment by NBC News to Mr. Kent. The terms of said payment are confidential.
>
> The events which occurred in August of 1992 leading to Mr. Kent's suspension and termination by NBC News

were exclusively the result of a contract dispute between the parties. They were not because of Mr. Kent's refusal to travel to and report from the former Yugoslavia. Indeed, immediately following the termination, Mr. Kent went to Bosnia as a reporter for CBC and BBC News, and produced the award-winning film, A VIEW OF BOSNIA.

Mr. Kent is an accomplished international news correspondent with a history of courageous reporting from war zones. Among the places Mr. Kent has reported from as a correspondent for NBC News are Afghanistan (with both the Afghan resistance and the Soviet and Soviet-backed forces fighting the resistance); China (at the time of the Tiananmen Square massacre); Romania (at the time of the fall of Ceauşescu); Berlin (at the time of the fall of the Berlin Wall); Moscow (at the time of the aborted coup); and later in Dhahran and the deserts of Iraq (at the time of the Persian Gulf War). In all of these assignments and in his many other reports throughout his tenure at NBC, Mr. Kent reported with professionalism and excellence, conducted himself fully in accord with his contractual obligations and distinguished himself as a member of the NBC News team.

Mr. Kent said the following about the settlement: "I did not bring this lawsuit to embarrass NBC News or to profit monetarily. I brought it to correct an injustice. Given the changes that have occurred at NBC News, I believe that injustice has been rectified."

NBC News' new President, Andrew Lack, stated: "We are pleased that this unfortunate incident has been laid to rest. Arthur Kent is and always has been a talented and courageous journalist who is highly regarded within the NBC News organization. We wish Mr. Kent every future success and emphasize that he is always welcome to return to NBC News."

A complete reversal of Michael Gartner's lies. And a terrific damage award. It all added up to freedom—freedom to go back to work on my own terms.

"Congratulations," General Randy House wrote soon afterwards. "It is always good to see the good guys win."

"It really was a victory," read the fax from Professor Peter Herford at Columbia University's Graduate School of Journalism. Peter was to have been an expert witness at trial. "I cannot remember a case in which a settlement was reached with such a public display of retraction."

"You *prevailed*," Richard Leibner shouted through the noise of our champagne celebration in New York.

And at the Peninsula Hotel in Beverly Hills, where O'Neill Lysaght and Sun laid on a wonderful party, Bruce Lilliston scribbled a Hollywood wisecrack on to my victory card. "So what have you done lately?" it read.

Exactly, I thought. What do I do with myself now?

* * *

We enjoyed good coverage of our win, and for weeks I carried the clippings in my briefcase–a pleasant counterweight to the bushels of bad press a year and a half earlier. Jack Carmody followed up on his initial coverage of the suspension by practically filling his column in the *Washington Post* with the settlement story. The *Globe and Mail* in Toronto gave us prominent play, as did *Variety*.

But it was Jane Hall writing in the *Los Angeles Times* who put it best, I think, writing that Arthur Kent "had agreed to an out-of-court settlement that provides him money and something he considered more important: his reputation."

The newspapers featured the key points of NBC's retraction–that the Yugoslavia affair had been nothing but a smoke-screen, that I had never, at any time in any place, breached my contract, and that I had always been a team player at NBC News. Peter Johnson in *USA Today*, who filed a great piece under the headline "Kent wins settlement, job offer from NBC," even managed to get through to Michael Gartner, who grumbled, "I always thought I did the right thing" in firing Kent.

Michael wasn't the only bad loser. Andrew Lack, after issuing our joint news release to the outside media, filed a face-saving few sentences in the NBC News computer that acknowledged none of the key points of the company's climb-down. It was pure denial, GE style, but laughably so. Andy's abbreviated in-house message clashed so remarkably with his fulsome praise for me in the newspapers that colleagues in the News Division could only shake their heads at yet another demonstration of corporate hypocrisy. Even in coming clean, management's priority was to hush things up. In such a culture, how could anything really change?

The greatest resentment towards us, of course, came from NBC's lawyers. The morning after the settlement, Mark Helm got on the phone to Brian Lysaght to demand that I hand over all copies of the deposition transcripts.

"Not part of the deal," Brian reminded him. "Arthur paid his way in this case, so the depositions are his." Prior to the news conference, both parties had signed a binding agreement guaranteeing the terms of the settlement. Nevertheless, Mr. Helm shouted down the phone at Brian, made threats.

"Well, if you're going to be difficult," Brian responded, "we'll see you in Judge Pfaelzer's court Monday morning to enforce the settlement agreement. It's up to you, Mark."

The NBC attorney hung up in a rage. He knew Brian's threat had teeth. Enforcement by Judge Pfaelzer would mean a public airing of every component of the agreement. Including the exact amount of the damage award—to NBC and GE management the most damning part of the settlement. Still, for two days, the angry NBC lawyers persisted. So I called Bill Wheatley.

"We signed an agreement, Bill. If the company's attorneys try to backpeddle on it, we'll all land right back in court."

"Don't threaten me, Arthur," he said in a cold voice.

"I'm not threatening you, Bill. I'm telling you that it's time for the company to start living up to its obligations. Right now it looks a lot like the same old dysfunctional NBC."

We had a heated exchange. Bill, I finally realized, was looking at our victory only from management's perspective. Had he lost face by failing to reel me in for less money, for less frank a retraction? I'll never know. We haven't spoken since.

That day, the feuding ended. I retain the transcripts. Richard Cotton forwarded NBC's payment to Brian on time—a single wire transfer for the full amount, delivered with a lot of complaints from Bob Wright's lawyer that the settlement coincided with big royalty payments for the network's National Basketball Association coverage, making "the bean-counters upstairs" all the more unhappy.

I never seriously considered returning to NBC News. Looking at GE's continuing transformation of the company, I saw nothing of the service I once worked for. In many ways "Dateline" had become NBC News. It was where Andrew Lack directed practically all the division's resources. The program found an audience—enough, even, to warrant three one-hour shows per week. But it did so, in my view, by bowing even more completely to Burbank's entertainment values. Today, many "Dateline" staffers will describe as tame and restrained the testimony here about Entertainment's grab for control of the show. "The sign over the door," one staffer recently quipped, "should read 'Ratings R Us.'"

From Long Island Lolita to the Menendez brothers, to Jeffrey Dahmer and his dad, and all the way to the most sensationally made-for-"Dateline" tale of all—O.J. Simpson—the program became the glossiest, slickest news/entertainment hybrid on the block. By 1995 the show was turning in most of the News Division's profit; Bob Wright had won a partial turn-around in his network's prime-time fortunes. But he had done it at the expense of real news.

"Dateline's" rise coincided with the further decline of international and domestic hard-news coverage at NBC. When GE backed the network's purchase of the European satellite broadcaster Superchannel, a daily world-news package had to be bought in from an outside broadcaster—Britain's ITN. Management's retooling of NBC News had left it short of both credibility and content.

That's a critical failing on management's part, since the shrunken News Division retains an extremely high talent ratio. In fact, proportionately, head for head, NBC News might still be the most capable, if also the most depleted, of the big three New York-based news divisions. But it would take seasoned news broadcasters to turn the place around now—journalist-entrepreneurs willing to put heavy investment into pure news. Sadly, that's not the kind of professional favored by NBC's mammoth parent. A joint venture into an interactive service with Bill

Gates' Microsoft has promise, but Gates is a visionary accustomed to exercising complete control. With GE-controlled NBC he has a corporate partner that jealously enforces its own unique business priorities–priorities that continue to cause miscues and gaffes.

In October 1995, for example, the Welch/Wright "company-without-boundaries" philosophy chalked up yet another fiasco. This time the object of management's confusion was a proposed interview with O.J. Simpson. In a blitzkrieg of advertising and promotion, NBC announced that Simpson, fresh from his acquittal on murder charges, was to be served up to the public in a probing one-hour interview by Tom Brokaw. It was a masterstroke for Andy Lack and his team. The interview the whole world was waiting for, a superscoop. Sure, some viewers would loudly object to Simpson's gaining further exposure. But the session would be a ratings giant-killer in the U.S., and NBC would gain worldwide notoriety by allowing foreign broadcasters a brief minute or so for their own news programming–provided the NBC logo was prominently displayed.

But suddenly, a hitch. Simpson's lawyers gave the chop to the whole idea. He was still facing civil charges, they explained, and an interview might jeopardize his chances in court. NBC's windfall evaporated. Now management was besieged by hostile critics. Once again NBC News was caught in a losing battle for damage control. And once again, the specter of Burbank loomed up through the smoke and debris.

This time it was in the form of Donald Ohlmeyer, NBC's Entertainment mandarin on the west coast. It turned out that the interview was Ohlmeyer's brainstorm–he was a close friend of Simpson's from their days together in sports broadcasting. It was revealed that the NBC executive had been a frequent visitor to the cells where O.J. had sat out the long months after his arrest for the murders of Nicole Brown Simpson and Ron Goldman.

"NBC is the laughing-stock of the industry tonight," declared Tom Shales of the *Washington Post* on CNN's "Larry King Live." In the absence of Simpson, everyone wanted to know more about Ohlmeyer. Had he exerted influence in the network's coverage of the trial? And if, as reported, News Division president Andy Lack had ruled out Bryant Gumbel as an interviewer because of the anchor's friendship with Simpson, why hadn't NBC ruled out Ohlmeyer* as an intermediary in setting the session up in the first place? And why had NBC's lawyers evidently failed to advise management that it wasn't O.J. Simpson who would decide where and when he would speak, but his lawyers? The attorneys, not Simpson, were in control of his words and actions now; why hadn't NBC consulted them before publicizing their client's appearance?

Meantime, Tom Brokaw sat in the spotlight. As a measure, perhaps, of how far the News Division had strayed from its hard-news traditions, the Associated Press broke the story of the interview's cancellation before NBC's executives finally got Tom on the air with their own carefully worded account of the situation.

Even for those of us who have left NBC, it was hard not to feel sorrow during this spectacle. The News Division had come a long way from the Berlin Wall and Tiananmen Square. A long way down.

(*Months after this controversy, while meeting with news directors from NBC affiliates, Entertainment chief Ohlmeyer was reported to have vigorously criticized the news executives for inaccurate coverage of stories like the Simpson case.)

"Is there a financial planner in the house?"

Watching people deal with a sudden superabundance of money
can be very instructive. Sudden wealth is a very difficult situation
to handle. It can be overwhelming...
> —from The Way of Real Wealth *by Mark Waldman, PhD*

THE TELEVISION INDUSTRY has a way of putting almost any
quantity of money into perspective. TV dwarfs money–soaks it
up, eats the stuff. Even the empire builders, the people at the top
of the business, have found that out as they chase those elusive,
expensive twin stars of television, production and global delivery.

So in my own little niche, way down the media food-chain, I
had no illusions about the new decimal places on my balance
sheet that spring of 1994. I had some big-time television ideas of
my own, and my Prairie Presbyterian consciousness was shouting
out for caution just as soon as the first images of documentaries-
to-be flickered through my mind.

There were, I admit, a few shivers in the direction of self-
indulgence, something like the cold sweats you get after a bout
with the flu. I felt this unusual sensation creeping over me on
the fine Caribbean beach that became the first haven for Debs
and me after peace had broken out with NBC. That house beyond
the swaying palms, I realized, could be mine. Along with the
gleaming white fifty-one-foot sailboat cruising by. And when we
eased her into her slip, an Aston Martin could be waiting just
outside the bar...

But then I thought: what would become of our time? Island

homes need living in. Cars and motorcycles need to be driven. And that hackneyed adage about boats is true–they're a hole in the ocean you pour money and time into.

So when the champagne mists cleared, I found myself back where I'd started–in Afghanistan, with a camera on my shoulder. It was a shiny new Sony Betacam 400AP, just what I needed to shoot videotape that would match the footage I had shot in the eighties. The camera and a documentary journey to Afghanistan seemed to me the best first investments after the settlement.

For some reason, within weeks of winning a whole new kind of freedom for the future, my mind came to attach great importance to the things I valued most about the past–the finest discoveries, I suppose, on all my favorite news trails. It wasn't about hiding there, or going to ground someplace comfortable and familiar. It was about starting over. And for me, the best place to do that was on one of the world's great jagged edges–the Hindu Kush. I wanted to track down Massoud's people in the Panjshir Valley of Afghanistan, profile their continuing struggle for survival, and get back to my reporting roots, my center.

The civil war in Afghanistan was dragging on that summer of 1994, fueled by interference by Pakistan and Iran–and by the steadfast refusal of the Russians and Western nations to press for peace. The foreign powers that had done so much to escalate the conflict in the eighties had turned away. And so had the Western media: no network, I was assured by my friends, would want to buy a documentary about the Afghans and their endless war. All of which appealed to me. The story had never been a cinch; the question was, would I still be up to it?

I made it to the Panjshir, and I wasn't disappointed. The valley's people worked their magic on me once again. As before, I discovered astounding determination and faith, and friendship. The families I had met during the war with the Soviets were rebuilding despite continued fighting in surrounding regions. I enjoyed their hospitality, and photographed their reconstructed homes. And I visited the graves of my friends.

In Kabul, eighty miles south, I managed to find Raz Mohammed, the boy who had lost both legs to the anti-personnel mine that had crippled his cousin, Lal, as well. Six years after our first meeting, I shot an update on his story as bombs and artillery shells thundered out a familiar backbeat to life in the city. I tried to help the family, realizing all the time that nothing I could do would prove to be enough. It hurt to see the country still bleeding uncontrollably after sixteen years of war, but tears and sympathy are not what Afghans want or need. They're a people deserving of real help. At least now I can finance our team's return there, year after year, to continue covering a story our networks have virtually forgotten.

The Afghan documentary was broadcast later that year as part of CBC's "Man Alive" series in Canada and on the BBC in Britain. Then, in 1995, a year after emerging from litigation, I decided reluctantly to leave "Man Alive" to return full time to my home in London and to reassemble, within a new company, the team from NBC Rome. Today, we're continuing to try to carve out a place for ourselves in the industry with our own style of news and documentary production. Briefly, in 1996, I returned to the daily news airwaves with CNN. It was a deeply satisfying experience—that is, until surgery to remove two benign growths on my vocal chords knocked me off the air. Thankfully my voice has returned, stronger than before (our voices are a unique part of human physiology: with careful therapy, vocal stamina and quality can be improved well into old age). However by the time I recuperated it was clear that my own company needed my complete attention. CNN management understood and graciously released me from my contract.

Still, when a big international story breaks, I often feel an old familiar hunger, a restlessness for the road. It's only a matter of time, I suppose, before the lure of hard breaking news draws me back to the big network circus once more.

* * *

Friends sometimes ask if I've been able to put the NBC dispute behind me. I tell them that I'm not so sure I want to—completely behind me, that is.

There's a definite satisfaction in knowing that each project our team undertakes is fueled, in part, by resources won from the General Electric Company; that at least some of Jack

Welch's wealth has gone towards genuine news. When I go to work at my own office in London, as the owner of the business, it's truly satisfying to know that this privilege comes as a direct result of beating one of the most competitive corporations in America, fair and square, in a proper legal arena.

But more than this, I feel that a basic faith in what journalists do for a living–a set of beliefs and goals and ambitions–has been restored and reaffirmed, at least for me and the colleagues closest to me. I view our case as an accomplishment, not just a means to an end. We discovered facts and attitudes and paradoxes that illustrate the need for vigilance in our craft, and in the broadcasting industry as a whole.

Recently, I watched *Quiz Show*, Robert Redford's motion picture about the infamous scandal over the 1950s TV game show "21." For veterans of NBC the film was an eerie journey to a not-so-distant past, and a foreshadowing of the turmoil and ethical crises at the network today.

"21" had been produced–and ultimately rigged–in the same studios at 30 Rock that I had come to know so well. The actors in that misadventure paced the same corridors, sweated out the final minutes before each show in the same familiar green rooms. The film depicted NBC's top bosses ducking blame when the curtain finally came down on the scam–they allowed the independent producer of "21" to take the fall for slipping the answers to contestants in advance. Management, at the last minute, had slipped the noose.

"I thought we were going to get television," a dejected government investigator says at the climax of the movie. "The truth is, television's going to get us."

To that dark prophecy, I would add this: only if we let it.

Good broadcasting is a responsibility, not a gift. Reporters, writers, drama producers, sportscasters–we all have to work at keeping our business clean. It's not a holy war fought by cloaked crusaders, but especially in the field of broadcast journalism, practitioners of the craft at every level have to take a stand. And they must do it every day, with each newscast, bulletin and program that goes out.

If the principles of reporting don't take precedence over the numbers–over ratings and revenue and greed–then there is really no craft at all. Just the hypocritical money machine that tarnished the Peacock's image in the fifties, as it has done again, four decades on, under General Electric.

Of course it would be wrong to say there should be no commerce in news broadcasting. There has to be profit, as much profit as possible without adulterating the product. I'm still young enough to remember the commercial news broadcasters who got me hooked on this industry in the first place. They proved that genuine news made real money, and lots of it. The profit motive is alive and well at our own company, where all of us realize that the way to produce more and better programming is by earning more—much more if possible—than we spend.

I can hear my old management adversaries now. Enough with the self-righteousness, they say. We paid for the business; we'll run it the way we see fit. Who are you to preach to us, anyway? A journalist? Give us a break—what makes journalists so special? What gives you any special right to preach to us about ethics?

The answer, the evidence, is there for all of us to see in the pages of our newspapers, and occasionally on TV. Sometimes it's bright and promising—a new insight into an old or previously unknown story, a revelation. Sometimes the proof is dark and horrible in its impact, like the two stories that ran side by side in Britain's morning papers the day of August 9, 1995.

In the former Yugoslavia, Croatian soldiers had shot to death a twenty-nine-year-old reporter for BBC Radio, John Schofield; his name joined seventy-six others in the list of journalists killed in the Balkans. Meanwhile in Algeria, Aicha Benamar, aged forty, had become the forty-sixth journalist murdered by Islamic extremists. Her body was found in the street near her home. Aicha's throat had been cut and she'd been left to bleed to death because of the words she had written.

All journalists have a special mission, whether they're working in life-threatening situations or explaining events at city hall. It's called accuracy: putting the truth on public record, no matter who that truth might offend. It's all about having enough courage to earn profits without distorting or dressing up the facts. Ethics do not constitute a handicap, as too many media owners seem to believe. They're assets, and when nurtured with care, they become vital ingredients to success.

This business is not just a balance sheet; it's a discipline. A discipline well worth the risk, and deserving of redemption.

Depositions in the case of Arthur Kent v. NBC, Inc
and Peggy Hubble, CV 92 6472-MRP (Ex)
U.S. District Court Central District of California

1. Arthur Kent was examined under oath by Mark B. Helm, attorney for the defendant, July 21, July 22 and November 12, 1993, in Los Angeles, and on February 4, 1994, at the offices of NBC, 30 Rockefeller Plaza, New York.
2. Steve Friedman was examined under oath by Brian Lysaght, attorney for the plaintiff, August 9, 1993, at NBC, New York.
3. Donald Browne was examined under oath by Brian Lysaght, August 10, 1993, at NBC, New York.
4. David Verdi was examined under oath by Brian Lysaght, August 11, 1993, at NBC, New York.
5. John Stack was examined under oath by Brian Lysaght, August 13, 1993.
6. Lisa Freed was examined under oath by Brian Lysaght, August 13, 1993.
7. Stuart Witt was examined under oath by Mark B. Helm, attorney for the defendant, November 16, 1993, in New York.
8. Richard Leibner was examined under oath by Mark B. Helm, attorney for the defendant, November 17, 1993, in New York.
9. Jeffrey Gaspin was examined under oath by Andrew Coombs, attorney for the plaintiff, November 17, 1993, at NBC, New York.
10. Joseph Alicastro was examined under oath by Andrew Coombs, November 18, 1993, at NBC, New York.
11. Jeffrey Diamond was examined under oath by Andrew

Coombs, November 19, 1993, at the New York offices of Ronald S. Konecky, attorney for the witness.

12. Warren Littlefield was examined under oath by Andrew Coombs, December 3, 1993, at the offices of NBC in Burbank, California.

13. Vincent Manze was examined under oath by Andrew Coombs, December 3, 1993, at NBC Burbank.

14. Peggy Hubble was examined under oath by Andrew Coombs, December 8, 1993, at the offices of Fredericks Jacobsen Reporting and Video Inc. in Austin, Texas.

15. Michael Gartner was examined under oath by Andrew Coombs, December 10, 1993, at the offices of Huney, Vaughn & Associates in Des Moines, Iowa.

16. Tony McGrath was examined under oath by Brian Lysaght, attorney for the plaintiff, January 27, 1994, at Denton Hall, London, England.

17. Garrick Utley was examined under oath by Brian Lysaght, attorney for the plaintiff, January 27, 1994, at Denton Hall, London.

18. Peter Sansun was examined under oath by Brian Lysaght, attorney for the plaintiff, January 28, 1994, at Denton Hall, London.

19. Nicholas Guthrie was examined under oath by Brian Lysaght, attorney for the plaintiff, January 28, 1994, at Denton Hall, London.

20. Timothy Miller was examined under oath by Andrew Coombs, attorney for the plaintiff, February 2, 1994, at NBC, New York.

21. Roberta Brackman was examined under oath by Andrew Coombs, February 2, 1994, at NBC, New York.

22. Gordon Manning was examined under oath by Andrew Coombs, February 3, 1994, at the Omni Berkshire Hotel in New York.

23. Bonnie Optekman was examined under oath by Andrew Coombs, February 3, 1994, at NBC, New York.

24. Tory Beilinson gave a sworn declaration for the record, January 20, 1994, at the Hay-Adams Hotel in Washington, DC.

25. David Miller gave a sworn statement March 3, 1994, in St. Petersburg, Florida.

Acknowledgments

THE RELIEF I feel at reaching this final passage is tempered with anxiety, because I can't hope to express adequately my thanks to all the friends and colleagues who have helped sustain the drive to see this assignment through to completion. This written account is the culmination of innumerable conversations over dinner tables and cocktail bars and long-distance phone lines. More than anything I've been motivated by the curiosity of others and their encouragement to set out our experiences for the record. For that support, thank you, to those both inside and outside the news business.

My eldest sister, Susan, was an invaluable ally and critic throughout this project. And Peter, Adele and Norma Kent have each demonstrated the most fabulous gift of family: the desire to help one another pull through. They were much more in evidence in this story than the pages reveal. Once again, our mother looks on as one of her kids accomplishes something that wouldn't have been possible without the others–or without her own inspiration and care. So thanks, Mother.

Laughter eased the bumps along the way, and no one has shown an ability to laugh, even at the worst of life's jokes, like Deborah Rayner. That her professional advice is invaluable, too, is yet another reason I must repeat: grazie, bella.

My editor at Penguin Books Canada, Jackie Kaiser, whose idea this book was in the first place, combined fun, creativity and purpose with an unwavering sense of discipline. She and the Penguin team across Canada made the publication of the first edition of this book a wonderful experience.

Mary Adachi deserves a five-star rating for cheerfully copy-editing this text, and Simon Chester bravely waded into storm-tossed waters to advise on finer points of law. Meanwhile, Stu Witt, my agent and friend, has somehow helped keep me on the air through all these adventures, even while my own signal has been split among many competing satellites—legal, personal, professional.

Dream teams? As you've read, I had the original: Brian Lysaght and Bruce Lilliston; Fred Friedman and Andy Coombs. All of them kept on course by the friendly, fastidious support team at O'Neill, Lysaght & Sun, notably Pam Brisendine—still with all the relevant documents at her fingertips—and at Bruce's office, Char Holliday, who tracks, on a daily basis, one of the busiest and most conscientious guys in Hollywood.

Finally, a special debt of gratitude goes to the many people who risked their jobs within NBC to suggest new directions, from time to time, in the hunt for facts. For obvious reasons, they cannot be named as of this writing. That they and hundreds like them continue to work at 30 Rock, keeping tradition and quality alive in some corners of the network, is a tribute to their dedication, and one of the reasons that many of us who've moved on still feel a sense of pride whenever the Peacock unfurls on the screen.

April, 1997

Index